DEFINING GIRLHOOD IN INDIA

DEFINING GIRLHOOD IN INDIA

A Transnational History of Sexual Maturity Laws

ASHWINI TAMBE

UNIVERSITY OF ILLINOIS PRESS
Urbana, Chicago, and Springfield

© 2019 by the Board of Trustees
of the University of Illinois
All rights reserved
1 2 3 4 5 C P 5 4 3 2 1
♾ This book is printed on acid-free paper.

Library of Congress Control Number: 2019025065

ISBN 978-0-252-04272-0 (hardcover) | ISBN 978-0-252-08456-0 (paperback) | ISBN 978-0-252-05158-6 (e-book)

To Anya

For the many ways you resist definition

Contents

Acknowledgments   ix

Introduction   1

1 Tropical Exceptions: Imperial Hierarchies, Climate, and Race   17
2 Adolescence as a Traveling Concept   35
3 Legislating Nonmarital Sex in India, 1911–1929   61
4 Early Marriage as Slavery: UN Interventions, 1948–1965   85
5 Population Control and Marriage Age in India, 1960–1978   101
6 Investing in the Girl Child, 1989–2015   121
7 Curtailing Parents? Marriage and Consent Laws, 2004–2018   142

Conclusion   151

Notes   157

Index   193

Acknowledgments

I've spent more than a decade working on this book, but it would have undoubtedly taken longer were it not for the love and support of many people and institutions.

First, thanks to the institutions that financially support critical interdisciplinary research of the kind seen here. At a time when the humanities are under pressure, such institutions help us to imagine and generate the many worlds that were and that could be. A grant from the Canadian Social Science and Humanities Research Council (SSHRC) enabled me to hire my wonderful research assistants Samantha Laforêt, Shama Dossa, Sumaya Ahmed, and Rajani Bhatia; fund my research trips to India; and organize a conference on transnational approaches to girlhood. A National Endowment for the Humanities (NEH) summer stipend helped me write chapter 6 using research on UN documents. A summer faculty grant from Georgetown University stoked my initial efforts—I came across the *Stree* archive while on an early research trip, and I later helped digitally preserve cover images and organize a traveling exhibit of *Stree* covers through a Toyota Foundation grant for cultural preservation. Research funds and a research leave from the Department of Women's Studies at the University of Maryland have made it possible for me to meet my writing deadlines and hire research assistants Sara Haq, Tangere Hoagland, and Samantha O'Donnell. I thank the UMD College of Arts and Humanities (ARHU) for supporting my Transnational South Asia colloquium. Anna Storti has rendered prompt and

ACKNOWLEDGMENTS

thorough assistance in the final stages of preparing this manuscript. To all my research assistants: much of your work was tedious, but I hope you're proud of the results.

Staying focused on writing was especially hard when I moved universities (and countries) midway through the project and took on a new role as editorial director of the journal *Feminist Studies*. I'll always be deeply grateful for the mentorship of Claire Moses, editorial director emerita of *Feminist Studies*, through this process. Her help with this manuscript has been a lifeline: her exemplary thoroughness as a reader and her prompt and thoughtful feedback helped me plug away with good cheer. Thank you, Claire, for your wise counsel on matters big and small—your friendship means the world to me. The University of Maryland writing group that Laura Rosenthal initiated has been vital to my intellectual health: I thank Holly Brewer, Jessica Enoch, Kristy Maddux, and Laura Rosenthal for asking probing questions, sharing outsider perspectives, and offering encouragement. Several colleagues and friends read prior versions of chapters. Debra Bergoffen and Evi Beck engaged generously with material now in chapter 4. Martha Bebinger made time to talk through ideas now in chapter 2. At the University of Toronto, Alissa Trotz offered crucial feedback on my early proposals, and Michelle Murphy offered stimulating engagement with my ideas on girlhood. I am grateful to Eileen Boris for her support for the NEH grant proposal and for inviting me to present parts of this book at the International Conference for Research on Women's History. Cara Kennedy helped me broaden my framing for nonspecialists.

I have gained much from presentations at conferences and talks; some of the most thoughtful contributions came from the global childhoods conference that David Pomfret and Richard Jobs organized at Hong Kong University; the transnational girlhoods conference I organized at University of Toronto; the European South Asian Studies panel on girlhood with Ishita Pande; the Northwestern University conference on writing histories of childhood organized by Sarah Maza; and my ongoing exchanges with Corinne Field and Nicholas Syrett—with whom I share so much excitement about age as a category of analysis. Participants in my seminars on transnational approaches to girlhood at the University of Maryland also offered opportunities for me to think carefully about why my work should matter to those outside South Asia.

Anonymous reviewers appointed by the University of Illinois Press read two versions of this manuscript and at both times with remarkable thoroughness, offering ideas for improving the book's structure, level of detail, and language. My manuscript is certainly the better for it. Dawn Durante at University of Illinois Press is a remarkable editor—her passion for promoting innovative scholarship in girlhood studies is transforming the field of women and gender studies. Her promptness, reassuring manner, and smart ideas make working with her a delight. Thanks also to Mary Lou Kowaleski for her very thorough copyedits.

The *Journal of the History of Childhood and Youth* published "The State as Surrogate Parent: Legislating Nonmarital Sex in Colonial India, 1911–1929" in volume 2, number 3 (Fall 2009), from which I drew parts of chapter 3; *Theory, Culture, and Society* included my article "Climate, Race Science, and the Age of Consent in the League of Nations" in issue 28, number 2, in 2011 and some of this article appears in chapter 1; and *Women's Studies International Forum*'s May–June 2014 issue contains my article coauthored with Bhatia, "Raising the Age of Marriage in 1970s India: Demographers, Despots, and Feminists," which I drew on when writing chapter 5.

Archives, libraries, and the people who fund them have been crucial to my work. I am thankful for the India Office collections at the British Library, the National Archives of India, and the social science and medical journal collection at the Robarts Library of the University of Toronto, Widener Library at Harvard University, the National Library of Medicine, and the library consortium of the University of Maryland system. At the Library of Congress, I especially thank the UN documents specialists for assistance over several visits. I drew on the late Mukundrao Kirloskar's personal collection of *Stree* magazines when taking photographs of covers, and I am thankful to him and to editor Vidya Bal for access and insights into this magazine's history.

And then there are those who made writing this book easier because they keep other parts of my work life sane. Karla Mantilla and Brittany Fremaux, my stalwart superhuman colleagues at *Feminist Studies,* come first. Karla's impressive work ethic and unbelievable eye for detail helps the journal in countless ways, and Brittany's cheerful and creative approach to publicity and business takes the journal in new and exciting directions. Thank you both for being my rock. And the *Feminist Studies* editorial collective is a stellar group of scholars who have animated my intellectual life throughout the writing of this book: thank you to Judy Gardiner, Leisa Meyer, Kathryn Moeller, Jennifer Nash, Uta Poiger, Minnie Bruce Pratt, Priti Ramamurthy, Matt Richardson, Lisa Rofel, Evie Shockley, Millie Thayer, Charis Thompson, Kamala Visweswaran, and Attiya Ahmad. My wonderful Feminist Legal Theory book group and fellow board members of the Potomac Center for the Study of Modernity are a steady source of great conversation. My smart colleagues in a small department— Alexis Lothian, Ivan Ramos, Michelle Rowley, Ruth Zambrana, Elsa Barkley Brown, Deborah Rosenfelt, Seung-kyung Kim, Katie King, Lynn Bolles, Carol

ACKNOWLEDGMENTS

Stabile, and LaMonda Horton-Stallings—bore added service burdens during my research leaves. Department staff members helped me hire research assistants and manage budgets: Angela Fleury and Meghan Sbrocchi at the University of Toronto, and Annie Carter, JV Sapinoso, Bobby Burgard, and Catalina Toala at the University of Maryland. My doctoral advisees Jaime Madden, Sara Haq, Cara Snyder, and Clara Montague each inspire me in different ways: their innovative projects, creativity in surmounting obstacles, and sense of humor have enriched my life at UMD—thank you!

My family in India teaches me how to love across time, space, and emotional distance—by renewing bonds every time they get tenuous. Thank you, Baba, for your pride and your help—from mailing me rare books to talking about my work with people I'd never know. Thank you, Abhi, for staying curious about what I do and reaching across the (yawning!) gap between our specializations to read my work. Your effort always touches me... and your music rocks. Thanks to Vatsala Vedantam for modeling persistence and to Gayatri Vedantam and V. K. Viswanathan for modeling a life of the mind and wise ways to navigate academe. Thank you, Mami and Mama, Aparna, and Ambu and Shalini for being beacons of comfort. Thank you, Shruti, Ganesh, and Kaka, for being lasting political and intellectual allies.

Finally, to those who have watched this project grow from up close: my daughter Anya's questions always perk me up and remind me why this work matters. Her self-sufficiency and empathy have made parenting a total dream. I hope you find this book more interesting to read than my others, Anya. Shankar Vedantam is a dynamo of a spouse—his heroism in meeting ridiculously high work demands while being a funny, attentive, and creative parent inspires me daily. Shankar: your curiosity about the world and its people has an infectious quality, and it always keeps conversations interesting—that is, when we're not talking schedules, bills, pickups and drop-offs.... I'm so glad to be sharing this ride with you.

DEFINING GIRLHOOD IN INDIA

Introduction

Age is a widely accepted category for organizing social and political lives. It plays a fundamental role in the apparatus of biopolitical states: schooling, voting, military recruitment, and social security, to name a few examples, are structured through age groupings and minimum ages of entry—and usually without controversy.[1] In the realm of sexual relations, however, minimum age standards have long been a source of conflict. Strong views dictate the ages at which one can consent to sexual activity, or marry, or transact in sexual services. Interestingly, the minimum age for each activity—whether for consensual sex, or marriage, or commercial sex—usually varies. And norms change across generations and regions, so lawmakers frequently face the challenge of laws misaligned with social practices.

Sexual age laws are complex matters largely because they are meant to signal social standards for sexual maturity. Age is usually a blunt metric for measuring such maturity, but the clarity of numbers—unlike vague visual markers or social status—makes it congruent with the needs of the law. The historically modern fascination with enumeration has meant that laws in our time center age as the criterion for inaugurating legitimate sex. Yet, efforts at devising common legal age standards for sex run the risk of not quite capturing what they seek to assure: numerical years are never fully adequate to the task of conveying the capacity for sexual judgment.

INTRODUCTION

Defining sexual maturity for girls is especially politically freighted, because it implies not just the potential for autonomous sexual activity but also pregnancy and motherhood. Around the world, sexual age standards have been defined differently for girls than for boys and debated with greater ferocity. This book focuses on legal standards for sexual maturity for girls in India and explores how and why these standards shifted over the course of the twentieth and early twenty-first centuries. I began research on this topic because I was intrigued by inconsistencies in the way the age boundaries were defined for girls. When studying the history of the sex trade for my book *Codes of Misconduct*, I frequently encountered laws on prostitution that demarcated a different age of consent than statutory-rape laws and marriage-age laws.[2] I was fascinated by what these discrepancies signaled about the meaning of girlhood. Why did understandings of sexual maturity vary in each context, and when exactly did girlhood end, then? Although my initial focus on India was driven by my specialization in South Asian studies, I found that it became necessary to engage intergovernmental actions and transnational expert discourses because of the pressure they placed on Indian debates. It became clear that most intergovernmental debates about child marriage as well as global development discourses about girls could not be explored without being routed through India. India has served both as a focal point in conversations about these topics as well as a source of new language and framing. In effect, this book tells a story of transnational circulation of ideas about girlhood with India at the center.

The stakes in defining age boundaries for sexual practices are particularly high in India. The country has served as a quintessential problem site in popular and scholarly narratives about child marriage. And rightly so, in a sense—nearly half of the world's girls who are married under 18 live in India.[3] It is also where some of the most dramatic shifts in the legal age of marriage have taken place in the twentieth century: from 12 years at the start of the century to 18 years by its end. The focus in this book is on the concepts that shaped these changes—the acceptance of adolescence as a sheltered phase, which was critical to justifying the deferral of marriage and adulthood; the imperative of population control, which propelled expert interest in the age of marriage; and moral hierarchies among nations, which shaped the tenor of intergovernmental debates on common age standards.

The changes in India can be linked to changes elsewhere: a striking upward shift in the legal age of sexual maturity occurred around the world over the course of the twentieth century. Spurred by women's movements, expanding industrial and educational systems, and international legal conventions, legislators across regions raised the ages of sexual consent, marriage, and prostitution.

As a result, early sexual activity has now come to be coded as a sign of social depravity. Like legal standards on other sexual practices, such as same-gender marriage and widow remarriage, the age of marriage has come to serve as an index of moral hierarchies among nations. This book demonstrates how age standards for sex came to bear the weight of representing the international reputation and moral worth of India. It recounts how norms about age of sexual consent and marriage emerged, shaped by colonial encounters, international conventions, circulating scientific discourses, and reformist social movements.

The story of the dramatic changes in India must be framed in a transnational light not only because transnational discourses influenced India but also because India was a site of expert discourses that influenced arguments, narratives, and terminology beyond its borders. India served not so much as a coherent cultural entity in this transnational context as an imagined category representing specific problems in expert conversations. As Matthew Connelly notes in his history of the population control movement, the phrase "countries like India" serves as shorthand for "poor countries with high fertility."[4] Beginning with the works of Thomas Robert Malthus, the first theorist of population, India has been a central preoccupation. India played an outsized role in public policy conversations also because it was the first country to adopt policies to reduce its population and the first to invite UN and US programs to establish clinics and projects testing new birth control techniques.[5] The knowledge gleaned from such initiatives traveled to inform policies implemented elsewhere.

Apart from being a focus in expert knowledge, global public attention to child marriage in India dates back to the 1920s, when scholarship and journalism about it appeared in the United States, Europe, and Asia.[6] In League of Nations debates in the 1930s, the Indian example was frequently cited in discussions about child marriage, as chapter 1 explains. When the United Nations first began to take up the age of marriage as an international problem in the 1950s, India again was a focus, with delegates from India playing an obstructionist role, as shown in chapter 4. Campaigns to invest in girl children and delay marriage were initiated in India in the 1990s and the first decade of the twenty-first century and spread to UN contexts, as chapter 6 shows.

The flows of influence in my account are thus multidirectional. Power operates in asymmetric ways within these circuits. In this sense, this book offers a distinctly transnational feminist perspective on international law. The book examines how international conventions, scientific discourses, and social reform movements created circuits of uneven power when exerting pressure to raise sexual age standards across countries. Efforts to harmonize the sexual age standards in international legal conventions confronted and sometimes reified problematic understandings of national differences and national culture. It is because sexual age standards had transnational genealogies that the chapters in this book deliberately alternate between geographical scales. The book shuttles back and forth between League of Nations and UN intergovernmental contexts and Indian legislative contexts and also European and American science and Indian science, thereby illuminating the interwoven influences. The emergence of the adolescent girl as a recognizable cultural figure in modern India, I suggest, cannot be fully understood without attention to such cultural flows: US understandings of adolescence moved to influence Indian psychology and consolidate understandings of adolescence. Influence also flowed in the opposite direction when a specifically Indian preoccupation with the "girl child" entered international intergovernmental discourse.

Implicit in my approach is a critique of how power operates within intergovernmental institutions. Such institutions have never been power-neutral venues, despite their lofty goals; they have been shaped by uneven relationships between national actors. Imperial discourses circulating in international settings made some parts of the world, such as India, disproportionately visible. I emphasize how local and imperial interests shaped international institutions (such as the League of Nations and United Nations) as well as transnational discourses (about population control and girl children). In so doing, I destabilize common assumptions about intergovernmental, national, and regional scales. I show how the intergovernmental sphere is neither culturally nor politically pluralistic and how it is frequently shaped by imperial and parochial interests. Conversely, I also show how advocacy at the national and subnational levels can be imbued with an ambitious cosmopolitanism. Indian legislators drew up legal age standards that were often an effort to manage national reputation or advance national development goals. It is vital to understand the culture of ideas and reputational imperatives that influenced such legal standards. Through engaging with such imperatives, I offer a fuller appreciation of how and why specific age coordinates emerged and shaped contemporary understandings of girlhood.

Given my expressly transnational feminist orientation, it may seem unusual that this book focuses so much on intergovernmental settings, such as the League of Nations and the United Nations. Transnational feminists typically deemphasize the significance of advocacy in these sites because national representatives were usually elite figures who were committed to their respective nationalist narratives.[7] As shown ahead, the League of Nations and United Nations did, indeed, reflect the nationalist priorities of individual national representatives. These intergovernmental organizations were less influenced by civil society groups in their early decades than they have been in recent years.[8] For this reason, scholars of the global turn in women's movements have also generally overlooked this early and mid-twentieth-century cross-border feminist advocacy and focused on the post-1975 period after the UN Year of the Woman.[9] Their reasons are understandable, but the earlier and less-celebrated genre of interwar and post–World War II international women's advocacy had important impacts. My account of League of Nations antitrafficking conferences and UN debates on the age of marriage offers a glimpse of such impacts while contributing to the broader project of tracing the history of age standards for sexual activity and India's place in this history.

Girlhood in South Asian History and Beyond

This book is primarily directed at interlocutors in South Asian history, girlhood studies, and transnational feminist theory, even as it is indebted to scholarship from many other fields, such as international studies and sexuality studies. The question of how life stages are imagined and demarcated has generated surprisingly little scholarship in South Asian history, compared to the vibrant debates in other settings.[10] Five decades ago, Philippe Ariès's idea that it was a modern notion to view childhood as a distinct bounded phase provoked a stream of counterarguments and research in childhood studies in Europe, North America, and Africa.[11] In the context of South Asia, however, there are comparatively fewer attempts to theorize the boundaries of childhood. While valuable scholarship exists on policy problems, such as child labor as well as son preference and female infanticide, the category of the child is taken for granted.[12] Indeed, as Satadru Sen argues, scholarship on South Asia has focused on children but could better problematize childhood.[13]

The child, is, of course, not free of gender. As historians of girlhood such as Catherine Driscoll, Crista DeLuzio, and LaKisha Simmons note, much scholarship on childhood has androcentrically treated the experience of boyhood as generically standing in for all childhood.[14] Even though Ariès acknowledges that girls were more likely to be treated as little women and denied the "specialized childhood" offered to boys, most early historians of childhood still devoted the bulk of their studies to boys.[15] Standard histories attribute the modern contours of childhood in the late nineteenth and twentieth centuries to a declining expectation for children to labor and to an increased insistence on children's schooling.[16] Historians of girlhood identify different expectations shaping girlhood in this same period. For girls, there have been fewer restrictions on laboring when one takes into account household work: girls were, and are, expected to learn and carry out domestic tasks from very early in their lives. Schooling also did not have the same vocational charge as it did for boys; girls' schools were framed as sites of personal cultivation. More often, it was marriage, with its attendant reproductive responsibilities, rather than a wage-earning job and the end of schooling, that marked the end of childhood for girls. So, in contexts where female puberty served as a marker of marriageable age, girlhood was a severely circumscribed experience. The treatment of puberty as a marker of marriageability meant childhood has been (and continues to be) cut short sooner for girls than for boys.[17]

The specific expectations for girls vary depending on history and place, of course. Scholarship on girlhood recognizes this point and tends to be organized along regional and cultural lines, with an emphasis on delineating specificities. Simmons, for instance, points out that black girls in the Jim Crow South were simply not expected to express rebelliousness as a feature of their adolescence; to the contrary, the mandate of respectability and threat of racial violence placed pressures on black girls to feign restraint.[18] DeLuzio similarly makes careful observations about how class mattered in US educational institutions focused on "reforming" lower-class white girls—such schools understood girlhood quite differently from the schools that upper-middle-class parents sent their daughters to.[19] In tracing the spread of the idea of the teenage girl, Driscoll limits all her observations to "Western cultures" and those shaped by Western discourses of girlhood.[20] Yet it is also the case that scholars of girlhood recognize the importance of linking multiple geographic sites. The Modern Girl around the World Project, for instance, explicitly attributes transnational corporate advertising and consumption practices with influencing the formation of a common interwar-era icon: the youthful, independent, stylish young woman.[21] The field of girlhood studies, then, is both attuned to the importance of regional specificity and open to recognizing links across geographic contexts.

The goal of this book is to contribute to girlhood studies and South Asian history a bifocal attentiveness to both the close-up details that make girlhood in India distinct as well as the wide transnational currents that shape its emergence. In Indian settings, as in other contexts, girlhood has been much circumscribed by marriage practices. Scriptural exhortations in the Rig Veda to have girls married before puberty indicate that this practice was observed in ancient times, although it intensified after the sixteenth century CE.[22] The key modern moments in expanding the length of girlhood were the raising of the age of marriage in 1891, 1929, and 1978, and in 2006 the effort to prohibit all child marriage. There is a wealth of scholarship on many of these efforts, especially about the pre-1947 colonial period, but while such scholarship convincingly shows that these legal debates reconfigured womanhood and nationalist politics, it is less instructive about how life stages were reconceptualized for girls.[23] Scholarship on the efforts to reform child marriage in the 1890s and late 1920s has explored how women's bodies became the terrain upon which nationalists articulated resistance to the colonial state.[24] But we still have much to learn about specific contours and sexual valence of the adolescent girl as a cultural figure.

Even less is written about how the Indian context shaped intergovernmental conversations in the twentieth century. My claim is that changes in India were a part of circulating understandings of girlhood in other parts of the world. The period 1880 to 1920 witnessed sharp changes in the age of consent in Europe as well. Until the late nineteenth century, the age of consent in most European countries was 13; in 1885 in Britain, the age of consent was raised to 16 years. In the early twentieth century, US legislators in individual states followed suit, sometimes raising it as high as to 18 years.[25] While holding up for examination the distinct case of India, this book simultaneously demonstrates how intergovernmental consensuses emerged and operated. Such an approach contributes to a critical feminist engagement with legal universals. As postcolonial feminist legal scholarship demonstrates, legal universals are rarely straightforward instruments of redress, and they frequently embed hierarchical social relations.[26] I advance this mode of understanding the law by examining the transnational conditions of production and reception of a specific legal universal, the age of marriage.

Many parts of this book focus on how age standards function as a prism for understanding how societies frame ideal heterosexuality. Increasing the minimum age for marriage is a form of "guarding the altar" from those deemed unfit to marry, as Michael Grossberg puts it.[27] Age of consent standards also implicitly desexualize normative girlhood. They project a vision of a society that not only protects its young from unsavory activities but also refuses to countenance early sex for those deemed future ideal citizens. For instance, there are differences in the age of consent for prostitution and marriage and for statutory rape: in the United States, where individual states range in their age of consent from 12 to 18 years, many states calibrate varying punishments for statutory rape depending on whether the female is of "chaste" character. Legislators have presumed that "unchaste" girls are less in need of state protection. In India, on the other hand, as chapter 3 explains, the age of marriage has long been lower than the age of prostitution because of how marriage is presumed to protect girls from the proverbial "fates worse than death."

This project is thus also of relevance to scholarship about childhood in sexuality studies and queer theory. A signature feature of modern childhood is the expectation that children be innocent. Innocence can mean both lacking in knowledge about sex and lacking in "sin" or "guilt." The romantic ideal of childhood inaugurated in Europe imagined children as innocent in both these ways: unaware of adult desires and blameless. Art historian Ann Higonnet chronicles visual representations in Western art that confirm this notion of children as lacking in sexual knowledge.[28] Yet this ideal of childhood sexual innocence is inherently vulnerable and relies on the adult fortressing of childhood for its preservation. As Kathryn Bond Stockton notes, it is a mistake to "take innocence straight"—she argues that childhood innocence is an adult creation, inverting what are considered adult attributes of knowingness and sin.[29] In other words, for Stockton, the way childhood is framed says more about adults than it does about children themselves. Following scholars such as Lee Edelman and Jack Halberstam, Stockton underscores how childhood is an adult projection focused on the goal of reproducing one's self. Furthermore, childhood is plotted along a linear trajectory headed toward an inevitably reproductive future for the child.[30] For all its provocative speculations, this line of thinking nonetheless remains attached to an understanding of the child as an abstraction, and it rarely examines the distinct features of actual girlhood. This study adds historical specificity to conversations about the construction of sexual innocence by exploring how legislators understood and posited innocence in debates about the minimum-age standards for girls' sexual activity in India.

Even if it is adults who are often the most anxious about preserving childhood innocence, the social entitlement to innocence is, all the same, distributed in unequal ways—it is deeply shaped by social class, caste, and race. The idea of childhood as a protected time devoted to play and characterized by innocence has been the prerogative of middle-class and racially dominant groups—in other words, those with the means to shelter children from the responsibilities of adulthood. Historians characterize the twentieth century as the period that stabilized and popularized this middle-class norm of the innocent child via state safeguards. Peter Stearns, for instance, argues that in the twentieth century, the association of children with innocence and vulnerability was elaborated through multiple institutions: the enforcement of schooling, stigmatization of their labor, and treatment as potential consumers.[31] Yet children of subordinate statuses have been consistently denied the luxury of protected childhood in this same period—the continuing prevalence of child labor underscores this point. Differing entitlements to childhood can even coexist within the same hierarchical household: in Indian household-servant relationships, the servant child has to role-play the persona of a playmate while recognizing, with an adult sensibility, that she or he is unequal in power to the mistress or master's child. (This frequently takes place alongside the infantilization of adults of subordinate status as "boys" or "girls.") Nazera Sadiq Wright has detailed how literary representations of black girlhood in the nineteenth century stressed their "premature knowingness," a sign of their violation by slave masters and mistresses as well as the economic hardships that forced them into early adulthood.[32] Social status, in other words, determines a child's access to the full experience of romantic childhood.

This section opened with the question of why childhood as a category has drawn relatively little attention in South Asian history. Perhaps the reason scholars are more comfortable focusing on problems affecting children (such as child labor) rather than historicizing the category of the child is that doing the latter risks unsettling the social consensus to protect children. Even if those who historicize the category of the child do not a priori question the principle of protecting children, their notion that protection is a historically contingent social mandate is deeply uncomfortable. There *is* an inherent tension between a deconstructive approach that asks how a social category emerges and a policy approach that seeks to ameliorate the conditions under which people affected by that category live. To the extent possible, the approach here is to focus on historical formations of categories while remaining attuned to their implications for actual girls. The structure of this book, for example, foregrounds moments of controversy across the twentieth and early twenty-first centuries that crucially defined life chances for millions of girls. Girls' ability to exert control over the trajectory of their lives and their sense of autonomy from parental and reproductive obligations are part of the stakes. This book explores the many tensions between actual vulnerability of girls and willful social control over girls' lives and celebrates social and legal victories of expanded life chances for girls while also staying attuned to the biopolitical interests fostering girls' reproductive futures.

The Contemporary Resonance of the "Girl"

Any effort to historicize the category of the "girl" must engage it in relation to the "woman." The term "girl" has long had a fluid but tense relationship with "woman." Both terms frequently index status and not just age. In the United States, until the women's movement in the 1960s and 1970s raised the issue, women across age groups described themselves in casual conversation as "girls" without much thought. More troubling, "girl" was used to infantilize racially or economically subordinate women: women in servile positions, such as domestic servants or secretaries, were addressed as "girls" well into their middle-age years.[33] Such historical indignities pushed feminists to claim the hard-won identity of "woman" as a counterpoint to the devaluation of women as "girls."

The hierarchical relationship between "woman" and "girl" has a specific inflection in India, where the term "girl" is associated with being unmarried: in common parlance, women in their twenties and thirties are not described as "women" until they actually marry. In fact, some Indian languages have the same root word for woman and wife—in the western Indian language Marathi, the word for woman, *bai*, is the core element of the word for wife, *baiko*. The norm of compulsory marriage conflates adulthood with married status, and a woman remains a "girl" unless she is married.

While some feminists have long been alert to how the word "girl" can be used to demean women, others, especially in Anglo-American contexts, have recently derived inspiration from the aura of "girl power." Some of the most energetic forms of countercultural music and art activism over the past three decades foreground the many transgressive possibilities of the "girl" as an identity. Punk music's Riot Grrrl movement, Guerilla Girls, and DIY zine culture, for instance, all highlight the rebellious register of the "girl." In contemporary US popular culture, it is easier to parlay feminist ideas in the name of girls rather than of women: books about feminism are peppered with the word "girl" in their titles—Sophia Amoruso's *#GirlBoss* (2014), Megan Seely's *Fight like a Girl* (2007), Lena Dunham's *Not That Kind of Girl* (2014), and Gwendolyn Pough et al.'s *Home Girls Make Some Noise* (2007).[34] In these instances where adult authors describe themselves as girls, the term "girl" functions as a spirited vehicle for relaying women's issues.

In social movement history, the boundary between girls' issues and women's issues has long been porous. Historically, women have advocated for girls, rather than claiming their identity *as* girls. Protecting girls, for instance, was a key plank of many women's movements in various parts of the world; in global abolitionist campaigns against sexual slavery and trafficking since the early twentieth century, women activists focused their energy on rescuing girl victims. Age is a dynamic identity and (cis)women have themselves experienced girlhood and possibly even mourned its loss.[35] The fluid social identification across the age categories "woman" and "girl" is therefore understandable. Many women activists who advocate for girls might even be advocating retrospectively for their former selves.

Understanding how girlhood is constructed is a timely and even urgent topic. Wherever we turn, we see girls presented as targets of well-meaning interventions: campaigns by intergovernmental agencies, development agencies, national leaders, and corporations alike advocate urgently for them. The 2010

INTRODUCTION

UN Foundation's Girl Up, the 2008 Nike Foundation's Girl Effect, and Canada's Plan International's 2010 Because I Am a Girl campaigns rally for a global focus on girls in the global South.[36] Sixteen-year-old Malala Yousafzai won a Nobel Peace Prize in 2014, a sign of the pervasive appeal of not just this girl but of girls as a cause.[37] When US President Barack Obama launched an antitrafficking initiative in 2012, he did it specifically in the name of girls, citing the horrors of enslaving "girls [his] daughters' age."[38] Even the otherwise-paralyzed US Senate in 2010 passed the International Protecting Girls by Preventing Child Marriage Act.

It is not just girls of any age but adolescent girls, specifically, who are the targets of such interventions. Adolescence is presented as a phase where much can go wrong and when special protections are called for. A reigning assumption is that adolescent girls are on an inescapable path to reproductive womanhood, and that investing in them, especially in their education, will delay and limit their childbearing and also improve the quality of their eventual parenting.[39] Such an orientation toward adolescent girls is at once protective and instrumental. Indeed, one could say that the figure of the adolescent girl has now replaced the figure of the hardworking Third World woman in nongovernmental organization (NGO) fundraising circles—after all, what donor can resist this combination of vulnerability and potential?

The contemporary celebration of the girl makes analytical attention to categories important. As suggested in this book, laws themselves produced the boundaries of girlhood rather than being formulated on the basis of a prior stable notion of girlhood. This argument continues the line of thinking that I offer in *Codes of Misconduct* about the social force of laws. Twentieth-century laws raising the marriage age in India were formulated in top-down ways, driven by nationalist legislators concerned about the reputation of the fledgling nation in the colonial period and by legislators enacting state-led population control and development priorities in the postindependence period.

Given the enormous social, cultural, and linguistic diversity within the unwieldy political entity that is called India, I do not aim to present an account of the experience of girlhood for all Indian girls. I am interested in exploring what forms of difference Indian girlhood represented in conversations about universal age standards. This book draws on my grounding in transnational South Asian history and international studies to tack back and forth among the context of India, intergovernmental conversations in League of Nations and United Nations settings, and European and American scientific discourses. Such an approach illuminates how a sense of Indian girlhood emerged across the twentieth century in relationship to a range of circulating ideas—about population and about slavery and not just about puberty and adolescence.

11

INTRODUCTION

Sources and Methods

Several chapters in this book have a foreground-background structure: they open with a dramatic episode and follow with the history of an undergirding idea. Such a chapter structure allows me to share genealogies I conducted over the course of this project. My initial question about the legal boundaries of girlhood provoked several spin-off questions that called for a genealogical approach: When did the idea of adolescence emerge? Where and why did the notion that climate shaped the age of puberty arise? How did the imperative of population control connect to marriage age? What is a girl child, and where and how did this locution gain power? Exploring these questions meant forays into scholarship in a range of disciplines: psychology, geography, biology, and demography, to name the most important. Following such histories of ideas might feel like detours from a central narrative about laws defining girlhood, but it is key to understanding intellectual legacies that have shaped our emerging present.

This book is therefore at once an intellectual history tracing the genealogy of concepts, a legal history that explains the social contexts shaping legal debates, and a cultural history that draws on popular visual representation. My choice of sources is heterodox because I show how concepts such as adolescence, puberty, and the girl child move across geographic spaces as well as disciplines, policy, and cultural arenas. Knowledge generated in the fields of psychology, medicine, economics, and sociology is brought into conversation with the events and debates excavated from legal files and bureaucratic records. Images from a popular magazine and websites of NGO campaigns are presented.

In many respects, the sources used in this book depart from dominant trends in girlhood studies scholarship. Girlhood studies has been strongly influenced by a cultural studies focus on subcultures, and as a result, scholars draw a great deal on oral histories and personal journals, in addition to literary, magazine, televisual, and filmic depictions of girls.[40] These sources effectively tend toward the study of historically recent and twentieth-century experiences. While my work also covers the same time period, my focus is not so much on the experience of girlhood as on legal shifts in conceptualizations of girlhood. I work outwards from legal debates to seek relevant expert discourses and, at times, popular-culture sources.

My most striking methodological departure from other histories of girlhood is in pursuing genealogies of ideas that are of indirect significance to girlhood. For instance, although the origins of the humanitarian interest in the "girl child" and the emergence of 18 as an accepted age boundary of girlhood are traced, I also ask how scholars in medicine, psychology, or public health have offered varied and problematic answers to such questions as whether climate affected the age of puberty, what adolescence means, and whether early marriage affects population growth. Focusing on such questions has meant following trails found in footnotes and bibliographic references across a wide range of disciplines. Working backwards has meant constantly asking, Who cites whom? And, given my transnational approach, where are they located?

The sources used are dispersed across four countries and housed in public archives, libraries, and private collections, alongside the many sources now found online. In the first two chapters about expert discourses on puberty and adolescence, I draw primarily from medical and psychology journals and books in the collections of the Robarts Library of the University of Toronto, Widener Library at Harvard University, the National Library of Medicine, and the library consortium of the University of Maryland system. Chapter 2 also draws from my work digitizing the covers of *Stree* magazine in Pune, India. The legal debates referenced in chapter 3 can be found in files at the National Archives in New Delhi and the British Library in London. Chapters 4, 5, and 6 draw on my research of United Nations records at the Library of Congress, Washington, DC, as well as online records in AccessUN and the Official Document System (ODS). Chapter 7 draws primarily on online NGO sources, print media, and parliamentary records about current legal debates.

Preview of Chapters

The book is divided into three sections. The first section examines expert discourses about the age of adolescence and puberty and explores the relationship between physiological and psychological notions of sexual maturation. I show how expert knowledge about puberty was steeped in conventions of scientific racism and how the notion that climate affected puberty enjoyed prominence in intergovernmental conversations. I also show how adolescence—a newly invented life stage that defers womanhood for girls—emerged and traveled between twentieth-century European and American contexts and Indian contexts.

The second and third sections focus on legal debates in intergovernmental settings and in India. The second section focuses more squarely on lawmaking practices, analyzing important moments in legal history from the 1920s to the 1970s. The third section grapples with the emerging present: I describe the efforts in the first decade of the twenty-first century to tighten marriage-age enforcement and "invest" in girls.

The chapters move back and forth across scales: Some attend to legal debates within India, and others examine broader contexts that feature India and shape

INTRODUCTION

India, such as European and American scientific discourses or intergovernmental contexts of the League of Nations and UN conversations. Each chapter in the book takes up distinct themes and periods.

Chapter 1 delves into the geopolitics of knowledge production about human puberty. I explore how the earliest efforts in the 1920s at the League of Nations to harmonize a common international age of sexual consent were undercut by ideas of racial difference in puberty, primarily expressed as climatic variation. Chapter 2 explores how adolescence as a concept was consolidated in early twentieth-century US psychology circles and sketches its very slow and uneven diffusion in Indian expert circles. Chapter 3 shows how nationalist reformers refused the idea that puberty arrived early in India and used League of Nations conventions and new understandings of prolonged girlhood to argue for a higher age of sexual consent. The chapter explains why differences emerged between the age of consent for sex within and outside marriage. Chapter 4 returns to the intergovernmental arena to examine another effort to harmonize a common age of consent, this time a UN-led universal age of marriage. Post–World War II conditions allowed for passing a 1962 UN convention on minimum age of marriage, even though Indian delegates resisted it. Chapter 5 examines how the age of marriage was finally raised to 18 years for girls in India in the 1970s. It presents the backdrop of international population control discourses that drove the change and traces the prominent role that India and Indian experts played in demographic writing in the 1950s, 1960s, and 1970s.

With the first section about genealogies of concepts and the second section more on legal disputes, the third section combines both. Chapter 6 traces the rise of the figure of the girl child in 1990s Indian discourses and then in UN discourses and shows the figure's efflorescence in state policies and corporate campaigns in the first and second decades of the twenty-first century. The chapter also describes government initiatives to directly transfer cash to families of girl children to ensure they remain unmarried until they turn 18. Chapter 7 describes a 2006 law banning child marriage as well as contemporary feminist dilemmas about lowering the age of sexual consent.

A key goal of this book is to trace how the figure of the girl is mobilized in instrumental ways. This figure serves as such an emotive and compelling mascot that it is easy for a variety of interests to travel under its sign: those asserting cultural supremacy, or class-based parental protectiveness, or even antiwoman agendas. Each chapter in this book details how ideas and laws that ostensibly focused on protecting adolescent girls were simultaneously aligned with the interests of other institutional forces, such as parental interests, national prestige, and imperial ideologies. For example, chapter 1 explains how scientific understandings about girls' puberty at the beginning of the twentieth century simultaneously embedded racial hierarchies between peoples and nations. Chapter 3 narrates how, when raising the age of marriage in 1929, parents and nationalist concerns came before those of girls themselves. Chapter 4 describes how, in the reconfigured post–World War II geopolitical landscape of the 1950s, girls' interests advanced primarily under the sign of antislavery advocacy. Chapter 5 explains how population control discourses had goals other than the well-being of girls, even if they contributed to raising the legal age of marriage. Chapter 6 describes NGO and corporate interests in the girl as a site of investment. Chapter 7 exposes how presumptions about the vulnerability of the adolescent girl can backfire when too much power is vested in parental hands.

In sum, the book elucidates the various peripheral interests that are served by an ostensible focus on girls. The vulnerability of girls can distract us from paying critical attention to such interests. To be clear, critiquing how girlhood automatically signifies vulnerability is not a denial of actual vulnerability. Adulthood certainly arrives early for too many girls because of a range of coercions that are economic, social, and sexual. But the voices and interests of girls themselves have been frequently ignored across multiple legal arenas. I hope that my exploration of how such sidestepping occurs can generate greater vigilance about how one can take girls more seriously.

1

Tropical Exceptions

Imperial Hierarchies, Climate, and Race

At what age do girls gain the maturity to make sexual choices? Until the twentieth century in many parts of the world, this question was answered using a physiological marker: the onset of menstruation. Menarche was treated as a threshhold marking the possibility of sexual activity both in religious norms and customary practice. The timing of coming-of-age ceremonies and customs, such as the *quinceanera*, *ritushuddhi*, and veiling, often coincided with this physiological change. In many instances, such rituals signaled sexual readiness and, as one attendant consequence, marriageability. While the level of choice that a girl could exercise in her sexual interactions certainly varied across contexts, puberty was generally assumed to mean a girl's sexual maturation.

A different sense of sexual maturity, however, was in evidence in 1921 in Geneva at the first League of Nations Antitrafficking Convention, when representatives of the International Union for the Protection of Girls suggested that the legal age of consent to prostitution be set at 21 years.[1] Only after reaching the age of formal majority, they said, did a girl have the requisite maturity to transact in sexual services. All countries around the world, they proposed, should share this same legal standard.[2] This far-reaching proposal met with immediate resistance. The most forceful objections came from the representative of British India: Stephen Meredyth Edwardes, an Englishman and former police commisioner of Bombay, declared that all "tropical colonies" and "Eastern countries" be exempt from any such common age standard. His reasoning was strikingly physiological: he argued that setting 21 years as the age standard would be in conflict with "established physical facts, it being well known that the climatic conditions of India result in maturity being reached at an earlier age than in Europe."[3] Indian girls and girls in tropical colonies, he suggested, reached puberty before European girls did and hence did not merit such a high age of sexual consent.

Two understandings of sexual maturity were in conflict here: Edwardes's rested on the notion of physical maturity, while antitrafficking advocates articulated a sense of mental maturity. Edwardes linked menarche with the capacity for engaging in sex, including transactional sex, while antitrafficking advocates presumed that such decisions were only possible after going through a longer period of mental maturation. These contrasting understandings of sexual maturity have been featured in other debates over legal age standards for prostitution, marriage, and statutory rape across multiple settings. This chapter focuses on the first sense of maturity—puberty—and explores why climate was presumed to affect it and how this notion shaped political debates.[4] The next chapter focuses on how the second sense of a longer phase of mental maturation, with an extended adolescence ending in adulthood, emerged in the nascent field of psychology. In both contexts, I show how expert knowledges were complicit in affirming imperial narratives about hierarchies among parts of the world.

Even more striking than Edwardes's focus on the physical marker of puberty is the meaning he assigned to early puberty: that it justified lower legal standards. Imperial ideologies deeply shaped this reasoning: the notion that menstruation and sexual maturation occurred earlier in warm climates was popular largely because it was consistent with the broader imperial narrative of the greater sexual proclivity of "tropical" people. Early sexual maturity was coded as a sign of fecundity, equated in prevailing ideologies with moral lassitude.[5] Describing "tropical colonies and Eastern countries" as sites of early puberty affirmed a link between sexual precocity and civilizational inadequacy. In this context of an antitrafficking convention, the attendant assumption was that warm countries, purportedly prone to greater sexual license, would not enforce stringent state control of prostitution.

The resistance that Edwardes offered in the name of India was not unusual for official imperial discourse; as postcolonial theorists have argued, a common "rule of colonial difference" treated colonies as exceptions to liberalism's universal norms.[6] But it is not just colonial officials who asked to treat India as an exception: representatives of independent India at the United Nations in the 1950s also asked to exempt the country when a common age of marriage was discussed, as chapter 4 describes. Refusing interference in social practices, particularly those that affected women and children, was presented as an expression of national sovereignty.[7] India, then, was held up as an exception to universal norms for both imperial and nationalist reasons.

Edwardes's utter confidence that climate caused geographic differences in maturity was a sign of how entrenched theories from race science had become. Climatology, a version of race science explaining differences between people based on physical landscape and temperature, had, over the nineteenth century, advanced theories that the age of puberty varied according to climate. Such theories continued to circulate in the early twentieth century: classic obstetrics textbooks from the 1920s, 1930s, and 1940s in the English-speaking world contain detailed descriptions of geographic variations in the onset of menarche in girls. Race scientists, it appears, were deeply committed to the idea that regions of the world differed in this way, and they even sought to compute the average age of puberty along national territorial lines. In League of Nations conferences and even later in UN conferences, delegates made frequent and unreserved references to climate differences between countries as the reason for differences in their sexual mores. This common use of climate as a shorthand for describing race raises interesting questions: What explains the appeal of climate as a category for expressing difference? And what is the trajectory of climate as an explanatory device in the intellectual history of "race"?

Over the several League of Nations antitrafficking conventions held in the interwar period, conversations slowly tilted away from physiological reasoning toward a moral reasoning when framing differences between countries in sexual age standards. The League of Nations debates and proposals are a useful case when exploring the thorny legal question of how to compare sexual practices around the globe, because they demonstrate how geopolitics can shape the formulation of abstract universal principles. The league ostensibly inaugurated a modality of intergovernmental relations based not on the principle of the absolute power of the imperial powers but on greater acknowledgment of the sovereignty of nations—the very order we have inherited in the twenty-first century. This new enterprise, premised on a liberal gesture toward the equivalence of nations, was, nonetheless, rife with attempts to establish implicit hierarchies among nations. Its proceedings also staged contests among competing imperialist nationalisms, apart from placing colonies in a subordinate role. In the 1920s and 1930s the minimum age for prostitution and marriage in various countries became a criterion for ascertaining their relative moral standing. In such a setting, climate emerged as a common way to index hierarchies in sexual practices. As the league's infrastructure developed across the interwar years into a concerted biopolitical project, seeking to map the age of marriage, consent, and even puberty in the name of ameliorating moral health, this hierarchical vision deepened.

The first section of this chapter describes the efforts of the League of Nations to harmonize the age of sexual consent across countries and how some delegates used climate-based reasoning to resist a common age standard. The frequent mention of climate in these debates prompts my excavation, in the next section, of the genealogy of climate as a category in race science. In the last section of the chapter, I reflect on how, as the League of Nations began to implement antitrafficking projects, it grew more and more focused on altering social practices in the name of morality. The league became increasingly biopolitical in its reach in the late 1920s and 1930s, tracking sexual age standards and more across countries—and geographic differences remained salient. In sum, the chapter traces how, in a context where imperial countries vied for power over each other and influence over other parts of the world, the national age of consent for sex—understood through both physiological and social lenses—became a plank for indexing hierarchies among nations.

The League of Nations Antitrafficking Campaigns

Legal age standards for sexual maturity are challenging enough to devise at the state or national level, but they are especially contentious at the intergovernmental level. In the twentieth century, efforts at setting common standards have often been dogged by arrogance on the part of those proposing standards and by misgivings on the part of those most affected.[8] The League of Nations case offers an example of an effort at universalizing age standards in a setting where tacit imperial hierarchies shaped relations among nations. In this context, I show both those who proposed and those who resisted universalizing efforts were complicit in advancing imperial ambitions.

The League of Nations Antitrafficking Conventions held in the 1920s were the first formal global intergovernmental context where a common sexual age standard was devised. Although earlier European conferences about white slavery (as European prostitution was called at the time) had specified a common age of consent, they did not bear the imprimatur of the league's formal interstate agreements nor its professed geographic reach; these agreements had been promoted by a loose alliance of voluntary organizations and European government officials who had instituted a bureau run by voluntary organizations.[9] The league took over the infrastructure of such agreements and gave it a universalist heft.

The institutional history of the League of Nations explains why it took up antitrafficking as a signature cause. The league was founded in the wake of World War I with the goal of preserving collective security, territorial integrity, and cooperation among nations of the world. It was prolific in setting up organizations that addressed important social questions of the time, such as refugee rehabilitation, labor rights, and public health, because such ventures in social terrains vastly enhanced the legitimacy of this new intergovernmental body. Its primary goal was to prevent a second world war, but through such organizations, it aimed to herald a new era of cooperation among nations.[10]

The purported aims of the league and its political structure were deeply at odds, though. While the league set out to offer a new model for international cooperation, it also was invested in preserving the power of imperial members. Its bipartite structure expressed the power of those victorious in the war: the permanent members of its executive body, the council, were the victorious Allied countries. As was common to many efforts at forming global institutions, "jockeying by competing colonial authorities" was a feature of its formation and functioning.[11] Yet it also presented a stage for the entry of new international actors, and India was one such actor. India held the unique position of being admitted to the league even though it was a British colony, because of its important contributions of soldiers to Allied armies, helping to end World War I; Britain, however, selected its representatives.[12] By the early 1930s the league's membership had reached an unprecedented sixty-three countries, including representatives from Latin America and eastern Asia, such as China, Siam, and Japan, which gave the league's ambitions and projects more heft. The story of its effort to coordinate a common age of consent illustrates the hazards of contexts in which coordination is attempted within deeply uneven power relations.

The first step the League of Nations took was to oversee the "supervision of the execution" of the 1904 and 1910 Suppression of White Slave Traffic protocols, as stated in article 23c of the Covenant of the League of Nations. It did so at the urging of several private organizations, particularly those of British origin, such as the Jewish Association for the Protection of Girls and Women, the feminist abolitionist Association for Moral and Social Hygiene, and the International Abolitionist Federation.[13] The league set up the Committee on Traffic in Women and Children, which focused on policies for dealing with cross-border transportation for the purposes of prostitution, discouraging tolerated brothels, and coordinating laws pertaining to the age of consent for prostitution. Through the 1920s this committee met in a series of international conferences and called on member countries to respond to regular questionnaires, submit annual reports, send delegates to conferences, and, ultimately, pursue the legislative changes that would harmonize laws across countries.[14]

When the first League of Nations convention on trafficking met in six public sessions in Geneva in the summer of 1921, it was attended by delegates of thirty-four states and fourteen organizations. The conference featured a standoff between those who sought to abolish prostitution and those who sought to preserve its licensed forms. The former included representatives of the International Association for Social and Moral Hygiene and the Dutch delegate; and among the latter were France, Greece, Italy, Rumania, and Panama.[15] The topic that galvanized the debate between these camps was a proposal to establish a common, and higher, age of consent for prostitution. Antitrafficking activists sought to raise the age of sexual consent for girls in an effort to establish an age below which entering prostitution would be illegal. Their goal was to prosecute as many traffickers as possible, and raising the age of consent allowed them to bring forward a larger number of cases.[16] Their ultimate abolitionist vision was to eliminate the possibility of any kind of consent to prostitution; this was realized in 1932 when the League of Nations Traffic in Women and Children Committee voted to eliminate the age limit.[17] In 1921 the Swiss voluntary organization International Union for the Protection of Girls made the formal recommendation to the league to raise the age standard to 21 years.[18] The organization's proposal implying that a woman below 21 was incapable of maturely consenting to prostitution gave rise to vexed debates among representatives about how age standards for sexual maturity differed across nations.

The most striking element in this debate was Edwardes's suggestion to exempt "Eastern countries" and "tropical colonies" from the age standards of the convention. Edwardes had served as both police commissioner and municipal commissioner of Bombay and demonstrated an abiding interest in surveying the sex trade in the city—he devoted sections of two of his books on Bombay to detailing the forms of prostitution in the city.[19] As police commissioner, he had overseen European brothels in Bombay and the registration of brothel workers and had little sympathy for abolitionist ideas.[20] Edwardes presented three connected reasons to not raise the age of consent in India to 21 years: It would offend the general body of conservative Indian opinion; it would be an "impolitic interference" by the state with religious and social customs of certain communities of India; and it would be in conflict with climate-based age standards for maturity in India.[21] The first two points—signaling the alignment between British ruling officials and Indian upper-caste elites—were actually established British imperial policy.[22] Edwardes was most vocal about the third point, arguing that "Eastern countries" in general be exempted from the age standards of the convention "owing to (their) climatic conditions and social and religious customs."[23] His formulation was accepted by other countries at the convention, such as Japan, Siam, and, particularly, France, which also decided to make an exception for "its tropical colonies." As a result, the League of Nations refrained from setting 21 years as the single age standard for every member, allowing for individual countries, such as India and Siam, to exempt themselves at the time of signing the convention.

This debate continued to haunt the deliberations of the trafficking committee throughout the 1920s and early 1930s. Even after the Advisory Committee on Traffic in Women and Children was divided into two separate committees in 1925—the Committee on Traffic in Women and Children and the Child Welfare Committee—the age of consent remained an issue discussed at their joint meetings. Edwardes's reference to climate as a key explanation for differences in the age of consent across countries was picked up consistently at these successive conferences on the issue. At the 1926 conference of the Advisory Committee for the Protection of the Welfare of Children and Young People, when the representative of the social section of the league secretariat opened the meeting with a report on an inquiry into the legal age of marriage and age of consent across countries, the first response from the floor was the emphatic declaration by the Polish delegate that the age of marriage varied according to "local custom and climate" and that countries that were "widely separated by climate and custom" could not be compared.[24] When the league secretary responded that the legal age of marriage was much lower in certain cold countries than had been supposed and, conversely, was higher in certain warm countries, the French delegate also declared that the legal age of marriage depended on "climate, habits and customs which were thousands of years old."[25]

At the 1927 joint meeting of the committees on traffic and child welfare, the Belgian delegate reasserted the view that the age of marriage "had to be determined by considerations of local interest, i.e., principally by climatic and physiological conditions."[26] The French delegate again reiterated his qualification that "climatic and physiological differences need[ed] consideration" when fixing a high age of consent.[27] The 1928 Joint Meeting of the Committees on Traffic and Child Welfare opened with the declaration that countries could determine the age of marriage "as seemed best to them, in accordance with the prevailing climate or moral conditions."[28] In 1930 the Italian delegate echoed the same view, noting that it was "unjust to fix an international age for minors, since social and climatic conditions tended to alter this age in different countries."[29] In each of these cases, the delegates yoked ideas of climate and custom together, as if to suggest that climate affected custom. It was insufficient to simply claim that countries differed in their sexual practices; "climate" lent a certitude to these justifications. These repeated invocations of climate as an explanation for variation in norms successfully thwarted other delegates' attempts to decree a universal age of consent for sexual relations.

The successful maneuvering by French, Belgian, Italian, and Polish diplomats raises questions about the intellectual milieu of the time: How did climate come to assume so much explanatory plausibility in an international legal setting in the 1920s?[30] What explains the remarkable confidence and receptivity to such an explanation? To what degree were the diplomats echoing, or overlooking, the scientific consensus of their time? In addressing these questions, it is useful to keep in mind Ann Stoler's observation that racial distinctions do not depend on the scientific credibility of understandings of race and can, indeed, thrive in the absence of science's authorization and certitudes.[31] Nonetheless, the authority with which the diplomats equated climate with sexual customs suggests that forms of climatological race science circulated in the realm of common sense. Although in many quarters of medicine and anthropology, climate had receded in importance as a category explaining racial differences, it continued to carry much weight in this setting.[32] The next section traces the mercurial status of climate in scientific discussions of racial difference. In trying to understand how climatological ideas bore so much plausibility in an international legal setting in the 1920s, I comment on the relationship between science and imperial expediency.

Climate, Race, and Science in Historical Perspective

The concept of the "natural" has served as a placeholder for describing human variation of various kinds. In many cases, framing variations as natural has implied their exemption from careful investigation. This is certainly true of variations in the age of puberty around the world. The vocabulary and conceptual constellations used to explain differences in puberty have shifted in the course of recent history. This section focuses on how race science naturalized differences in puberty via the category of climate.

Seventeenth- and eighteenth-century French naturalists and political theorists widely used climate as an explanation for human variation. In a period of imperial expansion and increasing European contact with climatically diverse regions, it is not surprising that territorial and human characteristics fused to form a singular axis for categorizing difference. David Arnold has argued that the very conceptual space of "the tropics" emerged as a consequence of European voyages of discovery in the fifteenth and sixteenth centuries and was consolidated through processes of "observation, mapping and classification" in the early nineteenth century.[33] He attributes this rise of scientific tropicalism to the work of European naturalists in this period who produced a common language of abundance to describe the diverse vegetation, fauna, and landscapes they encountered in the Caribbean, Southeast Asia, West Africa, and Northern Australia. Concurrently, a host of physiological, moral, and intellectual traits were crystallized and yoked to understandings of temperature zones and vegetation. Natural fecundity among flora and fauna in warm climates was equated with moral excess—that "people were incapable of appreciating the virtues of restraint and the curbing of sexual appetite."[34]

Eighteenth-century scientific tropicalists synthesized old and new ideas in formulating their understandings. They drew on the Greek physician Hippocrates's ideas about how climate determined temperament, and at the same time, they transposed onto human realms the growing knowledge base of naturalists who studied plant susceptibility to climate. For instance, Louis Leclerc, Comte de Buffon, the curator of the Jardin du Roi—the principal botanical garden of France—in the 1740s, cited Hippocrates in positing that every organism belonged in its proper climate; Leclerc was also one of the earliest naturalists to propound a theory of race, arguing in 1749 that climate was the "chief cause" of racial difference.[35] Montesquieu, Buffon's contemporary, also emphasized climate's effect on national character in his *Spirit of the Laws* (1748), drawing a direct link between climate and morals and also citing Hippocrates.[36] Both Buffon and Montesquieu also explicitly focused on the effects of warm weather on sexual activity, arguing that it led to sexual profligacy. When it came to the specific study of human sexual maturation, Swiss physiologist Albrecht von Haller held that climate affected the age at which humans attained puberty. In his discussion of menstruation in the classic *First Lines of Physiology*, he argued that the onset and the quantity of menstrual flow differed from country to country.[37] He expounded what came to be termed the latitude theory—that the further away from the equator, the higher the age of menarche.

Not all those who were interested in the topic agreed with this theory, though. Given the reductionism of the idea that warm climates led to earlier puberty, there were examples that did not fit. In the 1830s an Edinburgh-based medical scholar named John Roberton surveyed the average age of menarche in varied climatic zones in order to disprove the notion that warm climate quickened puberty. He based his argument on a number of sources, such as missionaries and doctors located in British colonies, such as India, Jamaica,

Antigua, Barbados, Labrador, and the protectorate of Corfu. A key plank of his argument was that the mean age of menarche was lower in India than in the West Indies, despite being, on average, colder than the West Indies.[38]

Despite such contestation, the link between climate and puberty grew more entrenched in the mid-nineteenth century, especially with anthropology's many somatometric projects focused on human variation.[39] English gynecological physician Edward Tilt's 1862 classic, *On Uterine and Ovarian Inflammation*, presents the dramatic culmination of scholarship on the relationship between climate and menstruation: Tilt produced a meta-analysis of various surveys of menstruation across world regions. He presented a table listing his results alongside those of other scholars, giving a snapshot of "the periods of first menstruation of 12,321 women in hot, temperate, and cold climates."[40] He attributed explanatory primacy to climate in producing racial difference, using as key evidence the differences in average age of menstruation across the different climates.

With Charles Darwin's elaboration in the 1860s of the concept of natural selection and hereditary adaptation, the relevance of climate to taxonomies of human difference shifted in crucial ways. Darwin's vocabulary of hereditary determinism produced a more rigid understanding of species distinctions. Whereas climatologists asserted that temperatures produced direct effects on temperament within one or a few generations, the Darwinian view was that racial traits were much more resilient to change and that among humans, natural selection could only be observed over millennia. The idea of hereditary rather than individual adaptation lengthened the time span over which human variation and, implicitly, racial distinctions emerged; this time span was considerably longer than what the climatic determinists had posited. Although Darwin did make references to climate and civilizational differences in his *Descent of Man*, climate receded from being seen as the primary cause of racial differentiation and subsequently served as one among several environmental features that affected the hereditary adaptation of humans. This shift in the explanatory apparatus of race coincided with the changing political and social environment of the North Atlantic world—intercontinental human movement and relocation were intense in the latter half of the nineteenth century because of colonial settlements, pogroms, famines, and steamship transportation. The notion that climate could directly alter, and degenerate, European character figured as a potential risk of settler colonialism, migration, and imperial expansion. The idea of hereditary determinism in place of climatic determinism insulated the construct of race from the possibility of immediate mutations caused by climate.

Yet despite the Darwinian shift away from climatological effects on individual humans, climate retained its potency in some quarters. It was particularly influential in French circles where Jean-Baptiste Lamarck's emphasis on environment was respected.[41] French colonizers' practical-advice guidebooks and how-to manuals continued to stress the role climate played in causing disease and degeneration in the tropics.[42] Another key setting in which the climate remained a central category of explanation was human geography. As a science of human-environment relations, geography was foundationally committed to the principle that environmental factors altered human experiences. In the first two decades of the twentieth century, leading tracts in the field, such as Ellsworth Huntington's *Civilization and Climate* (1915) and Ellen Semple's *Influences of Geographic Environment* (1911), posited that environment altered human traits.

Climate as a category also enjoyed a special influence in twentieth-century sexology. Iwan Bloch, often termed the father of sexology, put forth a direct link between climate and sexual practices, based on investigations into variations in sexual practices across regions. He reasserted the mid-nineteenth-century view that warm climates quickened sexual development and caused sexual profligacy: "Sensuality, polygamy, extravagant deviation, [all] correspond to the earliness of puberty.... [T]here can be no doubt that in the hotter regions of the earth, the normal sex impulse and the abnormal expression of it appear earlier and more intensely as well as more extensively than in the colder regions."[43] Writing as a medical professional, Bloch lent respectablity to the idea of entrenched and naturalizable differences among sexual practices in different regions of the world.

Prominent manuals of obstetrics and gynecology in the early twentieth century also circulated the notion that warm climates hastened puberty. H. S. Crossen and R. J. Crossen's *Diseases of Women* (1907), which was republished in seven editions until 1930, presented "as a general rule" that "the colder the climate the later the first menstruation."[44] It acknowledged research showing that "in some of the northerly tribes menstruation appears as early as in the tropics," but the authors broadly maintained that "the age at which the first menstruation appears varies in different races and under different environments" and that climate was the central influential factor.[45] In the United States, obstetrician John Whitridge Williams's canonical textbook (1903) declares that the "age at which menses are established varies in different countries, being earlier in warm and later in cold climates. In the temperate zone the first menstruation does not usually occur before the fourteenth or fifteenth year."[46] Similarly, Howard Kelly's *Medical Gynecology* (1908) also states that "it is well-known... that there is a wide difference between countries as to the age of first menstruation. For example, it occurs at the age of eighteen in the girls of Lapland and at eight to ten in the aborigines of Australia and in the natives of Southern Prussia, Egypt, Servia, and Sierra Leone."[47] Kelly cites "Age of First Menstruation on the North American Continent," George Engelmann's 1901 piece in the *Transactions of the American Gynecological Society*. Echoing the older latitude theory of von Haller, Engelmann divides the world into three climatic zones—the tropics, temperate zone, and cold climate—and correlates an increase in the average age of first menstruation with colder climate.[48] The authoritative tenor of such textbooks rendered global hierarchies in a language that was ostensibly neutral and reliable.

It is clear from these examples that climatological accounts were a prominent, if not dominant, current of race science that carried weight in obstetrics and gynecology circles in the first decades of the twentieth century and, therefore, influenced thinking about the age of puberty. It is also clear that there were many contradictions within the discourse: some scholars, such as Roberton, found evidence that refuted climatological certitudes; Darwin's ideas also undermined the influence that climate purportedly played. It was only in the late 1950s that arguments about climate and menarche came under serious critical interrogation, though. Climate was dethroned as an explanatory factor for the age of puberty in the post–World War II context, with the rise of public health research that emphasized the role of nutrition: better nutrition led to earlier puberty, it argued.[49]

Many researchers in newly independent India developed such new lines of thinking about the age of puberty. Perhaps because of the long association of early puberty with sexual precocity and civilizational inadequacy, Indian medical and demographic researchers sought to refute the link between climate and age of menstruation. For example, survey-based studies by K. A. Shah and by H. Peters and S. M. Shrikhande explicitly countered claims that the age of menarche varied between countries. They marshaled data demonstrating that the average age of menarche in various Indian regions approached that commonly assumed to be the average in Europe: 13 and 14 years.[50] Such research on the age of menarche, part of the incipient current of population and fertility research in the 1950s described ahead in chapter 5, was strongly motivated to refute racialized assumptions about early puberty in India.

In current scholarship, climate rarely appears as a variable explaining the onset of puberty. Work in nutritional studies proposes that the most important factor affecting the age of puberty is the quantity and quality of fatty foods consumed; indeed, in many warm countries, poor nutrition delays puberty.[51]

Still other research points to the influence of psychological stressors and endocrine disorders.[52] New research rejects the notion that bodily changes during puberty are only an endogenous process; it places the body in relation to its environment and also cultural expectations about what changes are normal.[53] A complex set of emergent factors, such as nutrition, psychological and endocrine stressors, and cultural expectations do contribute to variations across groups and individuals. However, they do not map onto the large geographic units that climate differences describe. In effect, contemporary research underscores the point that nations are not adequate units along which to measure variation in the onset of puberty, since nations encompass a range of social and economic groupings. From the vantage point of contemporary puberty science, treating climate or nation as a variable is thoroughly a relic of nineteenth- and twentieth-century race science.

The League's Imperial Biopolitics

When Edwardes and other delegates casually referenced climate in League of Nations debates, they were thus implicitly citing convictions that had been nurtured by race science over the preceding century. Even though climate was invoked in the initial meetings to obstruct efforts at setting down a universal age of consent, in successive meetings of the antitrafficking convention in the late 1920s, even those advocating common age standards appeared to accept the notion of geographic variation along national lines. Antitrafficking advocates sought to alter practices of states that either tolerated or licensed prostitution but could not do so without earning the cooperation of representatives of those states. To avoid the charge that their own standards were Anglocentric—a very real possibility given that many voluntary organizations carrying out antitrafficking were based in Britain—they conceded that national variation was important and sought to find ways to accommodate it, and in doing so also reified such differences.

The best example of this approach is that of Eleanor Rathbone, a leading voice of women's social reform and pacifism in the interwar years in Britain.[54] Rathbone had an outsized influence in League of Nations debates on trafficking in the mid-1920s; from the minutes of meetings, it is clear she, as "delegate of International Women's Organizations," spoke with authority alongside national delegates, offering ambitious proposals and drafting language for the text of resolutions.[55] Like many other antitrafficking advocates at the conferences, she carried out work under the banner of moral hygiene, the nineteenth-century movement to abolish prostitution and control venereal disease. Her goal was to shift the conversation away from thinking of variation in age-of-consent standards as based on inevitable natural differences, to imagining top-down interventions that "set high standards and produced a great moral effect."[56] Rathbone, however, did so without directly disputing the idea that differences in the age of consent were attributable to climatic differences. She, instead, stressed the social conditions, perhaps because those were ameliorable. The low legal age of marriage in Britain of 12 years—despite the country's cool climate—was, for example, an obvious anomaly in the climatological narrative. Rathbone explained it away by declaring that whereas the low age of marriage in Britain was not "a really serious evil," in India it needed raising because of the "deplorable evils" it produced.[57] This position was commonly taken by other British representatives, such as the delegate in 1926, Mr. Maxwell, who also defensively insisted that when it came to the British legal marriage age, "this age bore no relation to the facts."[58]

Given the vast and growing evidence of differences among countries in age standards, at the 1928 joint meeting, Rathbone conceded the possibility of not achieving a single common age standard and, instead, accepted differentiation across countries. But she did so by promoting a climatological notion of puberty rooted in geographic difference: she argued that an effective shared minimum age of marriage and consent across nations "should not be less than the age of puberty" and proposed that it should be at least "two years later than the average age of puberty in [each] country."[59] Devising such a standard presumed that the average age of puberty varied along national lines and that it could be measured. Her proposal certainly caused some discomfort: the delegate representing the British empire, Miss Wall, urged the group to not "enter physiological aspects of the question which could hardly become rules of law."[60] A medical expert, Professor Leon Bernard, agreed with Miss Wall and also expressed reservations about the possibility of an average age of puberty being measurable.[61]

Rathbone's fervent tactics were disputed by some delegates, but her idea that differences in the "age of puberty" existed across countries was quite consistent with the demographic imagination of the time and with the league's functionaries. Even before its first full year was completed, the committee had sent out a questionnaire to all member countries asking them to supply information about age standards. The committee's information collection reflected an awe about the promise of statistics. Rathbone proposed to arrive at a minimum age of marriage and consent through a process of calculation: she suggested that states could take on the goal of recording the age at which puberty occurred across their respective populations and then compute an average that served as a national index upon which a law could be formulated.

Such a proposal presumed a high degree of surveillance of populations; it expected that the sexual maturation of every body could be mapped. It also fused the idea of climatic differences with national boundaries. Effectively, the single parsimonious axis of climate provided an unproblematic grid upon which hierarchies were mapped onto nations, and then social reformist projects could be mounted.

Several facets of the league's approach were consistent with the rising demographic imagination of modern biopolitical states.[62] It conceived of populations across the globe as knowable and governable. Anthony Anghie notes that the League of Nations was unprecedented in its collecting of "massive amounts of information from the peripheries, analysing and processing this information" in an effort to construct "a science by which all societies may be assessed."[63] It was not just state actors who were included in these exercises; the league's reach in the arena of antitrafficking, as with the arenas of child welfare and obscene publications, incorporated actors from women's organizations, public health, and moral-vigilance agencies.[64] Indeed, all the antitrafficking efforts of the League of Nations could be characterized as a vast multinodal biopolitical effort. Even prior to the 1921 conference, the league sent out a questionnaire to all governments about their measures focused on trafficking and received ninety replies. In 1923 its expert committee, Special Body of Experts on Traffic in Women and Children, compiled information from twenty-eight countries, drawing on five thousand informants.[65] For the next decade, member countries, such as India, submitted annual reports that detailed the number of cases of trafficking that police investigated, as well as those encountered by voluntary organizations. In 1929 the League of Nations Assembly directed a more focused enquiry into trafficking in the "East," which required governments from the Near East, Far East, and Middle East (as constituted at that time) to respond to questionnaires enumerating laws, cases of trafficking, and broad patterns of recruitment of prostitutes. In 1934 the league's Advisory Committee on Social Questions undertook an inquiry into the rehabilitation of prostitutes, which involved asking "fifteen governments and six voluntary associations" to "fill in answers for 50 or more prostitutes . . . [who were] adult women and nationals of that country."[66] The advisory committee received 2,659 replies from women in twenty countries, and many of the respondents' narratives formed the text of the 1938 report.[67]

The committee's ambitious information collection left some delegates skeptical. Five years in, at a 1926 meeting, the delegate from Japan asked a cynical question: "Was it desirable to continue to collect statistics and proceed further in this matter? . . . It would be for the Governments and the Parliaments, in the light of the information collected regarding foreign laws, and with due respect to their own customs, to take such decisions as may be required."[68] The French delegate echoed him, reminding the committee of the relevance of "customs, climate, physical conditions, etc." in shaping laws.[69] Rathbone, however, shot down such hesitation, declaring that "it was of highest importance that the Committee should obtain full information on this question," particularly in helping girls understand the risks and options of traveling across national borders.[70]

Helping individual girls make travel decisions was not, however, the express purpose of such surveillance exercises; the exercises were primarily justified as information sharing that would lead to policy changes across countries. Greater knowledge about the bodily health and practices of populations was intended to generate legal changes, and in the Scandinavian case, it clearly did: the Danish delegate reported that the legal age of marriage in Denmark, Norway, and Sweden had been raised from 16 to 18 because an inquiry had "established . . . that . . . women in those countries did not reach maturity until 17 years of age."[71] National-level information was not expected to induce national policy changes in purely internal ways; the spirit of the league's effort was to cause change through the collective sharing of information—it was the comparing among countries that was expected to induce shame in those countries where the age of consent was deemed too low. For instance, in 1923 the expert committee tabulated the changes in laws carried out by a list of countries and then circulated it among all member countries, as if to suggest models to follow. It was an effective approach: as a consequence of such information sharing, Italy, France, Estonia, and Britain initiated measures to raise the age of consent and marriage.[72] Colonies such as India also felt the power of such potential shaming. As explained in chapter 3, some nationalist Indian legislators were keen to prove that their country's age standards were up to an international mark. The League of Nations thus initiated the formation of a slow consensus around the principle of raising the age of consent.

In many of these questionnaires, prostitutes were asked to specify the age at which they began this line of work. Although the committee was initially motivated to collect information in order to establish a common age standard, by the late 1920s the information collected began to be used to justify another, more ambitious abolitionist goal: to eliminate the age standard altogether. The reports that the committee compiled found that to avoid prosecution, traffickers were making false birth certificates to prove that women were not underage. In 1930 the British delegate proposed eliminating the age limit of 21 years, explaining that "girls over twenty-one years deserved as much protection as girls under that age."[73] Effectively, then, the league would be prohibiting prostitution in any form. Again, India, along with Siam, asked to make an exception for its national circumstance. These two countries said they would eliminate the age limit for "foreign traffic," but for "purely national traffic," they would allow prostitution over the age limit. However, since they had asked to be exempted from the 1921 convention, they were considered "outside the general regulation of the present Conventions."[74]

This ensuing 1932 amendment underscores how decisively the league oriented its actions toward abolitionist goals in the 1930s. The Traffic in Women and Children Committee continued to produce annual summary reports based on information received from various governments for every year through the 1930s and World War II until 1946, when the committee was subsumed under the United Nations mission. Even in 1938, as war loomed, the committee published a lengthy report on the rehabilitation of prostitutes, drawing on government and nongovernmental organization data.[75] The committee's persistence attests, in retrospect, to the reach of a moral-hygiene movement that successfully recruited state machinery to study and enforce an abolitionist vision. References to climate differences continued to appear as the grounds for objections to universal standards, but it was clear from the measures taken by the league that obstructions based on a physiological reasoning did not hold the same force they did in the early 1920s.

This slow but top-down process of norm setting was especially effective because the League of Nations was an environment in which imperial powers were *expected* to speak in a tutelary voice.[76] The league represented an attempt at a new internationalist world order: in its formulation of a mandate system, for instance, we see a retreat from forms of overt colonial domination toward a relationship focused on protective trusteeship.[77] This stewardship of many by a few great powers was premised on a naturalization of the latter's authority. This naturalization of authority functioned in two ways in liberal internationalist culture: first, imperial powers were portrayed as natural leaders; and second, colonies were presented as also having the right to *not* be dominated. In this context, a tutelary, rather than brute, form of imperial authority became the legitimate means for expressing power. In this tutelary relationship, colonies and former colonies had to *earn* this newly bestowed sovereignty through a display of civilizational adequacy. Enlightened laws on sexual consent were an index of this adequacy. At a time when colonies were calling for greater sovereignty through new kinds of relationships to imperial centers, such as mandates and protectorates, moral-hygiene campaigns focused on the status of women reasserted the moral authority of imperial centers and also became sources of anxiety for colonies. This dynamic was again repeated in the newly formed United Nations, as chapter 4 explores.

* * *

This chapter opened with two understandings of sexual maturity. Moral-hygiene advocates played a welcome role in delinking understandings of sexual maturity from purely physiological moorings. Although their efforts were salutary in moving the League of Nations antitrafficking efforts further away from race science–based narratives, theirs was nonetheless a vision based on British moral supremacy in the world. Their interest in age standards was not motivated principally by a desire to arrive at a better understanding of girls' capacity for exerting sexual autonomy; instead, their worldview could not countenance the possibility of girls or women consenting to prostitution. In order to criminalize all commercial sex, they pushed the League of Nations to ultimately abandon any kind of age standard.

A considerable body of scholarship on gender, empire, and nationalism demonstrates that matters related to sexuality have played a crucial role in articulating hierarchies of power.[78] This chapter shows how age standards for sexual maturity became instrumental in the imperial internationalist order the League of Nations enacted. In particular, it shows how such hierarchies were coded in physiological terms as effects of climate. The use of climate drew on a dubious mode of articulating human variation in the race sciences. As this exploration of the history of climate in race science demonstrates, the importance of climate rose and fell at various points. Even if dominant understandings of race in the 1920s did not center upon climate, variations in temperature were treated in circles such as obstetrics and gynecology as an acceptable explanation for the timing of menarche. This recounting of this history illustrates the uneven commerce between natural science, practitioner knowledge, and folk conceptions. The reference to climate at the League of Nations, although anachronistic, was useful because it offered an uncomplicated means to resist legal intervention. Because of how climate was moored in the realm of the irrefutable natural, it rendered differences among nations more explicable. An entire column of race science built on a climatological foundation was mobilized to refuse the idea of common age standards. Even though obstructions based on climate did not eventually hinder the functioning of the league, and it grew more ambitious in its reach, a modality of thinking about colonies as exceptions based on inherent flaws continued.

2

Adolescence as a Traveling Concept

"Girls over twenty-one deserv[e] as much protection as girls under twenty-one." This surprising remark, made by the British delegate at a 1930 League of Nations conference mentioned in the last chapter, uses the term "girl" quite loosely.[1] In describing those older than 21 as "girls," the delegate sought to depict them as vulnerable figures who needed the continuing cover of antitrafficking measures. His unusual phrasing "girls over twenty-one," though, signals an important cultural shift that was under way: that of seeing girlhood as lasting well beyond puberty. It was possible to refer to someone over 21 as a girl precisely because the age coordinates of girlhood were being reconfigured. A broad intellectual consensus was forming in the field of Anglo-American psychology in the 1910s, 1920s, and 1930s that menarche did not signal the end of girlhood. This delinking, which had deep implications for how girlhood was experienced in many parts of the world, was based on the idea that physiological maturity did not automatically produce intellectual and emotional maturity. This chapter focuses on how the distinction between these two kinds of maturity emerged and traveled as an idea, with specific attention to the United States and India.

The intellectual scaffolding for delinking girls' physiological and psychological maturity was provided by a concept that grew prominent among European and American psychologists in the 1910s and 1920s: adolescence, a life-cycle stage between menarche and adulthood. Adolescence as a concept expanded the reach of childhood, carving out a space during which a person prepared for the advent of adulthood while legally remaining a child. Although girls were not the primary focus of early writing on adolescence, they, like boys, were treated as children rather than adults well into their late teens, in this vision. Psychologists' new definitions of adolescence treated this phase as a period of vulnerability in which children were in continuing need of shelter and protection, thereby providing scientific legitimacy to a variety of efforts to raise age standards for sexual maturity.

The meanings of adolescence are, in our time, taken for granted. The long span of adolescence and deferral of adulthood are normative features of urban middle- and upper-class life around the globe. Most Indian languages, though, have no word for "adolescent," or, for that matter, "teenager." In English, the terms "adolescence," "teenager," and "youth" all refer to the phase between childhood and adulthood, each with slightly different connotations. As Catherine Driscoll describes these nuances, "adolescence" implies a process of development and maturation that is both physical and emotional; the term "teenager" refers to a phase marked by specific age coordinates, but it does not connote eventual maturation.[2] "Youth," the most abstract term of the three, is frequently used to refer to a class of people, and it extends to adults. In Sanskrit-based languages, there are terms for youth (*kumar/kumarika*) and a male young man (*yuva*), but none that specifically connote the years associated with puberty, and no fixed age coordinates (such as 12 to 18 years) anchor the terms that do exist. The closest word in use for a teenage girl in Sanskrit-based languages is *kanya*, which translates as "virgin" and usually connotes nubility, given the powerful role of marriage in defining sexual conventions and statuses.

This chapter shows how historically recent the idea of the adolescent girl actually is in India, by tracing its initial circulation in expert circles and its links to US psychology. The questions motivating my exploration are: How did adolescence first come to be defined as a life-cycle stage? When did it take root in Indian academic settings? My broad interest is in tracking how pre- and early reproductive years shifted from being conceived as a peak period in one's life—where beauty and romantic possibility are at their height—to a closely supervised life-cycle phase.

The next section opens by sketching the genealogy of the idea of adolescence in US psychology, describing how adolescence came to be articulated as a stage preceding adulthood and was consolidated in scholarly settings. Next, the chapter tracks how this idea traveled to India, noting links between expert circles in India and the United States in the mid-twentieth century. These links, I argue, took time to take root and were sometimes resisted. They were only consolidated with social changes, such as the rise in the legal age of marriage and compulsory schooling. The chapter closes with a visual speculation about how the adolescent girl became a recognizable identity in India, presenting a series of cover images from a popular women's magazine that mark a trajectory across the middle of the twentieth century.

US Psychology: Adolescence as a Threshold Phase

Although the term "adolescence"—from the Latin word for young man, *adolescens*—has been in used in English since the Middle Ages, its specific connotation as a distinct life phase emerged only at the beginning of the twentieth century.[3] The most forceful articulation of adolescence as a distinct phase between childhood and adulthood appeared in US psychology in the work of G. Stanley Hall, founder of the *American Journal of Psychology* and the first president of the American Psychological Association. Late nineteenth-century public health reformers and educators in the United States had begun framing puberty as a life stage requiring shelter and also called for compulsory schooling during this phase.[4] Hall's 1904 compendium *Adolescence* drew on such ideas and systematically formulated them across two volumes. He described adolescence as a phase that spread out over specific years, encompassing menarche and breast development for girls and facial hair and the breaking of voice for boys.[5] Others before him had studied phases of physiological development, but Hall was the first to collate these phases with emotional development and the first to vest adolescence with specific character traits that he believed existed regardless of class. In this respect, historian Joseph Kett argues, Hall "invented" adolescence.[6]

Crucially, Hall pronounced that physiological maturity did not signal intellectual and emotional maturity. The social and emotional preparation for adulthood needed more time than the physiological changes took, he argued; this maturity was not acquired synchronously with physiological maturation. Drawing on—and elevating—the insights of the nascent field of psychology, Hall insisted that psychological development was at least as critical as physical development and had its own distinct chronology. Although the end of childhood had historically been marked in many societies with a rite of passage that coincided with a physiological transition (such as menarche for girls or voice breaking for boys), the emotional transition now was spread out over several years from age 12 to age 18.

Hall was able to specify age coordinates for adolescence because of increased consciousness of chronological age and, indeed, of time consciousness by the close of the nineteenth century in the United States.[7] The numerical modes of measuring time inculcated during the 1860s and 1870s through the wider use of clocks and personal pocket watches as well as railway schedules had led to the increased use of numerical age markers for entering and grouping educational experiences.[8] Age grading in US schools became more common from the 1870s onwards.[9] It was in the 1910s that educators consolidated the standard that compulsory high school should extend until age 18, which, as Hall saw it, comprised the outer boundary of adolescence.

Hall's work consolidated significant new directions in thinking about this life stage. He argued that the social and emotional preparation for adulthood required a tremendous amount of time and supervision, especially in societies such as his own. In this respect, he expressed evolutionary thinking in his presumption that "the higher the species, the larger the proportion of life spent attaining maturity."[10] As Crista DeLuzio notes, Hall's was the first effort to express the developmental logic of evolutionary biology in psychological terms.[11] He also described adolescence as a period involving the expression of individuality and rebelliousness, in which the solidification of a person's sense of self was of primary importance. Finally, he expressed great anxiety around how to manage sexual impulses during the teen years. An entire chapter of volume 1 of *Adolescence* is devoted to the "dangers" of sexual development in boys. He gave elaborate justifications for segregated education and physical activity, influenced by Sigmund Freud's notion of sublimation of sexual energy via other activities. The combination of these features is what gave Hall's concept of adolescence a clear heft. His chosen constellation of features imbued this particular life stage with a specific character that psychologists and counselors then viewed as a blueprint for analyzing and assessing the problems of young people.

Historians of girlhood offer a mixed assessment of whether Hall paid adequate attention to girls. Most, such as Leslie Paris and Catherine Driscoll, agree that Hall's analysis was deeply gendered, in that he "feminized" adolescence in his romantic characterization of it as an emotionally turbulent time.[12] Others, such as DeLuzio and Simmons, argue that there is a paradox at the heart of adolescence for girls, since many of Hall's expectations of adolescent behavior—especially rebelliousness—were frowned upon if girls, especially middle-class white girls, expressed them.[13] DeLuzio goes so far as to depict Hall's analysis as "boyology."[14] Hall treated rebelliousness as a developmental requirement to express the full flowering of self. But there is no necessary physiological reason for holding that "storm and stress" and social rebellion *had* to accompany endocrine changes in the teen years. DeLuzio notes that in the seventeenth century, youth was experienced as a "relatively smooth" period in New England Puritan culture compared to Europe in the same period; youthful rebelliousness, she argues, corresponded more generally with social instability.[15] Anthropologists such as Margaret Mead also disputed the cross-cultural validity of the notion of stressful adolescence.[16] As Jeffrey Arnett observes, Hall's ideas about storm and stress have been widely repudiated as a myth by subsequent generations of psychologists, even if some of the physiological changes he tracked are still considered accurate.[17]

To be sure, Hall was aware that his own US context shaped his views on adolescence: he actually drew an analogy with US national character—he viewed the United States as an adolescent country and declared that "no country is as precociously old for its years." He feared that given the pace of social change in the country (via its "conquering nature ... leading the world in applications ... of science"), young people were "leaping rather than growing into maturity."[18] He was not alone in expressing such worries; as education scholar Nancy Lesko observes, much other writing about adolescence in the early twentieth century signaled anxiety about social changes, such as urbanization, immigration, and economic upheaval; she notes that the goal of commentators of that time was to "salvage" a pure stage of unsullied character building.[19]

Hall's work is significant to this project for three reasons: first, because of how it argues for deferring adulthood well beyond puberty; second, because of how it articulates a homology between notions of societal progress and physiological development; and third, because of how Hall's ideas circulated in the Indian context. The first, the justification for a deferral of adulthood, was critical to allowing for a longer period of girlhood before marriage in several contexts around the world. The second point is especially important to understanding the context of intergovernmental debates described in the other chapters in this book. Hall argues that those societies where adolescence was most fully expressed were also highest on a civilizational hierarchy; he states that the length of time spent attaining maturity signaled the evolutionary status of the society. He devotes an entire chapter of volume 2 of *Adolescence* to discussing what he termed "adolescent races," averring that "most savages in most respects are children, or, because of sexual maturity, more properly adolescents of adult size."[20] In this respect, he drew heavily on late nineteenth-century theories of recapitulation that held that individual-level biological development mirrored human evolution at the species level.[21] We can actually see Hall's ideas giving rise to the notion of adolescence as a marker of modernity; they underscored the idea that modern adulthood was so complex that it needed a separate life phase set aside to achieve it. Third, Hall's ideas were cited in prominent manuals and articles and even conferences in India, as shown ahead.

Hall's analysis was certainly androcentric. However, while he did not center girls in his analysis, he did not exclude them from his ambit either. It was not a new idea to measure societies by how they treated women, but Hall inaugurated an important inflection: whether a society provided girls with an adolescence came to be a crucial index of civilizational adequacy. The variation around the world in ages at which girls were granted an adolescence then became the justification for progress-based understandings of hierarchies among countries: those with longer life stages of adolescence were pegged as occupying a higher stage of development. Hall's ideas about adolescence built on the scholarship described in the previous chapter that codified geographic differences in puberty and naturalized them in scientific discourse. Countries with "early puberty" and where the attendant transition to adulthood was also made early were mapped as lower on a civilizational hierarchy. The intellectual infrastructure of race science and, specifically, climatology, which held that puberty arrived early in warm climates, rendered such claims more credible. Hall's ideas about psychological maturation expressed a similar and parallel hierarchy. The next section traces how European and American understandings of adolescence traveled to India and were transmitted and received in medical and psychological settings as an aspiration. The concept of a transitional phase called adolescence emerged, I argue, as a consequence of the circulation of scholarship from US psychology. This concept took root in the middle of the twentieth century as US scholarly hegemony expanded in the context of the Cold War.

Adolescence in Indian Social Science

Although adolescence was articulated as a distinct phase in the United States in the first decades of the twentieth century, its adoption around the world unfolded slowly. Adolescence appeared in other parts of the world through processes of circulation and US cultural hegemony in expert circles. Tracing its power in India is a story of encounter, diffusion, and reconfiguration. The term "adolescence" did not itself get entrenched in Indian psychology until the 1960s and 1970s, and even in recent times, literature in Indian psychology notes that adolescence is not a universally available experience in India and has frequently been absent. For example, Baljit Kaur, Shailaja Menon, and Rajani Konantambigi's 2001 depiction of the consensus view in Indian psychology is that a "clear understanding of what adolescence in India might imply is missing. For the vast majority of Indian children, childhood is truncated and adolescence is seldom experienced."[22] Jaya Sagade's 2006 book on child marriage states that in India, "rarely is there a stage of carefree adolescence in the life of girls."[23] So, any account of the idea of adolescence in India must acknowledge its necessarily partial impact.

No obstetrics and gynecology textbooks in India in the first two decades of the twentieth century specifically mention adolescence, even though they describe puberty and its average age. I. B. Lyon's *Medical Jurisprudence* (1904), perhaps the most widely cited text in Indian legal settings in its time, does not use the term. Kedarnath Das's 1914 *Handbook of Obstetrics* contains a discussion of girls' physiological development but does not include the term "adolescence." Other major foreign-published textbooks of obstetrics circulating in India, such as J. Whitridge Williams's canonical *Obstetrics* (1917) and Henricus Stander's *Textbook of Obstetrics* (reprinted 1945), also do not do so. Most of these early twentieth-century medical textbooks in India highlight the idea that puberty came early in India, and they underline differences between India and elsewhere and between races (a discourse of difference also explored in chapter 1 of this book). Lyon's textbook, in both its 1904 and 1921 editions, includes a table, "Ages of First Menstruation in India," that compares girls of different "races," such as "Europeans," "Eurasians," "Jewesses," "Chinese," and "Natives." The preoccupation was with menstruation as a threshold, but the idea of a longer period of psychological maturation that could be understood as a distinct life stage was not widely accepted.

In the 1920s social reformers began to propose a longer period of maturation. They questioned whether menarche served as an appropriate marker of readiness for marriage for girls. The historic Child Marriage Restraint Act (CMRA), passed in 1929 by the Indian central legislature, marked this shift: it legally extended the age of marriage beyond puberty and raised the age of marriage from 12 years to 14 years and in the process envisioned a longer phase of transition from childhood to adulthood for girls. In the years leading up to the passage of this law, social reformers and women's movement activists compiled scientific and sociological arguments for deferring marriage by increasing the span of girlhood. These arguments were articulated in the *Report of the Age of Consent Committee*, which sought to justify the passing of the CMRA. The report was written by a committee (nine Indian men, one Indian woman, and one British woman) of Indian and British social reformers, activists, educators, and medical practitioners, who toured almost all provinces across the country to interview witnesses and assess firsthand what marriage practices looked like.[24] It contains the results of an expansive survey that included four hundred respondents, doctors' testimonies, and scriptural literature, all making the case for raising the age of marriage. Importantly, it articulated girlhood as a time of "freedom and joy" and proposed raising the age of consent for marriage up to 15 years for girls (it was 12 at the time) and up to 18 for boys.[25] It argues that girls who had undergone puberty may have been physically capable of sexual relations but were "not worldly enough" to recognize the consequences of early sex and the possible outcomes, such as "social degradation" and "the likelihood of the birth of illegitimate offspring."[26] The report further notes that with the decline of joint families, independent running of households required "previous preparation," mothers had to be equipped with knowledge about how to conduct a home, and their bodies needed to be strong enough to bear the strain of childbirth.[27] The committee also presented a new vision of education as a means to occupy young girls' minds and to help them find vocations outside of marriage.[28]

The report's primary argument, framed in medicalized terms, draws on doctors' testimonies that puberty for girls occurred between 12 and 14 in India. It declares unequivocally, though, that a "physically mature body does not necessarily mean an intellectually mature mind" and calls for raising the age of marriage well above the age of puberty. It cites doctors who warned that children born to such young mothers would be weak. The authors pose an arresting question comparing girls with boys: "What man would expect a boy of 14 to do a full day's labor simply because his voice had cracked?"[29]

Apart from affirmation from medical sources, the report also relies on Hindu scriptural authority: "Menstruation is not a sign of bodily maturity.... It is not a sign of fitness for conception; and that the old Ayurvedic physicians realised this, is shown by the fact that Sushrut and Vagbhat categorically state that impregnation should not take place before a girl has attained 16 years, if healthy offspring is desired." The report highlights the variation between Hindu religious texts as a way to puncture the notion of a scriptural consensus supporting child marriage. It notes that the Rig Veda, for instance, represents marriage as taking place between fully developed adults, even though the later Smritis (especially the sage Manu's Smritis) claim that marriage had to occur for girls before puberty. The report uses this variation to underline the lack of clear scriptural support for child marriage.[30]

The authors of the report were also keenly attuned to geographic variation. They reference in detail the differences in age markers around the world. The appendixes, for instance, list the ages of consent in individual US states and juxtapose these ages with the Indian age of consent. In making comparisons, the authors sought to mobilize shame as a tactic to push for raising the Indian legal age of marriage.

The report does not use the actual term "adolescence" even though it clearly called for a distinction between mental and physiological maturity. Although the authors imagined the possibility of adolescent-like experiences for girls—such as a period of freedom from reproductive responsibility despite biological capability and also a period of psychological immaturity—the actual use of the term "adolescence" occurs through a process of diffusion of the influence of US and British psychology. It appears mostly via those in contact with such scholarship in the growing fields of social work, education, and counseling, apart from psychology. Scholars and publications in these fields played a key role in advancing the conceptualization of the period between 12 and 18 years as being an identifiable life phase with a name. Social workers, educators, and counselors focused mostly on sex education during this life phase; they strongly felt that sex was a topic that was not being adequately handled by parents in the face of numerous counterinfluences, such as peers and mass media.

Institutions that supported this goal of advancing sex education during adolescence combined two ideological leanings, abolitionist and eugenic. Abolitionism, as described in the previous chapter, was the name given to the early twentieth-century Anglo-American progressive movement to eradicate prostitution and venereal disease. Its infrastructure was vast and well organized. For instance, noted abolitionist Josephine Butler's efforts resulted in a strong network across British colonies and the United States under the auspices of the British Association for Moral and Social Hygiene. Pamphlets and books produced by US and British associations circulated in India, and members of the National Christian Council in India sent representatives to the British Social Hygiene Council in London and the American Social Hygiene Council in New York and Washington, DC.[31] Eugenics, the commitment to improving the genetic quality of the population, shaped many of these abolitionist institutions—they easily absorbed the antinatalist goals of promoting birth control and preventing early sexual activity in their approach to sex education. These became a key focus in the interwar period, on par with the founding goals of preventing prostitution and trafficking.

Institutions of these two persuasions actively carried out work promoting the idea of adolescence in India. An early example is J. Krishnan's 1929 essay "Sex Education for Children in India," which won a prize for the best essay under the auspices of the Madras branch of the Social Hygiene Council. His essay, which develops a schema for how sex education should be age stratified, mentions adolescence as the phase "between eleven and nineteen" when "development and appreciation for the sex instinct and a questioning attitude" emerge. Adolescence started at eleven rather than later because Indians "attain maturity earlier than in countries of a cooler climate." Krishnan, who mirrors Hall, describes adolescence as a "restless" period characterized by "emotional stir."[32]

CHAPTER 2

One of the first Indian journals in which the term "adolescence" appears regularly is *Marriage Hygiene*, founded by Bombay sexologist A. P. Pillay and published from 1934 to 1948 by Times of India Press. The journal regularly featured articles on birth control, sexuality, and marriage and promoted eugenic viewpoints. Its editorial board consisted of "a number of prominent Indian medical men," and its declared goal was "to secure a place for the science of conjugal hygiene" and to run a "eugenic clinic."[33] Its content reflects the crosscurrents of influence; in the 1930s its US editor was sociologist Norman Himes, and its UK editor was sexologist E. F. Griffith. The views of sexologists Havelock Ellis and Alfred Kinsey are featured in several articles. The *International Journal of Sexology* incorporated *Marriage Hygiene* in 1949, when Pillay was financially unable to sustain the enterprise.[34] The readership of this journal can be discerned from those who wrote for the journal—Indian academics writing in English, the dominant language of psychology research. Among its first articles is "The Age of Marriage," a 1934 contribution by a sociology professor from Bombay University, G. S. Ghurye, which argues for raising the age of marriage for girls as a way to prevent the number of possible children born per marriage "by curtailing the entire period available for reproduction."[35] Between 1934 and 1948, this journal regularly reprinted articles by prominent US psychologists and social scientists (such as economist J. J. Spengler) and Indian doctors and scholars (such as pathologist V. R. Khanolkar, the father of Indian pathology and medical research) who advocated birth control, increasingly presented as an urgent question of the time.

This journal frequently circulated articles explaining the concept and key features of adolescence. Examples include articles by European and US experts, such as Viennese existential psychotherapist Victor Frankl, "Erotic Problems of Modern Youth" (1937), and Lester Kirkendall, "The Sex Problems of Adolescents" (1948). Frankl was at pains to distinguish the sexual life of the adolescent from that of the child. Using psychoanalytic approaches, he describes the sexual development of an adolescent (and implicitly an adolescent boy) as proceeding from an amorphous urge to an impulse to an object-oriented desire. Frankl describes the ideal outcome of adolescence as being the fusion of the erotic (meaning "spiritual" in this case) and sexual desire, and he elaborates forms of sexual distress that adolescents suffer and that education should address.[36] Kirkendall presents the results of his quantitative analysis of "several hundred boys" in their mid- to late-teen years who underwent counseling; he outlines the urgent need for comprehensive sex education and counseling boys about the range of sexual behavior and appropriate vocabulary.[37] Clearly, Anglo-American social scientific knowledge in this period reckoned neither with its androcentrism nor its own cultural specificity; its aspirations for universality led frequently to generalizations about adolescence everywhere that implicitly centered the experience of boys of European descent.[38]

The long shadow that Hall's ideas cast on discussions of adolescence in the 1930s and 1940s is clear. But some Indian experts resisted Hall's ideas. Economist Radhakamal Mukerjee and psychologist N. N. Sen Gupta's article "The Evolution of Sex in the Individual" (1935), for example, presents skepticism about whether "the storm and stress of puberty and adolescence [were] inevitable accompaniments of the maturation of the reproductive system." They argue that the "tension" caused by sexual "awakening" could be "relieved by an adequate scientific knowledge of the normal course of sexual development." This tension could also be resolved by "placing before the adolescent person a new scheme of life or . . . a new status so that a configuration of ideas, feelings and obligations with their appeal as a novelty may successfully counteract the insurgent sex reflexes."[39] Although skeptical of Hall, Mukerjee and Sen Gupta, nevertheless, still centered boys' experiences, like Hall.

Indian social hygiene activists also sometimes resisted Western understandings of adolescence. The proceedings of the 1930 meeting of the National Christian Council show the social hygiene committee cautioning that, after reading "a large number of social hygiene books produced in England and America [they] do not find them wholly suitable for translation." The committee found that "social conditions, especially in the lives of adolescents are so different that books suitable for an American or English girl or boy would not suit an Indian girl or boy."[40]

Despite some initial skepticism from Indian psychologists, Hall's concept of adolescence did take root. A key example of the diffusion of the idea of adolescence in educational settings is a 1945 book, *A Study of the Problem of Adolescence in India*, by Moni John Mukerjea, who was an inspector of schools in the United Provinces in northern India. This 152-page pink booklet, published by T. C. E. Journals and Publications in Lucknow, drew on Mukerjea's education in psychology in England. It was intended as a manual for teachers, social workers, and parents on how to understand adolescent behavior, particularly that of boys. The booklet provides some insight into how ideas about adolescence traveled: it draws on Hall's definitions of life stages as well as Freud's notion of sublimation and John Dewey's notion of moral development. Mukerjea declares that "adolescence is more important than infancy, childhood or boyhood, because along with the growth of the youth, the personality takes the final shape. Personality is the supreme characteristic of all the human beings, the final goal of all the human development and the chief attribute of manhood." Adolescence, for Mukerjea, was a period when reason and the intellect develop but also when emotions intensify. Mukerjea replicated Hall's notion of adolescence as a period when one's individuality struggles to find expression. He exhorts teachers to avoid the "drudgery" of bookish education in these years and to enhance education with sports and a wide range of extracurricular activities, much along the same lines as suggested by Hall. Mukerjea even reiterates Hall's notion of recapitulation: "Direct inhibition of . . . tendencies [such as gang behavior] is harmful, for after all, the development of the child takes the course of the race in general."[41]

Organizations focused on social work, counseling, and education were also important to the dissemination of the idea of adolescence in the 1950s and 1960s. A key example is the Indian Association for Moral and Social Hygiene (AMSH), the offshoot of Josephine Butler's organization (the British Association for Moral and Social Hygiene), which organized educational activities through branches in every major state of the country. Through the 1950s and 1960s, it led missions to rescue women from brothels (its founding goal), but it also convened a series of conferences for parents, educators, and psychologists about sex education and family life. Many of these events featured presenters who explained the meaning of adolescence. Typically, they approached it as a didactic task, identifying key features of this phase and focusing on problems that needed to be addressed. Their definitions referenced broadly the same constellation of features that Hall had outlined: the rise of a sex impulse and the positive outcomes of sublimating the sex impulse. Their greatest anxiety was about how boys expressed sex impulses. The distinct added anxiety for many Indian educators, though, was the influence of Western media on ideas about sex and sexuality, as seen in descriptions of many AMSH meeting proceedings.[42]

The quarterly newsletter *Social Health*, published post-Independence by AMSH, reported frequently on events organized in Indian cities, explaining the features of adolescence. An early example was a 1962 "Seminar on Teen-agers" organized by the association in New Delhi on October 23, with the Union Health Minister Sushila Nayar serving as the chair. The speakers at this event focused on the value of sex education for adolescents and the need to "educate the educators."[43] The report also mentions that one foreign speaker named Dr. James (affiliation unnamed) had conducted research on the problems of adolescent girls and opined that "the most important problem of that age group was denial of the right to self-determination."[44] This event underscores the collaborative support that such initiatives received from the Indian government. Another event about adolescence also included government participants: a series of thirteen talks about adolescence from July 21 to August 27, 1965, held in New Delhi under the auspices of the Family Life Institute of AMSH, attended by nearly two hundred people.[45] One of the first presenters, Dr. A. K. Tyagi, was a senior scientific officer in the Ministry of Defense, and he spoke about the importance of parents understanding the physiological changes that children undergo during puberty. Among the other presenters were representatives and researchers at leading institutions in the fields of social work, education, psychology, and medicine: the Delhi School of Social Work, United States Educational Foundation, Central Bureau of Educational and Vocational Guidance, and the AMSH.[46]

What is striking about this event is the frequency with which adolescence is mentioned as a term and qualified with specific age coordinates. W. Mathur, convener of the conference, explained that the human body went through two intensive development experiences, the first during the prenatal stages and the second during adolescence; the latter took place "among girls from 9–11 to 13–14," and among boys from "13 1/2 to 15–16." He screened a 1955 American educational film, "Your Body during Adolescence," by Harold Diehl and Anita Layton that explained endocrinal changes during puberty. He stressed the importance of providing education that would prevent trauma and anxiety about physiological changes and "cultivate a wholesome attitude and responsible behavior towards the opposite sex." Following soon after, psychologist H. P. Mehta also stressed the fears and anxieties that adolescents suffered; he emphasized the excess of energy that had to be "let out through play or imagination." "At this stage," he noted, adolescents felt "the need to emancipate [themselves] from [their] parents," which parents found "difficult to accept." Theo Mathias, director of the Jesuit Educational Association, which oversaw numerous Catholic schools in the country, also described adolescence as a period of "hypersensitivity." Other psychologists present at this conference authorized the view that the goal of parents and schools at this stage was to assist in developing fullness of personality; sexologist B. K. Rao, for instance, called to equip adolescents "with the knowledge to understand and use sexual potentialities for the enrichment of [their] total personality."[47]

Apart from citing US experts or screening US films, such events often included participants who embodied cross-national intellectual exchanges about adolescence; one event in 1968 featured a speaker who represented US institutions, including the US embassy. It was a two-day course (or seminar) from January 16 to 18, 1968, titled Understanding the Adolescent, held at the Indian Social Institute (ISI) in New Delhi, a Jesuit institution that played a key role in promoting progressive intellectual currents in children's education. The conference was attended by "more than 100 parents, teachers, and youth leaders." It began with a panel, An Important Stage of Development, a discussion of what adolescence was, and went on to discuss the needs and common problems of adolescents, their relationship to school and home, advice on personal care, and sex knowledge. One of the early speakers was the social welfare attaché of the US embassy, Ruby Pernell, professor of social work at University of Minnesota. Other presenters included a professor at the Indian Institute of Public Administration and at the Delhi School of Social Work; the executive director of an Austrian-funded charity called SOS Children's Villages in India, Father Mathias; and a visiting professor at the All India Institute of Medical Sciences. Father Mathias declared that adolescence was a "time for the development of inherent talents." Pernell spoke about the features of adolescence and "dwelt at length on the physiological and psychological changes that take place during this period." She recommended "sublimating" the energy of adolescents through "games, debates, dramatics, etc." and upheld the value of coeducational institutions, where adolescents can mix with members of the opposite sex "in a natural situation." She noted the emotional instability of this phase: "Adolescents would sometimes behave like children and at other times like adults." She also warned parents "against fulfilling their ambitions through their children without caring for their interest, aptitudes and limitations."[48] Erna M. Hoch, a visiting Swiss psychiatrist at the All India Institute of Medical Sciences, suggested that "adolescents longing for sexual experience may have to be provided opportunities for sublimating and diverting their urge."[49] As these examples show, foreign experts were directly involved in transmitting ideas dominant in US psychology, such as those of Freudian sublimation. Such relationships are not surprising, given that seminars and lectures bringing US experts to India were part of the Cold War mission of enhancing US cultural power in India.

These events in 1962, 1965, and 1968 exemplify the general tone of articles published in the journal *Social Health* about adolescence in the 1960s. The articles stress the confusion experienced by adolescents and then present appropriate sex education, parental guidance, and counseling as a response. The fact that so many of the articles narrate adolescence so fully suggests that it was a concept that *required* fleshing out for readers in the fields of education and counseling. A particularly fulsome example is an article by Armaily Desai, a lecturer at the Nirmala Niketan College of Social Work in Bombay, which reads: "It is during adolescence that the youngster experiences pulls from opposite emotions and feelings, leading . . . to confused children and parents. He is utterly idealistic, loyal, almost puritanical as well as repudiate[s] and rebels against social norms. Erik Erikson, a well-known psychoanalyst, has very truly said that during this period there is a search for identity."[50] The citational practices of such articles indicate how currents in US psychology helped institutionalize sex education counseling and social work in India and, in the process, solidify ideas about adolescence.

The diffusion of the idea of adolescence—a life stage that implies psychological as well as physiological maturation—did mean that Indian experts could more readily recognize the need for a time gap between menarche and marriage for girls. But many of the scholarly articles described in this section imagine boys as central subjects in their elaboration of adolescence. This reflects the androcentric tilt of most social science research of the time, but it also underscores some of the genuine difficulties in extending the idea of adolescence to Indian girlhood, such as with imagining rebelliousness as appropriate behavior for girls this age. Instead, for girls, adolescence was understood to be a time when they learned how to be better disciplined as feminine individuals. An article by Anthony D'Souza in April 1969 makes this unequivocal point: "Sex is often considered as something we do, when it is actually who we are. We are male or female—man or women.... Sex education in its broad sense should... help[ ] us learn about being men and women."[51] Much of the anxiety reflected in the pages of journals such as *Social Health* is about chaos that might result from inadequate training of adolescents in gender-appropriate behavior and how to find outlets for sexual impulses. Adolescence for girls, then, was not simply about being sheltered but also learning appropriate ways to inhabit femininity.

Visualizing Adolescence

I turn now to a visual illustration of how the idea of adolescence for girls diffused slowly in India. I was provoked to more closely track such diffusion after noticing an odd absence when analyzing the iconic Marathi women's magazine *Stree* (*meaning* "woman"). The first exclusively women's magazine in the western Indian state of Maharashtra,[52] *Stree* was published continuously on a monthly basis from 1930 through 1986. Even though its title hailed women, the magazine was read by women and girls across life-cycle stages, and its contents regularly addressed interests across generations. A range of female figures appear on the covers of this magazine across its several decades of circulation: from trendy college students to bookish readers, from very young schoolgirls to romantic heroines to older women with several children. One absence in its early years that is noticeable to contemporary eyes, however, is images of what we would call teenage girls. In its first three decades, we see no such figures. For a magazine aimed at and read by readers of several ages—from young readers in their teens to grandmothers—this absence is striking. It suggests that adolescence was not something imagined as available to girls in the magazine's first two decades.

CHAPTER 2

A little context about the magazine is in order before viewing the images. *Stree* combined various genres: social commentary, literature, fashion, politics, legal advice, and women's movement reportage; its topics ranged from schooling to marriage to parenting and grandparenting. It is similar to other magazines in regional languages such as Hindi and Tamil and was part of a ferment in print culture in the 1920s and 1930s.[53] *Stree* was intended for a geographically broad Marathi readership: at the peak of its circulation in the 1950s, its thirty thousand subscribers could be found across urban settings, in semi-urban towns, and among the Marathi diaspora outside India. It influenced several successive generations of upper-caste middle-class readers, and Vidya Bal, who edited *Stree* from 1970 to 1986, described its readership as "intellectual, progressive, middle class."[54]

Stree's archive is appropriate to explore questions of representation given the vastness of this collection (twelve issues per year, over five decades) as well as the deliberate importance its publishers gave to its covers and their visual impact. *Stree*'s first editor was trained as an artist and often drew on renowned artists from the J. J. School of Art in Bombay to produce covers with vivid colors and high-quality paintings. In a context where literacy was limited, its covers performed important ideological work, signaling the fantasies of editors, artists, and readers and not simply the contents of the issue. Given that not every person within subscriber households could read, many covers had to be narratives unto themselves, suggestive of the lifeworlds that encased their personae. Much recent scholarship on visual culture in India powerfully recommends that we untether visuality from textuality, especially since the visual functions with different logics and wields a special power in a context of high illiteracy.[55] Such covers, then, can serve as a revealing window into the collective imaginaries and aspirations of their time.

I reviewed the covers of the magazine from 1930 through 1986 posing the question: how did it represent adolescent girls? To answer that question, I explored the subquestion: what were unmarried girls/women shown doing? Marriage seemed to be an appropriate proxy for age, since those who were married were likely to be at least beyond the legal age of twelve or thirteen, in this period. Marital status is possible to discern visually because in this part of India, it was a requirement for married Hindu women to wear the *mangalsutra*, a distinctive black-and-gold beaded necklace. Married women also often wore a red *kunku* (dot on forehead) and gold bangles. The cover in figure 2.1, from January 1957, is an example of a woman wearing a mangalsutra and bangles, applying a red kunku to her forehead.

Figure 2.1. Woman applying kunku, *Stree* cover, January 1957. Courtesy former editor Mukundrao Kirloskar

In order to discern how the magazine represented unmarried adolescent girls, I focused on young figures *not* wearing mangalsutras, red kunku, or bangles. There are very few examples of girls not wearing these—at least not until the late 1960s and 1970s. Before this period, the covers featured girls who seemed under twelve years without mangalsutras and married women with mangalsutras but very few who occupied a distinctive zone in between. Figures 2.2 and 2.3 are covers of figures recognizable as girls broadly under the age of twelve; the first (fig. 2.2) from September 1948, which is a photo of a smiling girl, and the second (fig. 2.3) from March 1955, a painting featuring a schoolteacher addressing a mother and young daughter (in an issue celebrating the anniversary of a famous girl's school in Pune).

But there were very few figures who were older but not quite adult whom we would call adolescents or teenagers today. The few examples I could find of figures wearing no mangalsutras often wore schoolgirl garb: their hair in two braids tied with ribbons, which was frequently a requirement with school uniforms, and the color white, which was a classic school uniform color and

Figure 2.2. Photo of smiling young girl, *Stree* cover, September 1948. Courtesy former editor Mukundrao Kirloskar

Figure 2.3. Girl visiting school with mother, *Stree* cover, March 1955. Courtesy former editor Mukundrao Kirloskar

rarely worn by married women because it was reserved for widows. Interestingly, though, their faces possessed features that we more commonly associate with those who are older than girls: elongated oval (rather than round) faces, elevated cheekbones (rather than full cheeks), and wise eyes suggestive of knowingness rather than wonderment. Figure 2.4, a painting from the cover of May 1956, of a girl with two braids, is an example of such a face: it is elongated, and the serious and knowing expression in her eyes creates the impression of a curiously older person than her clothing would imply. She wears no mangalsutra (or other jewelry), her blouse is white, and the plain sari (with no designs) suggests a uniform worn in the final years of high school or even college in India. Although she wears a red kunku, it is not large like the one the married woman in figure 2.1 is seen applying.

The April 1955 cover shows a girl in profile wearing a plain white sari (fig. 2.5); it is likely a uniform, since it has no designs. She has a placid, wistful gaze and reddened lips, which again suggests a figure older than what we might associate today with a schoolgirl.

The few other unmarried figures who seem to be adolescent but unmarried are also shown wearing saris, which were worn by all those who were past puberty and not little girls. There was not as yet any clothing style that was presumed to be a signature garb for adolescents, other than plain saris. All the

Figure 2.4. Young woman/girl with double braids, *Stree* cover, May 1956. Courtesy former editor Mukundrao Kirloskar

CHAPTER 2

Figure 2.5. Young woman/girl in side profile, *Stree* cover, April 1955. Courtesy former editor Mukundrao Kirloskar

figures are also shown engaged in activities associated with self-actualization, such as reading, the arts, or sports. They appear serious and self-possessed, rather than rebellious, bold, or joyful—qualities later associated with adolescence.

On the March 1938 cover (fig. 2.6), a girl with braids, no mangalsutra, and a plain sari is shown with a chivalrous badminton companion with upraised hat; her longer face and broad brow make her appear vaguely older than him.

In the June 1956 cover (fig. 2.7), we see a different variant of age confusion. A girl wears a sari and a necklace, but it is not a mangalsutra; her hair is tied in two braids; and her forehead shows a black (rather than red) kunku. Although she is unmarried, her heavy jewelry and hair decoration suggest she is dressed up. Importantly, she poses with a book and pen, evoking studiousness. The expression in her kohl-rimmed eyes and reddened lips is knowing and almost nostalgic. She looks like a lady playing at being a student or, conversely, a studious girl playing at being a dressed-up lady.

My goal in sharing these images is to speculate that the life stage we understand as adolescence was not always recognizable as such in the periods under consideration. During the 1930s, 1940s, and 1950s, the content of this life stage was still being elaborated. What Indian artists saw in that era was typically little women in the making. They all wore saris, the same garb as adult women. Their faces look oddly old, to contemporary eyes. The disjuncture between school uniform–style saris and older faces stands out, especially in figures 2. 4 and

Figure 2.6. Badminton partners, *Stree* cover, March 1938. Courtesy former editor Mukundrao Kirloskar

Figure 2.7. Young woman/girl holding book, *Stree* cover, June 1956. Courtesy former editor Mukundrao Kirloskar

2.6; the clothing and braided hair seem an effort to *dress down* the age shown in the face.

My reactions to these images might be reminiscent of Philippe Ariès's observations about the curiously old-looking children in premodern paintings; the children appeared to him to be mini adults since they did not possess the features typically associated with childhood.[56] The qualities that he had grown to expect—innocence and wide-eyed wonder and age-specific clothing styles associated with children—were found only in later eighteenth-century portraiture.[57] While several historians have taken issue with Ariès's evidence and conclusions, what is not doubted is that a specific sentimental notion of childhood emerged in Europe in the late eighteenth century, articulated by philosophers such as Jean-Jacques Rousseau and then by poets such as William Wordsworth, and consolidated through social and legal changes in the twentieth century. As Anna Mae Duane observes, the figure of the sentimental child—beautiful and perpetually endangered—permeated nineteenth-century European literature and went on to influence "social scientific child-saving movements of the late nineteenth and early twentieth century."[58] This romantic view treated childhood as a phase with its own distinct characteristics separate from adulthood: a sheltered state deserving protection from both the knowledge and responsibilities of adulthood.[59] Ideally, it was a time of play, wonder, and lightness. Sociologically speaking, access to this type of childhood could only be solidified through schooling. As compulsory schooling became more widely accepted, visual representations of such childhood grew more common.[60]

Such historiographies of childhood underscore two critical points: first, that there is no necessary set of qualities or traits that children universally embody; and second, that the qualities vested in children say more about the zeitgeist than children themselves. Extending this logic to understanding adolescence, it is not surprising that adolescence was not a prevalent formation on early covers of *Stree*; the covers do not offer ready examples. On some of the aforementioned cover images from the 1950s are faces of women dressed like schoolgirls, which suggests that at the time, the phase of being past puberty, unmarried, and not-yet-adult had no clear visual coordinates. In other words, the adolescent had no separate identity from either a woman or child but was an uncomfortable juxtaposition of the two.

Only much later, in the 1960s and 1970s, do we begin to see girls who are not wearing saris and whom we might today recognize as teenagers, such as on the covers in figures 2.8, 2.9, and 2.10. In each of these covers, the girls are wearing little to no jewelry and no mangalsutra, so they may be compared with the figures from earlier eras. In the last cover (fig. 2.10) from February 1976 of a girl

Figure 2.8. Photo of teen girl in skirt-blouse, *Stree* cover, June 1968. Courtesy former editor Mukundrao Kirloskar

Figure 2.9. Photo of teen girl laughing, *Stree* cover, July 1972. Courtesy former editor Mukundrao Kirloskar

CHAPTER 2

Figure 2.10. Photo of teen girl laughing with eyes closed, *Stree* cover, February 1976. Courtesy former editor Mukundrao Kirloskar

laughing intensely with an open mouth, we see joy and carefreeness, emotions that we do not find in the earlier images. The girls in the first two images from June 1968 and July 1972 (figs. 2.8 and 2.9) definitely reflect greater composure, but their open-mouthed smiles suggest not only a changing aesthetic about appropriate ways to smile but also a quality of ease. These are faces we might recognize as teenagers (rather than women dressed as teenagers) because their expressions convey a lightness and a sense of not being burdened by adult knowledge or woes. Of course, this sense of familiarity might be facilitated by the fact that the latter examples are photographs rather than paintings, but, nonetheless, a contrast between the expressions on faces and emotions conveyed is clear.

   These images underscore the point that adolescence as a recognizable intermediate identity category for girls is a historically recent formation. This phase, when girls continued to deserve sheltering and protection and an extended girlhood, was elaborated only slowly. Importantly, the girls in the photographs appear to be school-going. One is dressed in what could be a white-collared school uniform. The other is dressed in a *parkar-polka*, a blouse and long skirt without a veil over the breasts, that became an appropriate uniform for adolescent girls in place of the sari. These images reflect changed patterns in compulsory schooling: the Indian Constitution drafted after Independence in 1950 was committed to making education until age 14 compulsory in ten years (by 1960), although it did not initiate any forceful measures to assure this outcome (the state's greatest investments were in higher education in the technical sectors). Access to public schooling for girls until the tenth grade did, however, increase in urban areas across class and caste lines in the 1960s. Enrollment in colleges, which typically housed students in the tenth-to-twelfth-grade phase as well as in three-year degree programs, also increased.[61] The sheltered environment of schools and colleges, both usually sex-segregated, allowed girls in the age range of 12 to 18 to imagine themselves as free from reproductive responsibility. At the same time, even as the photographs from the 1960s signal more openness and ease with their identity as girls, they still embody conventional femininity: The girl in figure 2.8 poses with her hands demurely on her lap, and both figures 2.8 and 2.9 feature flowers in the backdrop.

Most important, the very possibility of adolescence being available to girls in India rested on the social shift toward later marriages. According to demographers, the mean age of marriage for girls in census data rose every decade from 1931 as follows: in 1931, the mean age of marriage was 12.69 years; in 1941, 14.69; in 1951, 15.59; in 1961, 15.9; and in 1971, 17.2.[62] The *legal* age of marriage rose very slowly over the course of this time—it was only in 1978 that it was raised to 18 years for girls, as chapter 5 explains. The legal raising of the age of marriage went hand-in-hand with imagining adolescence as a life stage for girls. A higher age of marriage rendered a girl more available for activities associated with adolescence, such as education, sports, and even social experimentation.

These shifts are in keeping with general ideas about the formation of adolescence in other geographic regions of the world. In an article reflecting on the construction of adolescence across the globe, John Caldwell, Pat Caldwell, and Bruce K. Caldwell argue that adolescence is hard for girls to access without changes in the age of marriage. The primary vehicle for girls' access to adolescence, they argue, is an "increase in age of first marriage and first childbirth from shortly after puberty to 20 years and beyond."[63] Changes in the age of marriage, which are discussed in later chapters of this book, were justified on the basis of new understandings of life-cycle stages.

* * *

The *Stree* cover images that close this chapter signal how the idea of the adolescent girl was a socially constructed formulation that took shape slowly and emerged most clearly in the post-1960s period in Indian settings. The idea of adolescent girlhood in India was influenced by conceptual innovations in US psychology and the cultural hegemony of US expert knowledge, and it was buttressed by key sociological shifts taking place in the latter part of the twentieth century, such as the raising of the age of marriage and increased access to high school and college education. Indian psychologists, social workers, and educators took to the terminology of adolescence enthusiastically in the 1960s, and a parallel identity category of the adolescent or teenager appeared in popular culture in the 1960s.

The images from *Stree* presented here telegraph the changes that unfolded over several decades, and they set up the chronological trajectory of legal reforms explored in the chapters to follow. Most important, they underscore the centrality of marriage in shaping the boundaries of girlhood. The images from the 1930s and 1940s struggle to simultaneously depict an unmarried postpubertal girl who is playful and mature. In the 1950s, such a combination becomes easier to depict with the notion of a college-going girl. It is in the late 1960s and 1970s that teenage girls actually appear, which is the era when the marriage age is significantly raised, as chapter 5 describes. Following this broad account of adolescence as an idea in US and Indian psychology, education, and social reform work, the next chapter describes how this new expanded understanding of girlhood went on to influence an Indian law restricting child marriage and raising the age of consent.

3

Legislating Nonmarital Sex in India, 1911–1929

In the 1920s in India, a double standard cleaved the legal definition of girlhood: while girls under 14 were readily defined as children in legislative debates about nonmarital sex, the same girls were simultaneously presented as mature and nubile in debates about the age of consent for marriage. Legislators saw no inconsistency in holding separate standards for sexual maturity within and outside marriage. When the Central Legislative Assembly debated in 1923 whether girls under 18 could legally consent to enter prostitution, Madan Mohan Malaviya, former president of the Indian National Congress and founder of the right-wing Hindu Mahasabha party, thoroughly rejected the idea. "It [is] outrageous that a child should be free to give herself away when she is not allowed to enter into a contract for 5 or 10 rupees," he announced, calling for greater protection of girls by the state.[1] Six years later, however, as the minimum age of marriage for girls was being raised from 12 to 14, Malaviya took a hostile view of state protection of girls, declaring that "the age of marriage should be fixed at 11 years.... Making marriage below the age of 14 punishable by law is a violent interference with the Hindu religion."[2] Malaviya's acceptance of early sexual intercourse in one instance and not in the other illustrates a central premise of this moment of legal reform in colonial India: "early" sexual activity for girls was not as severe a problem when it took place within the bounds of conjugal, patriarchally sanctioned settings as when it occurred outside them. Indeed, the boundaries of girlhood varied depending on whether sexual consent related to marital or nonmarital sex.

Indian law today holds 18 years to be the uniform age standard defining legal majority, consent to sexual activity, and consent to marriage. However, when these three categories were first codified in the late nineteenth century, there were major discrepancies between them. When the age of majority was codified in 1875, children (and implicitly boys) were declared to be of age when they turned 18; this was the age at which persons could represent themselves in owning property and signing contracts without the need for a guardian. But marriage was *not* among the contracts under consideration—in the same period, the age of consent for girls' consummation of marriage was set at 10. Raising the age of marriage for girls at the beginning of the twentieth century was a deeply polarizing issue. The two reforms of child marriage—raising the minimum age to 12 years in 1891 and then to 14 years in 1929—were moments of high political drama for Indian nationalists, religious conservatives, reformists, feminists, and British colonial administrators.[3] Interestingly, though, legislators raised the age of consent for prostitution with much less fanfare, well before the age of marriage was raised. A parallel minimum age for all nonmarital sex—which specified when girls could give their consent to sex with "strangers"—was steadily raised through the 1910s and 1920s to 16 in 1929. This shift has been relatively neglected by historians, and this chapter places both sets of legal changes within the same field of vision. I trace how the ages of consent in nonmarital and marital contexts were raised consecutively, exploring reasons for the success of the efforts to raise the age of consent for nonmarital sex and how such success related to marriage reform.

From a comparative feminist perspective, the distinction between the age of consent for marital and nonmarital sex in colonial India presents a puzzle. Generally speaking, the age of consent simultaneously marks the boundaries of childhood and the offensiveness of a given act. The higher the age of consent, the more offensive the state deems the sex act and, as a consequence, the greater the presumed need for state protection of individuals thereby marked as children. This premise, however, has been complicated in its application to young girls in prostitution.[4] States have typically deemed prostitutes unworthy of protection, and prostitution has frequently been assigned a lower age of consent than marriage, meaning girls could engage in commercial sex at an age lower than the official minimum age of marriage. Laws in some states in the United States and in Canada, for example, began to differentiate in the 1890s between "chaste" and "unchaste" girls, assigning "unchaste" girls a lower age of consent for sex.[5] In Britain, when the Criminal Amendment Act of 1885 raised the age of consent to 16, it made an exception for cases involving prostitutes.[6] This double standard, based on the "whore stigma" familiar to most feminist scholars, was certainly also present in India—legal reforms that affected marriageable girls drew much more public attention than laws affecting prostitutes.[7] It is hence worth pondering why, throughout the debates on child marriage in India, reformists consistently proposed a higher age of consent for nonmarital sex (and implicitly prostitution) than for marriage.

In approaching this distinction, the analytical fuzziness of the categories "nonmarital sex," "extramarital sex," and "immoral sexual relations" (used interchangeably in legislative debates) becomes immediately significant. The categories covered an array of acts of varying degrees of criminality and varying potential for consent: rape, abduction, kidnapping, and prostitution, as well as the more sensationalized "trafficking"— transporting across borders for prostitution. My analysis shows that by conflating these acts, an "age of consent for nonmarital sex" came to define all sex outside marriage below a certain age as criminal and akin to rape. In the process of nullifying sexual consent across such a range of acts at once, the boundaries of girlhood were solidified.

Two forces were responsible for raising the age of nonmarital sex in India. The first was international antitrafficking discourse. Debates in League of Nations settings, and Stephen M. Edwardes's refusal to apply League of Nations standards to India (described in chapter 1), influenced Indian deliberations. I argue that Indian legislators turned away from metropolitan Britain as a model in favor of emerging internationalist discourses. Spurred by international conventions, they transformed raising the age of consent for nonmarital sex into a nationalist and anticolonial cause. They actively drew on League of Nations conventions that proposed a universal age of consent for trafficking. These conventions became an impetus for reform though a complex route: while British colonial administrators argued that India should be an exception to the League of Nations standard, Indian reformists enthusiastically took to these universal norms, as the norms implied assigning India full civilizational "maturity." Indian reformists opposed colonial policy in the name of protecting India's reputation on a world stage. This chapter situates Indian reforms within an international circuit of influence, moving beyond analyses that focus on the dyad of British-Indian relations.[8] It thus incorporates a wider field of forces than is typically considered in histories of Indian social reform.

The other force raising the age of consent for nonmarital sex was parental resistance to the increasing mobility of girls in public spaces. Girls had growing opportunities for education and employment, and these changes provoked concerns about girls' marriageability and the declining control of parents. In a context where parents overwhelmingly arranged marriages, the "age of marriage" effectively pertained to when parents could set up marriages rather than when girls could exercise sexual choices. Raising the age of consent for marriage, as was proposed in the 1920s, carried risks for parents—they had to wait longer before they could consolidate marriage matches—and the likelihood that girls would choose mates on their own was now greater. Raising the age of consent for nonmarital sex served as a safety valve against such anxieties: girls who chose mates that parents disapproved of could now be declared victims of "rape" or "abduction." I argue that in raising the age of consent for nonmarital sex, legislators presented the state as a surrogate parent as a defense against the erosion of parental control.

The focus in this chapter rests on changes in legislative politics and on how Indian legislators appropriated international antitrafficking standards. The chapter follows a series of legislative debates held between 1911 and 1929 and shows the influence of international antitrafficking discourse, beginning by discussing the Dadabhoy Bill, the first formulation of a distinct age of consent for all nonmarital sex, which was partially provoked by conventions drawn up by the International Society for the Suppression of White Slave Traffic. Next, the chapter examines how Indian Legislative Assembly members in 1922 and 1923–24 responded to the claims Edwardes made to League of Nations delegates justifying a lower age of consent in India. Then I turn to the 1929 abolition of child marriage, focusing on its effects on sexual consent outside marriage and the resulting anxieties about parental control. I offer a fuller analysis of the *Report of the Age of Consent Committee* (*Report*), the official sociological report leading up to the 1929 CMRA, which chapter 2 introduces. The text of this report, which conveys deep-seated parental anxieties, allows for an analysis of the forces shaping the 1929 law constraining child marriage. Although this 1929 law is widely considered a key moment of Indian social reform, I argue that it was facilitated by prior and concurrent measures that fixed a higher age of consent for nonmarital sex. These measures entrenched parental control over daughters' sexual practices and ultimately limited the implications of marriage reform.

A Backdrop

The realm of lawmaking was a distinctly limited, yet intensely contested, arena of competing authority between Indian nationalists and British colonial officials. For Indian nationalists, legislation symbolized greater self-determination, even if the colonial government did not always enforce controversial laws rigidly in the interest of social stability. The Central Legislative Assembly was a site where Indian legislators exercised what legal theorist Upendra Baxi terms a "fantasy of power."[9] In the public eye, the declarative and symbolic power of lawmaking outstripped its role in regulating concrete practices—public attention was often more focused on the scandals prompting changes in legislation than on the extent of general enforcement. It was often presumed that laws—particularly, those on age of marriage, widow remarriage, and prostitution—would not be enforced in such a large and diverse country.

Nonetheless, the British colonial state, particularly in the late colonial period between 1857 and 1947, facilitated the control of women's lives via a multifaceted structure of legality. In the name of preserving moral order, it endorsed the household as a separate arena in which male property rights in women reigned, and the state designated an edifice of "personal law" to rule this arena.[10] British colonial officials upheld a stance of declaring noninterference in all matters pertaining to personal law, terming it the province of custom and religion.[11] But implicitly, this new colonial structure granted greater power to religious doctrines to govern marriage and family relations, and specifically to religious elites; the latter now had a newfound authority to define religious doctrines in the fixed, universal terms of the law. Furthermore, it also generated an emphasis on the nuclear family as the aspirational norm for households.[12] The colonial state also authorized a decidedly male-dominant sphere of lawmaking in the Central Legislative Assembly by granting men who were legislators the power to speak on behalf of women of "their" communities; they thus reified women's identities along the lines of such religious/ethnic communities. Women's access to legislative forums was, at best, strained: they were elected in the 1920s to municipal and provincial councils but not to the Central Legislative Assembly.[13] Women's organizations therefore exerted pressure largely from outside the assembly through organizing public rallies, petitions, and sponsoring resolutions pertaining to vital legislations.[14]

Laws on the status of women in colonial India were often coded as cultural change writ large and were a key staging ground for political conflicts.[15] Indian legislators at the Central Legislative Assembly level who proposed reforms argued that reforms signaled the incipient nation's purported civilizational maturity.[16] Those who opposed reforms presented tradition, most often Hindu and Muslim religious practices, as sacrosanct structures under threat. Although British legislators were ostensibly committed to reformist positions, many tacitly encouraged orthodox ideological positions in debates.[17] Their support for religious elites was fueled by strategic imperatives: Indian legislators who took orthodox positions commonly came from landed agricultural classes from whom the colonial state drew revenues; the colonial state extended protection to them in the interest of preserving social stability.[18] In the power struggle between agricultural and mercantile/industrial classes in the early twentieth century, the British colonial administrators presumed the landowning (*zamindari*) classes to be natural leaders, and the state relied on support from the provincial governments that the landowning classes dominated. The support to such classes was premised on a policy of noninvolvement in customs, except where land and property relations were at stake.[19] This imperative partially explains why British colonial administrators so consistently encouraged the positions of religious elites in the Central Legislative Assembly and sought positive responses from provincial governments before passing laws.

Adopting orthodox positions with respect to social reforms also preserved British racial prestige. Distinctions between Indian and British laws reified ideologically crucial distinctions between Indian and British subjects. The purported lasciviousness of Indians was a central plank that distinguished the two groups, and child marriage was seen simultaneously as a cause, effect, and symbol of Indian sexual promiscuity.[20] Although English evangelicals viewed child marriage as remediable and attacked it in the first part of the nineteenth century, administrators in later stages of colonial rule often attributed an unchangeable quality to the practice, with the aim of preserving a distance between English and Indian subjects.[21] In line with the currents described in chapter 1, the administrators relied on climatological explanations for early marriage in the late nineteenth century: puberty was argued to arrive much earlier in the tropics than in Europe; the hot weather was said to have produced, over the centuries, effects in the Indian character that were not subject to legislative transformation.[22] Even though Indian reformists challenged the notion of unchangeable Indian traits, such ideas were the backdrop against which debates over the age of consent were conducted in the late nineteenth century and then the 1920s.

The most politically dramatic of these debates, in 1891, concerned raising the age of sexual consent to consummation of marriage. The 1891 act raised the age at which child brides could be forced to cohabit with their husbands or "consummate marriage" from 10 years (set in the 1860 Indian Penal Code) to 12 years.[23] Although this move only indirectly eroded child marriage, it galvanized public debates and met with furious opposition. Hindu religious revivalists denounced British colonial administrators for appearing to violate the sanctity of marriage customs. Nationalist B. G. Tilak in Maharashtra argued that the colonial state had infringed on the authority of the Hindu husband and branded Indian reformists supporting the act, such as Behramji Malabari, traitors. This controversy successfully produced a long silence on marriage reform: the chastened colonial state did not entertain any further legislation on this topic for nearly twenty years.

The 1911 Debates

Whereas reformist legislators quailed at taking on the topic of the age of marriage, they showed no such hesitation in addressing another age of consent in this period, the age of consent for "immoral sexual relations." In 1872, even before the feverish 1891 debates concerning the age of consent in marital settings, the age of consent in cases where a child was bought or hired for purposes of prostitution was set at 16 years.[24] Satadru Sen finds that conservative officials from provincial governments in Bengal drew a distinction between girls who were not already prostitutes and those who belonged to that profession by caste or "habit."[25] The officials set a lower age of consent of 13 years for girls who were born into the profession, thereby rendering an entire section of the native population less worthy of state protection. In other words, even before the crucial debates pertaining to sex within marriage took place in 1891, there was already a variegated legal conceptualization of which girls deserved protection from prostitution.

In the first decade of the twentieth century, an even higher age of consent was proposed in the context of campaigns to address "white slavery"—generally, the sale of women into prostitution and, specifically, the transporting of European women to work in colonial brothels.[26] In 1910 the International Society for the Suppression of White Slave Traffic, which convened cross-national conferences in 1899, 1904, 1910, and 1913,[27] proposed a prototype for future conventions against trafficking when it specified that a "woman" was a female over the age of 20 and defined trafficking of all girls below that age as an offense.[28] It assumed that girls under 20 were incapable of grasping the consequences of consenting to being transported to distant locales to engage in prostitution. This measure provoked attempts to harmonize laws on age of consent in India.

The colonial Government of India did not accede to the 1910 convention because it viewed setting the age of consent at 20 years as impossible, given its vast difference from 16 years, which was the age of consent for girls sold into prostitution under the Indian Penal Code.[29] Although the international convention only met with India's partial acceptance, its contents were echoed in two 1911 proposals that private members introduced in the Imperial Legislative Council: the Dadabhoy Bill and the Madge Bill. The legislative debates on these bills reorganized the elements of the discourse on early sexual relations and forced the conservative stance of the colonial state into the open.

CHAPTER 3

The 1911 proposal by Manicekji B. Dadabhoy, a respected Parsi advocate and industrialist from Nagpur, took aim at a range of nonmarital sexual relations such as rape, dedication of girls to temples, and concubinage.[30] Borrowing from the 1910 international convention, the Dadabhoy Bill, which proposed to invalidate consent when it had been "gained by fraudulent means,"[31] also adopted provisions from an English enactment on the protection of female children from prostitution.[32] The Dadabhoy Bill was circulated as a set of measures aimed at "legislating immorality" along with another bill that called for deporting those who trafficked foreign Asian women. The new "age of consent for immoral sexual relations" applied to a host of relations—from the relatively stable, such as concubinage, to single coercive acts such as rape by strangers. This was the first time that an age standard for such a wide range of sexual relations had been grouped together under a single label. The standards otherwise were treated under different sections in the Indian Penal Code: sections 359 through 368 focused on forms of kidnapping and abduction; sections 372 and 373, the sale and purchase for the purposes of prostitution; section 375, rape; and section 498, adultery.[33] In using the term "immoral sexual relations," the Dadabhoy Bill initiated a distinction in legislative debates between the ages of consent for legitimate and illegitimate sex; it also valorized marriage by defining sexual activities only in terms of their relationship to marriage.[34]

Given that "immoral sexual relations" was a catchall term, there was difficulty in agreeing upon a suitable age of consent. We might rightly pose the question: why was delimiting an age of consent even necessary for kidnapping, rape, and abduction, since these were by definition nonconsensual acts? One possible answer is that reformists aimed to establish, once and for all, an age below which all nonmarital sex could be defined as statutory rape. This redefinition would bring a range of customs reformers deemed offensive—the dedicating of daughters to temples as dancers, guardianship of children by prostitutes, transferring of wives, and concubinage—under one prosecutable classification. Some legislators sought to assimilate the law on statutory rape to that in England, where sexual intercourse under the age of 13 was considered rape. However, given that the British colonial state accepted child marriages below that age among its Indian subjects, all sexual intercourse under 13 could hardly be banned. (The mean age of marriage for girls in 1891, for instance, was 12.54 years; in 1901, 13.14 years; in 1911, 13.16 years; and in 1921, 13.67.)[35] A large segment of girls in the country were married by the time they were 13. As a result, the carefully worded proposal emerged: "All sexual intercourse with girls (except wives) up to 13 would be rape, as in England, with ten years' imprisonment."[36]

For reformists, the maturity that qualified a girl for marriage was defined more leniently than that for nonmarital sex. Legislators felt that "obviously a difference" existed between "seducing a young girl under 15 and living with a wife under that age."[37] The missionaries of the Society for the Protection of Children in Western India made it clear that it was sexual relations with underage girls "outside the pale of recognized wedlock" that was abhorrent.[38] The 1891 nationalist outcry against raising the age of consent for consummation of marriage appeared to have taught legislators a lesson: to avoid the appearance of interfering with marital relationships. The Dadabhoy Bill specified that the age of consent being discussed was not related to marriage; in almost every clause the bill clarified that sexual relations with girls by all *except* their husbands was under consideration. The reformer N. B. Divatia viewed this emphasis as the bill's strength, noting "there is no possibility of the cry 'Religion in danger' as this bill [does] not concern itself with marriage."[39]

The boundary marking a child from an adult, which should have been a key issue, remained vaguely formulated. In trying to decide the age at which a girl became capable of consensual sexual relations, reformists were not helped by the confusing and at times conflicting laws. The age for entering legal majority, declared as 18 by the 1875 Indian Majority Act (Act IX), had made a clear exception in all matters related to marriage, divorce, dower, adoption, religious rites, and usages following a mandate from Queen Victoria in 1858 against interfering with religion. Section 552 of the Criminal Procedure Code held that abduction or unlawful detention for immoral purposes of "a woman or every female child under 14" was punishable; this was interpreted by the viceroy's secretary, Henry Wheeler, to mean that "every female of 14 and upwards [was] reckoned as a woman."[40] With the age of consent for marriage set at 12 years in 1891, any girl over 12 could also be defined as a woman, further complicating the definition of childhood.

These legal discrepancies exemplified a confusion surrounding what constituted maturity for girls, and the tension between physiological and intellectual notions of maturity. The line defining marriageability was based on physical maturity: the age of consent for marital sexual relations had been set at 12 years in 1891 in the belief that puberty occurred at that age. This notion continued to be circulated, as seen in the following confident statements of a Bombay attorney to the Judicial Department: "Puberty is a sign which shows that the girl is fit for cohabitation," and "native girls according to the best medical authority attain puberty between 12 and 13 years of age."[41] However, when trying to raise the age of consent for concubinage, which occupied a gray area between marriage and prostitution, reformists had to disconnect their argument from such physiological reasoning. In proposing to have concubinage subject to a higher age of consent than 12 years (the age of consent for consummation of marriage), Dadabhoy assumed a different definition of sexual maturity: one premised on an intellectual capacity to distinguish a moral from immoral act. Along with other reformists, he argued that because children were "not capable of giving valid consent for an ordinary contract in life till attaining the age of majority, i.e., the age of 18," they could not be capable of disposing themselves and their reputations to "strangers."[42]

This gesture toward children's moral agency appears facile, however, when one remembers that it was parents who regularly arranged marriages and sometimes during a girl's infancy. It is not unreasonable to assume, then, that for most brides, husbands were *also* usually strangers and often significantly older strangers. The entity conferring consent was effectively the parents and not the child; it was the assent of parents that overwhelmingly construed a union as legitimate and moral.[43] Needless to say, when reformists doubted children's ability to make mature decisions, it was regarding "illegitimate" strangers rather than those to whom the children were betrothed. The disjuncture between acceptance of marital and nonmarital sex was most glaring when debating concubinage, a long-term sexual relation mimicking marriage but which Dadabhoy hoped to redefine as prostitution.[44] Orthodox religious legislators opposed the Dadabhoy Bill by casting concubinage as a timeless and widespread custom in various communities. For example, Vishnu Raghunath Natu from Bombay declared in broad terms that concubinage was akin to marriage: "[T]here are various forms of marriage in the complex societies of India.... [T]hese forms are sanctioned by long-standing customs, as concubinage itself was by the ancient in all countries."[45] A. B. Desai, also from Bombay, argued, "To this day, concubinage prevails largely in this country, even amongst people who are rich, influential and otherwise very respectable."[46] Although such legislators sought to preserve concubinage in the name of community and religious identity, reformist legislators rejected such formulations. Ganesh Vyankatesh Joshi, for instance, declared that "intercourse . . . with girls of tender years . . . is detestable and revolting to the general moral sentiment of the country" and that "the age of consent in the case of concubinage . . . should be . . . 18 years."[47] Yet these same legislators simultaneously accepted sexual intercourse between husbands and brides well below that age. Rather than debating the ability of girls to resist early sexual relations, the political struggle centered on the legitimacy of nonmarital sexual relations that competed with the dominant form of marriage. The Dadabhoy Bill received much publicity and was circulated widely to various provincial governments, from whom surprisingly positive responses were received. The Government of Bombay suggested that any sexual intercourse (except by husbands) with girls under 16 be considered rape.[48] The Governments of Bengal and the United Provinces both suggested this age of consent be 14.[49] The colonial Government of India was clearly taken aback by this reformist enthusiasm and concerned about alienating orthodox Indian constituents. It had not even expected to assimilate the law on rape to that in England, where the age of statutory rape was 13 under the Criminal Law Amendment of 1885, and the common law age of marriage for girls was 12.[50] In a letter to the secretary of the state for India, the Judicial Department stated that "a higher limit than [that] in England" was something they were "certainly not prepared to endorse."[51] The implications for notions of civilizational supremacy were clear: raising the Indian age of consent higher than that in Britain would puncture British prestige. Thus, in spite of the recommendations of several provincial governments, the "age of consent for immoral sexual relations" was not raised from 12 years. Although the Dadabhoy Bill did not successfully raise the age of consent, its collating of categories such as kidnapping, rape, concubinage, and prostitution was an important prelude to changes that occurred in the 1920s.

Aspiring to International Legitimacy, 1921–1924

The political climate in India became more conducive to social reform after the 1919 Government of India Act set up a Central Legislative Assembly premised on the principle of greater self-governance by Indians. This assembly, which for the first time had a majority of Indian legislators, became a vital arena for elected reformists to push for new laws; they authored a series of bills on the age of consent. The Women's Indian Association (WIA), a leading national women's organization founded in Madras in 1917, lobbied intensively in favor of these consent bills.[52] The efforts to amend the Indian Penal Code produced the first codified age of consent for all nonmarital sexual relations.

The initial provocation for raising the age of consent for nonmarital sex came from the League of Nations. The league's various measures described in chapter 1 pertaining to trafficking spurred sympathetic responses among Indian reformist legislators. One of the earliest tasks that the League of Nations secretary-general took on, in December 1920, was to send a questionnaire to member countries, asking them to list the measures they took against trafficking. The Indian response to the questionnaire was prompt, pointing out that parts of the Indian Penal Code dealing with kidnapping for illicit purposes (IPC section 366) and with the sale of girls into prostitution (IPC section 372) both set down 16 as an age of consent.[53] The league's antitrafficking mission began ambitiously with a single goal: to standardize the age of consent for prostitution across countries. But Edwardes—the British government's Indian representative to this 1921 meeting—sought to exempt India from raising its age of consent. His efforts to rally on behalf of "tropical" colonies met with success, as described in chapter 1, and the League of Nations refrained from setting 21 years as a single-age standard, leaving it to be negotiated instead by individual countries at the time of signing the convention.

Although Edwardes met with success in Geneva, he incited fury among legislators in India. He was no longer in service in India and was likely sent by the British government to Geneva to represent India because he then resided in England. In 1922 the Central Legislative Assembly in India met to discuss the International Convention on Trafficking, and several members took exception to the claims Edwardes had made in Geneva. Taking their own role as elected legislators to heart, Indian members complained that Edwardes had spoken without the consent of the assembly.[54] N. M. Joshi, a trade union leader and Labour nominee from Bombay who took a liberal universalist stance on matters relating to women, argued that girls in India did not attain maturity any earlier than elsewhere, and he put forward a proposal for India's adherence to the age standard of 21, overruling Edwardes's stand.[55] This bill to adjust Indian law to the League of Nations recommended standard age of 21 was a clear indication of the nationalist stakes in the debate over the age of consent.

The British colonial government's approach to N. M. Joshi's proposal to raise the age of consent was predictably cautious. William H. Vincent, the British Home Member who explained the bill in the Legislative Assembly, trod very softly. He asked the assembly "not to bind itself to legislate on a subject of such importance ... without consulting public opinion."[56] He inflated the importance of the bill, warning that banning the procuring of girls under 21 would also lead to the banning of sexual intercourse with girls under 21; he wondered aloud if such measures could be "dangerous in the present circumstances."[57] Like Edwardes, Vincent, too, was near the end of his service in India and took conservative positions on political issues. When some Indian members welcomed the international convention as a means to prevent Indian women from being trafficked outside the country, Vincent downplayed the possibility of such trafficking. He warned, in an alarmist tone, that the scope of the League of Nations articles went beyond trafficking between nations and that all acts within India would be penalized as well.[58] Reformists in the Legislative Assembly disregarded Vincent's warnings and insisted that India should prove itself "equal" to other countries of the League of Nations. As Harchandrai Vishindas, member from Sind in Bombay Presidency, put it: "If we in any way lower the age-limit, we lower ourselves in the estimation of other nations, who will have to think that we are not quite capable of rising to the height to which other nations are capable of rising."[59] He was echoed by N. M. Samarth, member from Bombay city, who declared, "As a self-respecting citizen . . . I would certainly not be a party to any lower age than that which has been accepted by other nations."[60] We see here the unfurling nationalist logic of the reformist position: The age of consent was a marker of national advancement, and the League of Nations was a world stage upon which India, a fledgling nation, was being evaluated.

Some conservative Indian legislators stressed a more conventionally patriarchal reason for approving the bill: the protection of women. Pyari Lal, member from Meerut, a city in the United Provinces, held that women between 16 and 21 "are much sought after . . . in this period of life" and "required protection of the State to no small degree."[61] J. Chaudhuri, member from Chittagong in northeastern Bengal Presidency, argued that Indian women, lacking in education and "mental maturity," needed *greater* protection from procurers than European women. If European women were being protected up until the age of 21, then the law needed to be applied with greater force to Indian women. He warned that procurers would otherwise take advantage of the lower age limits in India, making the country "a hunting ground for this nefarious trade."[62] Although in this instance reformists featured Indian women's cultural difference—rather than similarity—with other women, they still used a competitive framework, equating a high age of consent with greater national honor.

Orthodox Hindu and Muslim legislators also invoked religious and community identities, although in a different, defensive direction—they saw changing the age of consent as an infringement on particular traditions. C. S. Subrahmanyam, an orthodox Hindu member from Madras, characterized the bill as "far-reaching" and "far in advance of public opinion."[63] Muhammad Shafi, education member, reiterated the colonial view that girls became adults much sooner in India than in Europe and reminded members that according to High Court rulings, a girl in India was presumed to reach puberty by age 14 unless proven otherwise.[64] British members of the assembly, such as Vincent, encouraged conservative Indian members to air their religious objections. Such a move preserved an illusion of the colonial state's noninterference with local customs—a tactic used by British legislators in several contexts.[65] A variety of conservative members were able to raise fears about religion being under attack by emphasizing the threat to marriage-related customs. Ultimately, British members of the assembly voted en bloc against N. M. Joshi's bill, along with conservative Indian legislators. This combined vote of British members and orthodox Indians defeated Indian reformists. The Government of India therefore signed the international convention after substituting 16 for 21 as the age below which trafficking was illegal.[66]

The indefatigable N. M. Joshi, unfazed by the failure of his previous bill, introduced another bill to raise the age of consent for kidnapping and abduction to 18 years in the Indian Penal Code.[67] This initiative also applied articles of the League of Nations' International Convention for the Suppression of Traffic in Women and Children. The act was passed by a slim majority of three in the legislative assembly. Because of the close vote, the colonial government asserted that it was doubtful if the law would be "upheld by public opinion generally" and prevented its passage.[68]

British legislators repeatedly raised the specter of threats to marriage each time Indian reformist legislators proposed changes to the age of consent for nonmarital sexual relations. When Rai Bahadur Bakshi Sohanlal proposed another bill in the legislative assembly session of 1922 to raise the age of statutory rape to 14 in IPC section 375, Vincent, the presiding member, stipulated that "if the bill did go to a Select Committee, it could only go on the distinct condition that the section did not apply to marital relations, and that in the case of girls over 12 and under 14, the punishment should be materially reduced and placed on a similar level to that which obtained in England."[69] Despite the fact that the offense clearly did not pertain to marriage, Vincent's reference to marital relations reminded legislators that religious customs would be eroded by the bill; this subtle framing goaded conservative legislators into opposing it. His insistent reference to age standards in Britain also presumed it could set the limits of possibility for Indian social reform.

Newspapers were highly critical of the foot-dragging by British legislators in the 1922 legislative assembly session. The *Indian Social Reformer*, on April 28, 1923, carried a piece indicting the "self-regarding cautiousness" of the Anglo-Indian government as "one of the greatest obstacles to progress in social matters in India." The colonial government's refusal to recognize that reformists were the majority among Indians in the assembly also looked undemocratic. The April 7, 1923, *Sind Observer* lamented that government did not accept the lead given by the assembly and instead took "refuge behind orthodox opinion." Such criticism of the colonial government indicated that the tide on the issue of age of consent was shifting.

When the next legislative assembly session commenced in 1923, N. M. Joshi moved yet another bill to increase the age of consent for "selling and buying women for the purposes of prostitution" and "enticing them away from guardians." Joshi's bill met with much resistance, particularly, from orthodox Muslim and Hindu members. Both groups claimed that the bill attacked marriage customs because girls could be enticed away from guardians for legitimate reasons, such as marriage, and that girls could also be legitimately bought and sold into marriage. This objection was, to an extent, made in bad faith, because the bill targeted child prostitution. The legislators, nonetheless, preferred to publicize all perceived threats to the autonomy of religious communities in controlling the domain of marriage.

The political factionalism in this session was more pronounced than in previous ones. The Congress Party upheld the reformist agenda as an emblem of resistance to Britain's obstructionist policy and to colonial rule, in general. The high point of the debate on N. M. Joshi's bill was the feisty exchange between the key political figures Mohammad Ali Jinnah and Malaviya.[70] As mentioned at the opening of this chapter, Malaviya espoused raising the age of consent for prostitution. Jinnah, who had recently ascended to the position of president of the All India Muslim League, led another faction in the assembly that objected strongly to this move because it included a clause concerning "enticement of girls."[71] Jinnah declared that prostitution and enticement of girls were not the same, asking the pointed question, "Why can't a girl of 16 peacefully walk away with anyone she likes, provided it is not for immoral purposes?" and more forcefully asked, "We are to enact a penal section to meet the sentiments and feelings of parents? That she cannot marry till 18?"[72]

Jinnah's questions marked a rare occasion when a legislator distinguished the interests of parents clearly from those of daughters; the two were otherwise seen as synonymous *both* in reformist and conservative discourses. In highlighting the agency of girls to make decisions independent of parents and religion, Jinnah was articulating opposition to the bill on grounds different from those of legislators in his faction who supported early marriage for religious reasons. Personal circumstances may well have fueled his unusual position: in 1918 his wish to marry 17-year-old Ruttenbai Petit met with severe opposition from her father, Parsi industrialist Dinshaw Petit. Dinshaw Petit opposed the marriage on the grounds of religious difference as well as the age gap (Jinnah was over 40 years). He issued an injunction against Jinnah, keeping him away from Ruttenbai; Jinnah could only marry Ruttenbai after she turned 18.[73] Although Jinnah's comments had the potential to undermine both the established positions in this debate, they were ultimately absorbed by his faction's general opposition to the bill on religious grounds.

The British member who led the discussion, Malcolm Hailey, maintained an aggrieved posture throughout the debate as if to imply that the colonial government's yielding to reformist opinion had led to unwarranted chaos. Hailey was known to be an "authoritarian" administrator, as John Cell notes; at this point in his career, he had served as chief commissioner for Delhi.[74] He claimed that the government had introduced this bill to not appear "reactionary and opposed to social advance" as it had in the previous assembly session. His own position was actually far from that of a neutral bystander. He did not dispute conservative members who redirected the debate to emphasize threats to marriage customs. As a result, although the assembly voted to raise the age of consent to 18 for girls who were "bought and sold" for the purposes of prostitution, it did not do so for girls who were "enticed away from guardians" for the purposes of prostitution.[75] This distinction implicitly set apart daughters from professional prostitutes, who were "bought and sold," from those who were "enticed away" from more respectable "guardians."

Despite the dilution and obstruction of several bills, reformists continued to assiduously pursue their legislative agenda through repeated proposals. Their new legislative prominence emboldened them to begin raising the question of sexual relations within marriage. In the 1924 assembly session, Hari Singh Gour, an attorney with a record of pursuing marriage reform, introduced a bill to raise the age of consent for both marital and nonmarital sexual relations to 14, terming all sex by husbands with wives under 14 as rape.[76] However, the government's select committee appointed to review the bill recommended that the age of consent be reduced from 14 to 13 years when a husband committed the offense, thereby shying away from interfering with "marriage customs." Gour's original proposal came with the support of major women's organizations: the Women's Indian Association (WIA) in the south and the National Council of Women in India (NCWI) based in Bombay enthusiastically promoted the measure, organizing publicity meetings and sponsoring resolutions on its behalf.[77] Ultimately, an overwhelming majority of the legislative assembly voted 65 to 22 to raise the age of consent in nonmarital cases, although only a narrow majority, 45 to 43, agreed to raise the age standard with respect to "marital rape." The colonial government responded in a predictable fashion, by opposing its final passage and declaring the bill "unsafe" to put in practice. The defeat of Gour's bill led to strong protests from women's groups; as Mrinalini Sinha notes, women's activists such as WIA founding member Dorothy Jinarajadasa (an Irish feminist married to a Sri Lankan theosophist) now campaigned in Britain and called on British women to pressure the colonial Government of India through the British Parliament.[78]

This strong response from women's groups and reformists, who were now a majority in the council, moved the government to capitulate, and in 1925 Home

Member Alexander Muddiman proposed a bill identical to Gour's, fixing 14 as the age of consent in "extra marital cases" and 13 for "marital cases." Indicative of the rising support for reform, this bill was passed by 80 votes to 11.[79] Muddiman's bill is marked as a major step in the dismantling of child marriage, but it also put into law a clear double standard for the age of consent within and outside marriage—an aspect that passed almost without note in legislative debates.

On the whole, the 1923–24 debates may be seen as a success for reformists, because the very question of raising the age of consent had drawn fire since the 1891 controversy. This success may be attributed to the introduction of international age standards to the discursive field and the nationalist narratives that these standards provoked. To not raise the age of consent was for India to not be on par with other nations. English legislators found it increasingly hard to resist such a logic of national advancement. Even though British legislators, such as Hailey, openly encouraged orthodox Indian resistance, the Indian reformist majority in the council could not be easily silenced, particularly in the face of resolute members, such as Joshi and Gour, who repeatedly issued bills despite rejection. This dynamic laid the ground for successful attempts to raise the age of marriage in the late 1920s.

Reconstituting Marriage, 1924–1929

The next few years witnessed hectic activism against child marriage, which, in turn, produced changes in the age of consent for sex outside marriage. The increasingly vocal women's movement led the way in pushing reforms related to marriage. The three national women's organizations, the WIA, the NCWI, and the All India Women's Conference (AIWC)[80] all grew in prominence through their activism on the age of marriage.[81] As Mrinalini Sinha notes, they successfully mobilized women as a political category independent of the dictates of religious and caste communities and reconfigured the relationship between social and political questions.[82] In promoting a higher age of marriage, middle-class feminists and nationalists upheld the construct of an ideal female citizen who was educated and not subjected to early motherhood and who served as a guardian of the moral polity.[83] The ideological linking of women's delayed sexual activity with the nation's civilizational maturity acquired a specific urgency with the publication of Katherine Mayo's *Mother India* in 1927; this book argues that India would be incapable of self-rule as long as child marriage persisted.[84] The book incited a defensive nationalist response, propelling legislative action against child marriage.[85] The Child Marriage Restraint Act (also called the Sarda

Act) was passed in 1929, banning marriages of girls under 14, and was widely acclaimed as an historic law. Less noticed was a concurrent provision that the age of consent for sex in "extramarital" cases be raised to 16. The remainder of this chapter explores the reasoning and silence on this second, vital, change.

Although it appears that the 1929 raising of the age of consent for nonmarital sex was buoyed by changes in the age of marriage, the link between them was not straightforward. The reformist rationale for a higher age of nonmarital sex was distinct from the rationale for a higher age of marriage; these distinct rationales become clearer when examining Malaviya's position as a prominent dissenter in the 1929 debate about child marriage. Whereas he had supported 18 as the age of consent for nonmarital sexual relations in the 1923–24 debates with Jinnah, he now declared that the age of marriage for girls should be fixed at 11 years, saying that he "considered it [his] duty to strongly oppose" the Sarda bill.[86] His written comments represented the orthodox Hindu view in the minutes of dissent for the final 1929 act. For Malaviya, having a high age of consent for nonmarital sex defused the concerns of parents anxious about daughters who remained unmarried past puberty. Once the age of consent for nonmarital sex had been raised, parents could classify any alliance their daughters independently formed as an abduction, kidnapping, or rape—offenses under the synonymous classifications "nonmarital" or "extramarital" sex. This was a logic that both reformist and orthodox legislators shared.

This logic becomes even more obvious when examining the recommendations of the Age of Consent Committee, which was established to produce a report on nationwide marriage practices. As mentioned in chapter 2, this committee presided over a massive sociological study that used six thousand surveys, the testimony of four hundred witnesses, and a tour of twenty cities and ten villages.[87] Even though the committee's *Report* focused on raising the age of marriage, it also recommended a parallel rise in the age of consent for nonmarital sex. While suggesting raising the age of marriage to 15 years from the existing 13, it also proposed that the age of consent for nonmarital sex be raised to 18 in cases of extramarital sex.[88] It applied the new age of consent to a variety of extramarital sexual offenses listed in separate Indian Penal Code sections, including rape, prostitution, and abduction. Although these were vastly different acts, the offenses that the committee found most objectionable were situations where a marriageable girl's status was altered, such as cases where "a stranger [could have a] connection with a girl of 14 with her consent in the very house of the guardian."[89] The committee formulated a clear distinction between the age of consent for nonmarital sex and marriage. In doing so, it made more palatable its general recommendation to raise the age of marriage.

The higher age of consent for nonmarital sex became a buffer allowing parents to retain control over marriageable daughters' sexual relationships.

The text of the *Report* provides insights into the rhetorical positioning of parents vis-à-vis the state. The committee strongly voiced parental anxieties in sections dealing with the age of extramarital sex. The following passage illustrates their call for the law to "step in" to protect Indian girls when parents could not do so:

> As clerks and typists in offices and as factory workers in big industrial centers, girls below 18 are employed in much larger numbers today and such employment has necessarily placed them in a position where they need utmost protection. The migration to cities and the gradual loosening of the ties of Joint Family . . . have also placed girls of a tender age, both married and unmarried, in a less sheltered position than before. Under these altered circumstances of society, it has become increasingly necessary that law should step in and afford greater protection than it has so far given. The age of 18 does not appear to err on the side of excess in light of these circumstances.[90]

The social transformations in the 1920s were indeed substantial, particularly among poor families. The number of female factory workers employed in this period rose sharply; as Radha Kumar notes, women began to form up to a quarter of the labor force in cotton textile factories for the first time in the 1920s in cities such as Bombay.[91] This was also a period of greater women's visibility in the labor movement. Women workers stood at the head of picket lines during strikes in Bombay and Calcutta, and there were prominent female leaders of railways and textile workers in Bombay.[92] In Madras, the WIA, the first major women's organization, developed associations of women millworkers because of their urgent demands.[93] Women's access to higher education had also rapidly expanded in the decade preceding the age of marriage reforms, with the spread of colleges, industrial schools, and even universities for women. In 1914 there were 16 colleges for women in major cities; in 1916 Shreemati Nathibai Damodar Thackersey Women's University (SNDT Women's University) was set up in Poona; in 1919 the Calcutta University Commission opened postgraduate classes to women.[94] Although many upper-class parents were enthusiastic about such opportunities in the hope of improving their daughters' marriage prospects—based on the premise that well-educated grooms sought well-educated brides—many poorer parents also saw value in the incomes their educated daughters could bring in through employment in schoolteaching, spinning, embroidery, and lacemaking.[95] The Age of Consent Committee thus cited girls' capacity to be employed before marriage as an ideal and relied on the prevailing images of expanding female educational and employment opportunities.[96] It proposed a new vision of womanhood, emphasizing the seeking of "equal opportunities" and the value of education as a way to occupy young girls' minds, and presented education as a means to increase women's worth: "A capacity for earning must exist in a woman to ensure her a more vivid recognition by the husband of the woman's share in conducting a home."[97]

Girls' increasing access to higher education institutions and new types of employment fostered a potential erosion in parental supervision; it also offered opportunities to interact with nonfamilial males. It was in the context of these changing horizons for girls that the committee framed its anxieties. Referring to the statements of witnesses from across the country, the committee noted some "expressed apprehensions . . . about girls in rural areas and working in factories" and warned that an Indian girl who embarked on an illicit sexual encounter may know "the physical nature of the act" but was not worldly enough to recognize the consequences of sexual relations with men other than those her parents chose. The committee listed the following as certain outcomes: "social degradation," "utter aloofness," "likelihood of the birth of illegitimate offspring," and "grave consequences to her whole future existence." The committee's rationale for a high age of consent for nonmarital sex was framed in no uncertain terms as parents' ensuring the marriageability of their daughters: the *Report* states that regardless of whether a girl consented to or resisted the "offense" of nonmarital sex, "it is very difficult *to secure for her* a suitable husband."[98] The committee's adoption of a parental voice is clear in this last sentence: the state and parents were presumed to speak as one. Reformists, then, were arguing for state protection of girls using terms similar to the orthodox argument *against* raising the age of marriage: preserving female honor and consolidating the legitimacy of marriage. The parental (and indeed paternal) state was being asked to assist parents in securing daughters for marriage.

In advocating an age of consent for nonmarital sex that was higher than the age of consent for marriage, the committee implied that decisions about marriage did not require the same mental maturity as engaging in nonmarital sex did. This distinction is demonstrated in the choice of words used to describe the girls in question. When it discussed consent to nonmarital sex, the committee described any girl under the age of 18 years as "an infant"; she would be "incapable of entering into a binding contract for the disposal of her property . . . and [her] own person." No such mention of "an infant under 18 years" appears in the *Report*'s chapters on age of marriage; a girl could, for the committee, experience the condition of being married to a stranger, engage in sexual intercourse, and bear children well before this age. So committed is the *Report* to the sanctity of the married state that it coins the rather forgiving term "marital misbehavior" for the offense of husbands having sex with wives under the age of 14. In its section on nonmarital sex, however, the *Report* declares that "a girl at 14 is not fit for the sexual act"; sex with strangers for girls under 14 is deemed "rape."[99] This discrepancy between marital and nonmarital sex underlines the fact that for legislators, the party conferring consent was the parent.

Despite the Age of Consent Committee's contradictory definitions of girlhood within and outside marriage, it did promote a change in the general construct of girlhood consistent with shifts in the 1920s. It articulated girlhood as a time of "freedom and joy," as mentioned in chapter 2.[100] In suggesting a change in the age of marriage from 12 to 14, the committee sought to distance the age of marriage from the age of menstruation, arguing that the onset of menstruation did not signal full bodily maturity and that pregnancy entailed physical hardship: "Why should women, the weaker sex, be exposed at a tender age to the strain, not of one day's hard labor . . . but to the nine months' strain of the growth of a foreign body inside them followed by the intense exertion of labor, which even in the easiest cases throws a great strain on the heart and kidneys?"[101] While such attention to the plight of young mothers is noteworthy, it is clear that this issue entered the nationalist agenda largely because of the eugenicist arguments of the era that linked the health of the "race" with the age at which girls became mothers.[102] The first two arguments that the *Report* presented for raising the age of consent were "physiological and eugenic" reasons, and the *Report* clearly outlined the importance of ensuring the health of the progeny of legitimate mothers.[103] Mothers had to be equipped with "enough knowledge to conduct a home and to bring forth and to rear children . . . and those below 16 could not have had the time to acquire such 'minimum' knowledge," it argued.[104] With the decline of joint families, the independent running of households "necessitated previous preparation."[105]

Comparisons between maturity standards for boys and girls were generally rare, and there was a striking taken-for-grantedness about ideas concerning boys' physical and emotional development. For boys, marriageability was clearly delinked from the onset of puberty and linked instead to the legal age of majority, 18. The law deemed boys under this age incapable of entering into a binding contract for the disposal of property and, by extrapolation, marriage. Although boys did get married before this age, as implied in Ranglal Jajodia's 1924 attempt to penalize marriage of boys under 16, the idea that boys delay marriage until the end of their teen years was socially acceptable. The 1929 CMRA's decree that boys could not marry until they turned 18 met with less protest than its measure that girls could not marry until the age of 14. In fact, the *Report* propagated the view that boys under 18 were emotionally immature. It argued that boys younger than 18 years—an age that the *Report* termed "tender" for boys—needed protection against "the blandishments of girls over 16" and "designing girls" who could lead them to be "penalized" for acts for which the boys were not wholly responsible. Here it presented a distinction between "chaste" and "unchaste" girls, defining a separate category of girls who sought to entrap men.[106] Thus, many contextual variations and contradictions in the concept of girlhood were elaborated by the committee.

In passing the 1929 Age of Marriage Law, legislators addressed an audience both within and outside India.[107] The *Report* called for extending the span of childhood for Indian girls but did so while comparing their physical maturity with girls of other "races." The *Report* references and reproduces in its appendix a League of Nations document that lists the age of consent in countries of Europe and individual states in the United States.[108] In so doing, the *Report* mirrors the tendency among women's organizations to frame the status of women in India in comparative terms as a means to spur change.[109] Women's organizations of the era adopted internationalist angles on many of the social problems they faced and looked beyond Britain as a model. Although the very idea of a legal age of consent was popularized through British cultural hegemony and remains an Anglocentric formulation, British law, because of its own low age of consent, was not the principal referent for Indian legislators.[110] British common law had for a century held that a girl over 12 was capable of marriage. Indeed, activism in India stimulated the codification of marriage law in Britain: in the spring of 1929, the British Parliament passed an Age of Marriage Act rendering void any marriage of children under the age of 16. The activism of British women's organizations interested in the CMRA in India directly contributed to the momentum for raising the age of consent in Britain through key figures, such as Eleanor Rathbone, who also lobbied for the passage of CMRA.[111] As Stephen Cretney notes, the 1929 law in Britain was passed without much prior campaigning and seemed motivated largely by threatened British "national prestige."[112] Indian consent laws were not so much modeled after those in Britain as forged in response to notions of Indian inadequacy on a world stage.

An irony in the legal wrangling over the age of consent for nonmarital sex is that it grew far removed from its original referent, prostitution. The term "immoral sexual relations," which was consolidated in the context of efforts against the sale of girls into prostitution in 1911, became a different kind of legal standard by 1929. In the *Report*, the chapter on age of consent for nonmarital sex mentions girls in prostitution as a separate subcategory, but the main constituents were the "ordinary classes who lead a normally chaste life" and girls who experience "the horror of ravishment by a stranger."[113] In other words, prostitute girls, the initial targets of such measures, were no longer worthwhile victims for legislators. Laws raising the age of consent for nonmarital sex ultimately had less to do with prostitution per se than with the state's channeling of sexual activity toward marriage.

* * *

My story here offers a counterpoint to the triumphalism that is sometimes associated with the 1929 banning of child marriage: I have argued that this moment was not as transformative as it appears if one considers changes in the age of consent for nonmarital sex. In exploring why the age of consent for nonmarital sex was raised earlier and higher than that for marriage, I have linked two processes: the international valorization of raising the age of consent and the increased parental control enabled by such laws regulating nonmarital sex. The 1929 CMRA responded both to sociological shifts—incorporating the aspirations for female education and employment—and to the outward-directed political imperative of national prestige but only while staving off the perceived dangers of increased sexual autonomy for girls.

British colonial interests were consistently conservative on this issue. As seen in legislative debates from 1911 to 1929, the colonial state thwarted several attempts to raise the age of consent for nonmarital sexual relations. British administrators justified their reticence by arguing that Indians were resistant to change and by essentializing Indian physiological and cultural traits. The colonial government's nurturing of religious orthodoxy shows its active effort to shore up a civilizational difference between India and Britain—a prerequisite for the colonial government's stated civilizing mission.

Indian reformist legislators who sought to overcome such colonial obstructionism received a boost from international conventions against trafficking: these antitrafficking measures buttressed local anticolonial politics. In their measures to raise the age of consent in sections of the Indian Penal Code dealing with procuring, rape, and concubinage, reformists incorporated the 1910 convention and League of Nations standards. This chapter effectively traces Indian legislators' international turn. Unlike the 1891 controversy, when religious revivalist opposition to raising the age of consent had the aura of a nationalist goal, it was reformists in the early twentieth century who were able to couch their struggle in anticolonial terms. Contesting the colonial narrative of Indian "backwardness," they turned the Indian age of consent into a matter of national honor. They were able to redirect international antitrafficking discourse, itself emerging in an imperial context, to serve a nationalist agenda.

Their effort was successful because it elevated concerns about protecting respectable Indian women. As with other controversies over social reform, such as widow remarriage and sati, female honor was the terrain on which the political struggle among colonial administrators, reformers, and religious revivalists was carried out.[114] Unlike these other controversies in which religious revivalists and nationalists were arrayed against anglicized Indian reformers, the debates on the age of nonmarital sex evinced fewer ideological camps. Religious nationalists who opposed reform of the age of marriage also supported bills to raise the age of nonmarital sex. Reformists—simultaneously nationalist *and* orthodox *and* modern in this case—managed, ultimately, to have the state serve as a supportive surrogate parent that prevented "undesirable" marriages by setting a higher age of consent for nonmarital sex. Even as "late" marriages appeared to challenge social orthodoxy, the state secured the legitimacy of such marriages through a stricter regulation of nonmarital sexual relations. The next chapter moves the focus back to the intergovernmental setting, exploring how the age of marriage (rather than prostitution) emerged as a site of international debate after World War II.

4

Early Marriage as Slavery

UN Interventions, 1948–1965

Many scholars of women's legal rights are only barely aware that in the mid-twentieth century, the United Nations presided over an international convention—or multilateral treaty—to prevent early marriage. This 1962 convention, titled the UN Convention on Consent to Marriage, Minimum Age of Marriage, and Registration of Marriage, long remained an unpublicized international legal instrument until it more recently became a plank in the campaign to legalize same-sex marriage, because it enshrines the human rights principle of freedom of marriage.[1] The 1962 convention on marriage had 16 original signatories and then 55 countries that ratified it, and today more than 120 countries are party to it. This chapter describes the process by which the UN formulated its interest in standardizing marriage practices around the world and in preventing child marriage. It traces how cultural variation in marriage age and sexual consent again became a matter of international contention, with India figuring in the debates as a problem site and Indian delegates playing an obstructionist role. The chapter explains how the final intergovernmental agreement for a common age-of-marriage standard of 15 years for girls was passed.

The 1962 convention is typically narrated as an accomplishment of women's advocacy groups.[2] I argue, however, that it is because UN delegates framed forced marriage as akin to slavery that the convention came into being. In this sense, the success of the 1962 convention may be attributed to the rhetorical force that antislavery discourse had in the geopolitical reconfigurations of the post–World War II period. Much of this chapter focuses on how age standards became a means to express geopolitical hierarchies, and it includes attention to the role that Indian delegates played in attempting to obstruct the convention, amidst a very public reckoning with the problem of child marriage in India.

At first glance, it is surprising that the UN addressed the question of what an appropriate age of marriage should be around the world while it was still a fledgling organization. Founded in 1945, the primary goal of this intergovernmental association was to prevent global conflict, but like its predecessor, the League of Nations, the UN also took on an array of social and economic goals. It could be argued that the UN was significantly more successful on these other fronts than in preventing conflict. It founded several bodies to attend to social and economic goals, such as the umbrella Economic and Social Council (ECOSOC), the Food and Agricultural Organization (FAO), the World Health Organization (WHO), the International Court of Justice (ICJ), the UN Development Program (UNDP), and the UN High Commission on Refugees (UNHCR). It was ECOSOC, a body with representatives elected by the General Assembly (the main deliberative organ of the UN with members from every country), that targeted the question of marriage and its forms. The timing of the UN's interest in marriage appears incongruous—this was long before the UN Decade for Women (1975–85) and well after child marriage had been publicized as an Indian problem in the 1920s. So why did this issue emerge at this moment?

The chronology of UN interventions detailed in this chapter follows this rough order: in 1951 the question of marriage practices as slavery was raised in the Ad Hoc Committee appointed to report on slavery. In 1956 the General Assembly approved a ban on forced marriage and over the next several years, debated legal instruments specifying a minimum age of marriage. In 1958 the assembly proposed an international convention to prevent early marriage. In 1962 the assembly approved the text of the Convention on Consent to Marriage, Minimum Age of Marriage, and Registration of Marriage and opened it for signature and ratification. This document recommended, among other matters, that all countries set a minimum age of marriage. While the treaty was being signed by various member states (it formally entered into force in 1964), it was supplemented by a formal recommendation specifying a minimum age of marriage, of 15 years, which was adopted in 1965. The questions explored in this chapter are: What was going on? Why and how did an intergovernmental organization of this scale in its tentative years—its first decade of existence—pursue marriage-age standards and adopt a stance on what was bound to be, and what, indeed, turned out to be, a contentious issue?

The official explanation, as recounted by Boutros Boutros-Ghali, UN secretary-general in the 1990s, is that the Commission on the Status of Women (CSW) was the prime mover in spearheading this legal instrument.[3] The CSW, an intergovernmental body formed in 1946 to promote the goal of women's advancement, consisted of national representatives appointed by governments and of representatives of nongovernmental organizations (NGOs).[4] Early in its life, relying on the energies of its constituent groups, such as the International Alliance of Women, the CSW placed marriage-related laws on the UN agenda. In 1954 it urged the UN General Assembly to pass a resolution (Resolution 843 IX) to take measures to "abolish customs, ancient laws and practices limiting the freedom in the choice of a spouse, the practices of bride price, and the betrothal of young girls before the age of puberty."[5] The CSW also facilitated the passage of the 1957 Convention on the Nationality of Married Women, which enabled women to retain the nationality of their choice after marriage to men of other nationalities. Concomitantly, the CSW gathered information on marriage practices around the world and the extent of free consent to marriage and child marriage. According to Boutros-Ghali, the CSW reported that the practice of "giving girls away in marriage between the ages of 11 and 13 was widespread" and therefore pressed for an international instrument that would cover the minimum age of marriage.[6] The resulting 1962 Convention on Consent to Marriage, Minimum Age for Marriage, and Registration of Marriages remains, according to him, one of the "only international agreements on women's rights relating to marriage adopted by the United Nations."[7] Devaki Jain, a pioneering scholar of women's advocacy within the UN, also notes, "As early as the 1950s, the UN confronted the prototypes of what later would be called human rights violations against women and children."[8] In her account, the case of child marriage is one of the few where "the UN responded to abuses through legislation,"[9] and it did so by means of the CSW's efforts.

Although women's organizations such as CSW played a major role in this process, I suggest that the success of this 1950s effort may be attributed to the specific framing used in that moment: rather than efforts in the name of women's status, it was the abolitionist energy around ending slavery that propelled questions of early marriage and age of consent to the forefront of the UN's agenda. The countries that sought to redefine marriage practices as slavery, such as Britain and Spain, were current and former imperial countries that had been perpetrators of the transatlantic slave trade. The next section details the specific political appeal of championing antislavery for such countries.

CHAPTER 4

The Context of Postwar Abolitionism

In the late 1940s and early 1950s, the UN General Assembly entrusted ECOSOC with studying the problem of slavery. In 1926 the League of Nations had passed a slavery convention aimed at establishing agreement among all countries to prevent slavery and, specifically, the traffic in African slaves; the new UN body ECOSOC now considered it part of its mandate to continue to guard against this social problem. In 1949, in the aftermath of the signing of the Declaration of Human Rights, the General Assembly requested that ECOSOC report on the problem of slavery at the next assembly session, calling on ECOSOC to assess the "nature and extent" of slavery and "other institutions and customs resembling slavery" and "to suggest methods of attacking these problems."[10] On May 4, 1951, the Ad Hoc ECOSOC Committee appointed to examine this topic reported that "apart from slavery in its crudest form, a number of institutions or practices analogous to slavery or resembling slavery in some of their effects still existed in various parts of the world." The committee listed a number of institutions it considered to be analogous to slavery, such as (the more familiar) debt bondage, serfdom, and customary forced work; it then included forced marriage and child marriage.[11] The intervention of the CSW appears to have been crucial at this point, Jain observes:

> In 1952, ECOSOC, acting on the recommendations of the CSW, asked member states to "abolish progressively ... all customs that violate the physical integrity of women and which thereby violate the dignity and worth of the human person as proclaimed in the Charter and in the Universal Declaration of Human Rights." ... Though female genital mutilation was the most publicized issue, several others fell under the general rubric of violations of the bodily integrity of women and girls, such as child marriage, bride price, and dowry.[12]

ECOSOC declared that the 1926 League of Nations Convention on the Abolition of Slavery needed to be updated since it did not cover all such practices, and it proposed that a supplementary convention on slavery be prepared and adopted. This antislavery convention, the 1956 UN Supplementary Convention on the Abolition of Slavery, first proposed regulating the age of marriage.

Even though it was the CSW that proposed attention to marriage-related practices, it was the rhetoric of antislavery that drove the momentum toward the 1956 Supplementary Convention on the Abolition of Slavery. Egon Schwelb, a notable Czech-born human rights lawyer who served as deputy director of the Division of Human Rights of the UN Secretariat, confirms this argument by describing the UN agreement on marriage to be "the most recent upshot of the international struggle against slavery."[13] In the immediate aftermath of World War II and the rawness of the horrors of genocide and fascism, the UN had crystallized opposition to state authoritarianism in the form of the 1948 Universal Declaration of Human Rights. The highly individuated language of human rights facilitated the condemnation of multiple forms of force exerted over an individual, whether by tyrannical states or tyrannical social and economic customs. The enslavement of one individual's will to another's became the abstract blueprint for a range of offenses. When the UN General Assembly set forth an unusually strong resolution about marriage practices on December 17, 1954, it cited the force of this 1948 universal declaration: "Certain customs, ancient laws and practices relating to marriage and the family were inconsistent with the principles set forth in the UN Charter and in the Universal Declaration of Human Rights." It called on all states to ensure "complete freedom in the choice of a spouse, eliminating completely child marriage and betrothals of young girls before the age of puberty, establishing appropriate penalties where necessary and establishing a civil or other register in which all marriages will be recorded."[14] Interestingly, the General Assembly glossed over "slavery in its crudest form," or chattel slavery (the most commonly understood form of slavery), and instead expounded in bullet-point detail the new practices that would be incorporated into the scope of slavery, such as forced marriage and child marriage. These practices then became the locus of intergovernmental discussions under the rubric of antislavery action.

The expansion of the definition of slavery unfolded thus: in August and September of 1956, the United Nations convened a Conference of Plenipotentiaries to discuss a supplement to the 1926 League of Nations Convention on Slavery, with a focus on "institutions and practices similar to slavery." This Conference of Plenipotentiaries consisted of delegates of fifty-one states, including several countries that had imperial histories, such as Britain, France, Spain, Portugal, Netherlands, Italy, and Belgium, as well as several former colonies, such as Argentina, Haiti, Guatemala, India, Pakistan, Canada, Australia, and the Philippines. These delegates adopted a resolution expanding the definition of slavery to include several new clauses about forced marriage as well as debt bondage and child labor. In order to clarify what "free marriage" meant, the delegates agreed that individual consent to marriage distinguished it foundationally from "slave-like marriage." It now became paramount to establish an age at which consent was possible. For this reason, article 2 of the resolution recommended that states adopt a minimum age of marriage, although no specific age was mentioned. It is clear that the process was fraught: UN records note that when a phrase specifying the minimum age of marriage as "preferably of not less than 14 years" was introduced in 1956 Supplementary Convention, there were twenty abstentions.[15] The final version of the supplementary convention did not include mention of the age 14.

Apart from opening up the question of age as it related to forced marriage, the 1956 Supplementary Convention on Slavery also constructed new clauses defining force in marriage. It defined "servile marriage" as comprising three objectionable practices that it called on states to progressively eradicate: when a woman, without right to refuse, was promised or given in marriage for payment; when a husband or conjugal family or clan sold a wife; and when a woman was inherited by another person after the death of her husband. In outlining each of these specific scenarios, the formulators were clearly applying an understanding of slavery rooted in the ownership of another human being and extending it to this context of marriage.[16] They were also transplanting a terminological apparatus related to slavery when using words such as "servile marriage," "servitude," and "slave-like marriage."

There were certainly grounds for drawing links between marriage-related practices and slavery. Both slavery and traditional marriage involved persons entering a lifelong relationship with no right of subsequent refusal.[17] In addition, both slavery and marriage explicitly involved classifying a person as belonging to another. Indeed, the husband's legal "ownership" of the wife was reinscribed through such practices as changing the wife's last name. The relationship was also defined both technically and culturally as involving servitude, since wives were expected to tend to the needs of their husbands. Finally, there were certainly many contexts in which wives were treated as transferable property: when husbands sold wives to others or upon the death of the husband, when wives were transferred to the husband's brother (called levirate marriage). The UN effort to draw on abolitionist energy to intervene in marriage was therefore not, in analytical terms, misplaced.

This likening of marriage to slavery has a long history in feminist discourses in many settings. In Britain, Aphra Behn's 1676 play *The Rover* drew this parallel,[18] US abolitionists and suffragists in the mid-nineteenth century famously made this connection in the 1848 Seneca Falls Declaration, and early twentieth-century Indian writer Rokeya Sakhawat Hossain, especially in her 1905 *Sultana's Dream*, draws the analogy between marriage and slavery.[19] Some have complained that this analogy could be stretched too far—for instance, Angela Davis has noted that when all marriage is likened to slavery, it potentially trivializes the violence of slavery.[20] Anna Mae Duane has also observed that the "use of the term slavery to account for a host of practices, with different levels of consent, coercion and harm, diminishes the horror of chattel slavery."[21] Nonetheless, it is the case that marriage has too often been cast as a private sacrament, allowing its abuses to be exempted from legal scrutiny. So, the effort to broaden the analytical cast of marriage in this instance was a welcome development.

When the postwar abolitionists called for banning those forms of marriages that were close to slavery, they were also calling for more faithfully applying the Declaration of Human Rights of 1948, which in article 16 laid down the freedom of marriage. But because the terrain the UN was entering was so controversial and the potential for failure so high, it had to proceed carefully. Making marriage, a religiously sanctioned custom, analogous to slavery, a practice that had gained universal opprobrium in the mid-twentieth century, could provoke outrage. As a result, a plethora of meetings, statements, memos, and even a large-scale study were conducted under the auspices of the UN in the late 1950s on the topic of marriage, all of which appear frequently when one searches the archives of the UN's ECOSOC for this period. This multitude of discussions show how slow and highly deliberative the 1956 supplementary convention was.

A contrast is instructive here. Around the same time as it worked to define early and forced marriage as slavery, the UN General Assembly decided to relegitimize the 1924 Geneva Declaration of the Rights of the Child, just as it had done with the 1926 League of Nations convention on slavery. The process for relegitimizing the rights of child declaration took far less time: within a year, in 1959, the assembly was able to formulate and adopt an expanded version, adding ten principles to the original five. However, the debate on defining early and forced marriage as slavery stretched out over at least nine years, exercising the energies of numerous bureaucrats and nongovernmental advocacy organizations.

There is another way to frame this effort to redefine marriage. This newly expanded definition of slavery—to focus on child marriage, bride price, and dowry—deflected attention away from European states, who had been the principal perpetrators in the transatlantic slave trade as well as in Nazi slave labor camps, the most recent examples of slavery.[22] The focus now was placed on many newly independent states or former colonies that were presented as principal sites for the perpetration of slavery-like practices. In displacing abolitionist attention onto former colonies and onto how their states regulated marriage, the 1956 Supplementary Convention on Marriage rehearsed a familiar theme about the civilizational inadequacy of these countries.

A closer look at how slavery's definition was expanded would support this interpretation. It was the United Kingdom that submitted the draft on which the initial text of the supplementary convention was based.[23] Repeating a dynamic from the 1921 debates at the League of Nations (described in chapter 1), the British delegates presented themselves in a tutelary relationship to other countries' delegates. Again, in parallel to 1920s League of Nations conversations, the other former imperial European powers—France and Portugal—did not immediately sign in 1956 the amended version of the 1926 convention.[24] The United Kingdom, in other words, assumed the mantle of speaking on behalf of the cause of antislavery, while other European powers expressed caution about the applicability of universal standards concerning marriage. Neither of these impulses—to claim a tutelary role nor to obstruct in the name of cultural difference—were politically innocent. British claims to moral authority on this ground were disingenuous, because British law itself was not especially trendsetting on the matter of marriage age; the legal age of marriage had been 12 until 1929, lower than several other European countries, and child marriage had a long history in the country.[25] British colonial officers supported lower ages of marriage in colonies in order to garner the support of local orthodox constituents. As chapter 1 mentions, S. M. Edwardes, the British delegate representing India at the League of Nations conference on trafficking, obstructed the attempt to harmonize a common age of sexual consent. In the UN context as well, the South African delegate (representing the white population of South Africa) was the only one of two voices from countries in Africa who expressed reservations about intervening in marriage practices; other delegates from Africa were vocal in calling for changing marriage practices.[26] Interestingly, then, it is not the case that representatives of all newly independent states were, prima facie, opposed to interventions in marriage practices. And those who opposed the imposition of a universal standard, such as Portugal, Belgium, and the Netherlands, were likely more motivated by the exigencies of governing smoothly in colonies and opposing Britain's attempt to claim moral authority rather than an impulse to uphold the interests of girls and women. Again, Lauren Benton and Lisa Ford's observations about how competitive jockeying by nineteenth-century imperial powers shaped international law can be extended to this context, especially because this case underscores how imperial contexts have shaped international law.[27]

The 1956 Ad Hoc Committee appointed to examine the draft of the supplementary convention (the draft the United Kingdom initially submitted) held twenty plenary meetings; it consisted of delegates from Australia, Ecuador, Egypt, France, India, the Netherlands, Turkey, Union of Soviet Socialist Republics (USSR), United Kingdom, and Yugoslavia. The most heavily debated items in the draft included the subject of article 2: how to establish and record the free expression of the consent of both parties to a marriage. Marriage practices varied widely and did not always entail the formal expression of consent between the wedded parties, so to some delegates from non-Christian countries, the expectation of recording consent itself seemed ethnocentric.[28] Thirty countries signed the 1956 Supplementary Convention on Slavery, compared to the forty-six for the 1926 Convention on Slavery—and at a time when the number of independent countries (and potential signatories) in the world had actually increased.[29] Following the adoption of the 1956 supplementary convention, the members who had participated agreed that a separate and deeper discussion of the variation in marriage practices around the world was required. They recommended to ECOSOC that its members prepare a report that would draw "attention to the desirability of free consent of both parties and of the establishment of a minimum age of marriage, preferably of not less than 14 years."[30] In other words, the mandate of this ECOSOC study was to generate material that would confirm the desirability of establishing 14 as the minimum age of marriage.

The Longer Debate, 1958–1965

The CSW took the lead in generating the information for the ECOSOC study and consulted with scholarly sources and national delegates. The fifteen members of the CSW hailed from countries that were not just members of the Security Council; they included Mexico, India, Guatemala, Costa Rica, China, Turkey, Venezuela, and Syria.[31] The CSW submitted a report of the nearly two-year study to ECOSOC in 1958. The twenty-one-page report, "Consent to Marriage and Age of Marriage: Report by the Secretary-General," offers a brief survey of the kinds of marriages practiced across the world along with the criteria of consent and age.[32] The first chapter proposes four main types of marriage based on descending degrees of consent: only the consent of the spouses matters; the consent of spouses holds authority above a certain age, but below this age, consent reverts to the parents; the groom's consent after a certain age is required but not the bride's, and parental consent is always required; and the consent of neither spouse is required, and parental consent is sufficient.[33] This world tour of marriage, so to speak, also went into some detail about Islamic and Chinese "systems" (while still oversimplifying the complexity of these contexts), drawing from both scholarly sources as well as accounts presented by national delegates. India figured prominently in the section detailing child marriage, with a spotlight on the role that parents played in arranging marriage matches.

The second chapter summarizes how countries varied in their laws on the age of marriage, with a detailed appendix of the minimum ages of marriage for girls and boys. Across the world, the report found, societies encouraged a lower age of marriage for girls than for boys and that the age of marriage for girls often was lower than 14 years. The most significant aspect of this document is how it details the range of marriage practices without passing judgment and at the same time reveals a fault line in the politics of the UN between the United States and European countries and the nonaligned bloc, several of which were newly independent countries. This fault line, now termed the North-South divide in the post–Cold War era, has persisted across several arenas of UN action, which Jain notes in her history of the UN and women.[34]

Even after this report was compiled, the UN continued its fact-finding mission on marriage in order to elucidate the precise contours of the problem and classify it by scale. The UN secretary-general sent out a three-page, multiple-choice questionnaire to all member countries, laying out in detail the various scenarios under which marriage occurred: whether consent had to be granted by wife, by husband, by both, or by parents; what the minimum age was below which a marriage was considered invalid; and whether marriages were registered.[35] The question format intended to cover all possible conditions and was also admirable for its eye toward specifying, and potentially creating, specific legal instruments. For instance, question 4 in section 2 (on the age of marriage) reads:

> What is the effect of the non-observance of rules concerning age of marriage on
> a) the validity of the marriage
> b) the liability (i) civil or (ii) criminal of the persons concerned?

Such a question pushed states to consider whether their enforcement of age of marriage laws needed to be strengthened by instituting criminal, and not only civil, suits against offenders. This questionnaire is an example of how the UN contributed to norm creation by mobilizing the language of shared expertise.

The questionnaire was also distributed to NGOs holding consultative status, who became the loudest advocates for raising the minimum age of marriage. St. Joan's International Social and Political Alliance, a Catholic UK-based suffrage organization with consultative status to the CSW, in 1957 recommended a minimum universal age of marriage of 16, after starting with proposing 14 in 1956. In a 1958 statement, St. Joan's Alliance observed that member states of the UN were unduly cautious in calling for "evolutionary processes and educational measures to take effect" when considering marriage age. Too many governments, they felt, were unwilling to direct this kind of social change and instead let norms shift on their own. But "[t]oo much caution means leaving countless children to suffer," St. Joan's observed, noting also that "laws never actually overhauled tradition and that changes occurred slowly anyway."[36]

The Antislavery Society for the Protection of Human Rights, another British NGO, founded in 1839 and with a long history of participating in abolitionist causes, also submitted a forceful statement to the secretary-general about women's status in marriage law, calling for a ban on marriages between people below the age of puberty in the interest of establishing genuine consent as the basis for marriage. This organization also paid considerable attention to the practice of monetary exchanges accompanying marriage, such as bride price, given its focus on slavery. The group's statement inveighed against marriages that were "entered into as a purely commercial transaction between the parties to the marriage or between the parents of guardians of parties to a marriage."[37] The statement upheld an ideal of "marriage as a partnership of equals, the only basis on which a marriage can be founded with significance to both parties and with hope of enduring value to them, the children and the community."[38] It presented Britain as the moral touchstone in these matters—ignoring centuries of arranged marriages within the aristocracy—when noting that "even in societies such as the British where women's social equality of status is substantially accepted ... the concept of the husband as the head of the family persists."[39] Despite positioning themselves as NGOs speaking for all women, these organizations frequently reverted to their national allegiances in praising British practices.

The International Alliance of Women, a nongovernmental group with consultative status to the CSW and founded by US suffragists in 1902, was also bold in calling for a common standard age of marriage. In 1961 the alliance supported 16 years as the minimum age of marriage, in a statement submitted to the ECOSOC. This statement sought to balance the dual goals of preventing too-young girls from marrying as well as preparing girls for successful marriages. It accommodated the standard psychological reasoning about adolescence: "the age of 16 should allow for some settlement of normal emotional disturbances that arise from puberty; provide some safeguard against too early marital relations; and further provide an opportunity for better education in preparation for marriage, since the mother carries a heavy share of responsibility for the well-being of child, family and nation." This NGO hoped for an even higher age of marriage, as its statement registered "pleasure that certain Governments clearly regard[ed] the age of 15 as too young."[40]

Debate continued in the UN about whether girls matured earlier in tropical countries and whether the marriage age should be correspondingly low there, echoing arguments voiced during League of Nations deliberations in the 1920s (examined in chapter 1). St. Joan's took a strong stance against tropical exceptions: "The very countries where climate was used as an excuse for being content with a lower marriage age are now in the forefront of progress," and noted that in Brazil, Ethiopia, Jordan, and Tonga (where the climate was warm), the age of marriage for girls was over sixteen.[41] Members of this NGO observed that there remained "ninety-four countries where the marriage age was under fifteen" and that these "were not primarily tropical or semi-tropical countries, but include three of the States of Australia, Ireland, Newfoundland, Quebec, and four states of the United States of America."[42] Such examples powerfully countered the narrative that tropical countries required a lower age of marriage.

From these examples, we see that British and US NGOs contributed vital voices to debates in the period from 1958 through 1961 about drafting the convention on marriage. At one point, when it appeared that no agreement would be reached on a minimum age of marriage, the International Federation of Women Lawyers (also having consultative status) weighed in, expressing "deep concern" and calling for a "definite mention" in article 2 of the convention of a minimum age of marriage for all countries of "no less than fourteen years."[43] The contentiousness of setting a common age is evident from the following detail: the first draft of the Convention on Marriage, submitted in 1959, left a blank space where a number should have been entered because naming an actual age was so sensitive. (The draft also contained two alternative provisions for its article 1: the first provided for a different age of marriage for women and men, and the second provided the same minimum age for both.)[44] Those who worked on the draft must have felt that mentioning a specific age would stir up opposition and doom the prospects of the convention as a whole.

The delegate from India played an obstructionist role in the process of setting a common marriage age, not unlike the role Edwardes played in the 1920s. Rather than expressing unease about specifying an age, as happened during the League of Nations debates, the Indian delegate in 1961 proposed an amendment to the convention that weakened the idea of consent itself: he asked to qualify article 1 concerning "free and full consent" by bringing into the picture the voices of parents. "For [the] purposes of this article," he requested, "'free and full consent' in the case of minors shall mean and include not only the consent of both parties to marriage but also the consent of the guardians of such minors."[45] This statement demonstrates the extent to which the practice of parents arranging marriages was entrenched in India; the Indian delegates imagined it was possible to make the guardian, or parents, count as an important party to the marriage. Given the prominence of India as a problem site where early marriage was widely practiced, it is not surprising that this proposal was not accepted. Another Indian delegate, Nemi Chandra Kasliwal, chair of the Third Committee drafting of the 1962 convention, also played a clearly obstructionist role: he downplayed the importance of the Universal Declaration of Human Rights by changing the wording in the preamble's opening sentence from "*Recognizing* that, as stated in Article 16 of the Universal Declaration of Human Rights" to "*Recalling* that Article 16 of the Universal Declaration of Human Rights states that." This change in phrasing allowed countries to not feel bound by the language of the declaration, according to Schwelb.[46] India was thus not only a problem site when it came to child marriage; Indian national delegates actually stymied international efforts to eradicate child marriage.

Notwithstanding Indian opposition, the General Assembly approved the Convention on Consent, Age, and Registration of Marriage on November 7, 1962, and opened it for signature and ratification by countries on December 10, 1962, which was, significantly, declared Human Rights Day.[47] The document specified that all states that signed the convention "shall take legislative action to specify a minimum age for marriage" and seek to "eliminate completely child marriages and the betrothal of young girls before the age of puberty."[48] In January 1963, U Thant, the Burmese secretary-general of the UN from 1961 to 1971, issued a memo to the CSW asking the commission to consider new text to add to the convention specifying the age of 15 as a minimum. The draft text he proposed reads, "No marriage of any person under the age of fifteen shall be legally entered into except where a competent authority has granted a dispensation as to age, for serious causes, in the interest of the intending spouses."[49] It is noteworthy that U Thant took this bold step of calling for a specific age of marriage; a few years later, he also declared the importance of the right of parents to decide the number of children they would have—his positions were, as Alison Bashford notes, clearly aligned with promoting contraception and population control (explained in greater detail in the chapter 5).[50]

In March 1963, and in response to the secretary-general's draft text, the CSW discussed the implementation of the 1962 convention. Many CSW delegates worried that signatory countries were not implementing it in good faith; the Netherlands delegate bemoaned the fact that countries were able to "formulate reservations on any of the clauses, even substantive ones." Two specific problems were under consideration at this meeting: "marriage by proxy," which was the practice of having a girl's consent to marriage communicated by a representative, usually her guardian, a practice that delegates from Spain, Argentina, and Indonesia, in particular, wanted to continue to allow; and specification of a minimum age of marriage. Unlike the nongovernmental women's organizations described in previous paragraphs, national delegates to the CSW tended to be conservative about accepting a higher age of marriage. The UK delegate felt that "fifteen was a suitable age, for too high a minimum age would cause difficulties for countries where girls reached puberty early and did not continue their education after the age of fifteen." We see from this statement that national and geographic variations in the age of puberty figured in conversations into the 1960s. The USSR delegate recommended not specifying the age of marriage because "very different views were held on it."[51] Even though many of the official delegates to the CSW were women entrusted with advancing the status of women, they tended to remain loyal to their national narratives in ways that were not starkly different from male national delegates. It is the voices from advocacy-oriented NGOs that exerted greatest pressure in pushing this convention to declare a common, and higher, age of marriage.

The final version of the convention was put into force in 1964, after the period of open signatures was completed. This final version, *Convention on Consent to Marriage, Minimum Age for Marriage, and Registration of Marriages*, enshrined marriage standards that form the common sense of our time in intergovernmental settings: that marriage requires the consent of both parties (article 1); that the marriage of girls under the age of puberty should be eliminated; that countries should stipulate a minimum age of marriage, with a nonbinding recommendation (added in 1965) that the age of marriage be no less than 15 years unless a competent authority agreed that there were serious reasons to provide otherwise (principle 2); and that all marriage should be registered by a competent authority (principle 3). Although only thirty countries initially signed on to this supplementary convention (the *1965 Recommendation on Consent to Marriage, Minimum Age for Marriage, and Registration of Marriages*), today, more than 120 countries, or 64 percent of UN member states, are parties to it.[52] India did not sign the convention; its delegate Mr. Sahae claimed that the "multi-religious and multi-racial" composition of the Indian state made any kind of uniform legislation for all its different communities "unfeasible."[53] To the present day, India continues to receive criticism for this stance.[54]

One of the most curious puzzles in the process of setting an international minimum age of marriage was its apparent lack of connection to conversations around the 1959 Declaration of the Rights of the Child. The general spirit guiding this document was to enshrine the ideal of a happy childhood and to set out rights and freedoms imagined for all children, such as the right to health, free and compulsory elementary education, and freedom from exploitation. Even though the protections inherent in this document had consequences for the convention on marriage, it was adopted with far less acrimony than the latter. This is perhaps because the idealized vision of childhood in the declaration is not one that any country can easily dispute or shun. India was a signatory, in this case. The "child" in this 1959 document was imagined in the masculine using masculine pronouns; this was a standard grammatical custom at the time. Yet it is possible also to surmise that the needs of girls were not specifically on delegates' minds when discussing or signing the declaration. The attention to girls and the "girl child," which only gathered momentum in the 1990s, is elaborated in chapter 6.

* * *

This chapter narrates how the UN came to formulate an international standard for preventing child marriage by enshrining the principle of consent and a minimum age of marriage. Although marriage is conventionally understood as a feminist issue pertaining to the status of women, the chapter documents how the trajectory of UN involvement was shaped by another commitment, that of abolishing slavery. It further shows how antislavery discourse was mobilized in the service of maintaining Eurocentric hierarchies. The focus on child marriage, bride price, and dowry turned the discussion of slavery away from the United States and European states, which had historically been the principal perpetrators of the transatlantic slave trade, to states of what is termed the global South. In displacing the gaze away from the British slave trade to newly independent states, the UN discourse on marriage shifted moral responsibility for enslavement from historically culpable nations to many of those oppressed by them. A colonial logic thus informed efforts to raise the age of marriage.

The process of deciding on a minimum age of marriage was itself enormously challenging; even women delegates to CSW and committed advocacy groups hesitated to define a common age that was acceptable to all states. Many resisted the goal of a universal common age, instead opting for loose formulations, such as "of full age" or "the age of puberty." The 1956 supplementary convention on slavery condemned "betrothals of young girls before the age of puberty," and the 1962 convention on marriage repeated the same principle. It was only in 1965 that 15 came to be accepted as a recommended minimum age.

Although the outcomes may seem weak to our eyes today, the conventions as well as the surveys and reports that the UN deliberations set into motion actually continued the information-based groundwork established by the League of Nations for shaming countries where objectionable practices prevailed. The UN deliberations entrenched the use of sexual practices as an index for hierarchically ordering societies. In this instance, the mobilization of the powerful language of antislavery buttressed the logic of recapitulation (detailed in chapters 1 and 2): the logic that in some societies, when sexual adulthood comes early, it corresponds to the society's lack of civilizational stature. The mobilization also allowed the global racism generated by the Atlantic slave trade to be entrenched in new institutional forms: formerly exploited colonies were now the targets of international opprobrium. India, one such colony, did little to dispute such opprobrium. Instead, Indian delegates defended the institution of child marriage by asserting the right of parents to control children's marriages.

In subsequent years, the role of the UN in influencing marriage age shifted in a distinct new direction: its funding and support for population control measures and the rise of expert bureaucrats pushed the conversation away from slavery toward a new discursive context, that of demography. The principle of raising the age of marriage became much easier to uphold using the framework of population control. The next chapter traces this shift.

5

Population Control and Marriage Age in India, 1960–1978

For much of the twentieth century, the legal age of marriage for girls in India hovered below 15 years. Although Indian officials strenuously refused to follow intergovernmental motions to harmonize a higher common age of marriage in the 1960s, the Indian government finally raised the minimum age of marriage for girls to 18 in 1978. The change happened not because early marriage was framed by the UN as slavery or because of women's advocacy on behalf of girls; it happened in the interest of meeting demographic targets. In the two decades leading up to this legal measure, population control experts popularized the idea of raising the age of marriage as an instrument for curtailing birthrates. Attention shifted away from how early marriage harmed girls to how later marriage benefited populations as a whole. This shift, which made feminists deeply uneasy, exemplified a split between the principles of population control and reproductive autonomy. India and Indian experts figured prominently in this shift. While British and American scholars such as Thomas Robert Malthus and Paul Ehrlich, are famously associated with promoting population control, Indian scholars such as S. N. Agarwala and research in India such as the Mysore Study influenced the trajectory of global population studies in the reverse direction and specifically concerning the topic of marriage age. This chapter recounts the process by which demographic certitudes about marriage age were established and implemented in India and were simultaneously contested by Indian feminists.

CHAPTER 5

Exploring how the age of marriage became entwined with population control reveals many twists in demographic writing in the 1960s. Both US and Indian experts participated in popularizing the idea that delaying marriage reduced population, and the idea took root in India very quickly, even as Indian feminist demographers dissented from their field's new orthodoxies. Revisiting this historical moment makes clear the broad power of population control discourses in shaping the destiny of girls' bodies.

* * *

When, in 1978, the Indian parliament raised the age of marriage to 18 years for girls and 21 years for boys, the measure created barely a ripple. What was at stake was remarkable: since 1929, when the Child Marriage Restraint Act (CMRA or Sarda Act) had set the age of marriage as 14 for girls and 18 for boys, the age of marriage had not been changed except for a minor amendment to 15 for girls in 1949.[1] The age of marriage was being dramatically raised after three decades, but few legislators marked the moment as noteworthy. As a February 22, 1978, *Times of India* (Mumbai) article observes: "Even though the measure [was] of vital social significance, the attendance in the chamber was poor," the debate was "lackadaisical," and "a bell had to be rung to draw in enough members to fulfill a quorum for passage."

This lack of interest in the measure is mirrored in scholarly writing: only a handful of books and articles actually focus on this event.[2] The neglect of this episode appears genuinely surprising when contrasted with the scholarly treatment of two prior occasions when the age of marriage was raised, in 1891 and 1929: these are treated as watershed moments in Indian social history. Feminist historians of India might even agree that the loud debates leading up to the 1929 CMRA and the polarized positions associated with the 1891 Age of Consent debates are among the most studied events in their field. This chapter accounts for the relative quiet among feminist historians and activists on the legal change in the 1970s, underlining the contrast between the interests at play in the 1920s and in the 1970s.

Any effort to understand the 1978 historical moment must begin with an acknowledgment of the power of the era's discourse of population control. Whereas the most vocal advocates for raising the age of marriage in 1929 were social reformers, particularly women, during the 1970s it was professional demographers and policymakers who were the prime movers. Whereas preventing the violence of forced sex and forced household responsibilities at an early age was what 1920s reformers highlighted, it was the specter of fertile girls causing booming population counts that occupied 1970s demographers' minds.

The reigning consensus crystallized in zoologist Ehrlich's 1968 popular book, *The Population Bomb*, was that the world's human population stood poised to outstrip its resources and that "overpopulation" had to be curtailed to prevent famines. This international climate of alarmism around population growth was particularly germane to India, which had become a training ground for international population research and programs after its independence in 1947. The world's earliest government-sponsored family planning program was initiated in India, and research derived from studies in India shaped the growing field of population studies throughout the world. So, the questions are, Just how did international population control discourses frame the age of marriage, and how did this discourse become the impetus behind the 1978 law that raised the age of marriage in India? What is the relationship between the age of marriage and other instruments of population control? How did the political leadership and women's organizations within India react to this change? And what does this moment tell us about the evolving relationship between feminism and population control?

Feminist engagements with reproductive rights have long been confused with population control. During the first half of the twentieth century, some birth control advocates certainly contributed to this confusion by their conflation of feminist, eugenicist, and Malthusian goals. For instance, Margaret Sanger's desire to prevent women from enduring multiple pregnancies grew indistinguishable from her eugenic efforts to prevent the reproduction of people she deemed inferior—in the United States as well as in countries such as India.[3] Several early Indian feminists were also motivated by elitist impulses of enlightening and reforming poor women's health practices.[4] In their push to ban child marriage and rally for the passage of the CMRA in 1929, many adopted positions that were eugenicist in perspective. Yet in the 1970s Indian feminist activists were not among the vocal factions calling to raise the age of marriage—feminist and Malthusian population control interests did not converge. This apparent feminist indifference on the question of age of marriage in the 1970s is explained ahead.

Population Institutions, the UN, and Age of Marriage

The idea that postponing marriage reduced population was not invented in the twentieth century; Malthus had, in the early nineteenth century, advocated delaying marriage as a means to limit births.[5] He did so in a culture that frowned upon interfering with sexual activity within marriage and curtailing births; in his time, postponing marriage was the presumptive means to reduce sexual activity. Later in the nineteenth century, demographers' attention turned to more directly managing sexual activity and developing contraceptive methods rather than postponing marriage, per se. In the 1950s, though, with a vigor fed by statistical tools, US demographers revived Malthus's ideas about delaying marriage: they began to mathematically project the effect of specific changes in age of marriage on birthrates. The belief that the legal age of marriage could be manipulated as part of national population policy grew dominant. What began as a largely scholarly discussion quickly graduated to an international policy conversation in the 1960s amid growing concern about world population growth and the establishment of UN bodies focused on population control. Influential demographers backed by the Milbank Memorial Fund and the Rockefeller and Ford Foundations, among others, theorized that a shift from high to low birth and death rates could be engineered in developing countries.[6] The primary architects of this idea, which came to be called demographic transition theory, were Ansley J. Coale, a demographer at the Office of Population Research at Princeton University, and Frank Notestein, also a Princeton demographer and the first director of the UN Population Division, one of two UN bodies dealing with population matters that preceded the establishment of the UN Fund for Population Activities (UNFPA) in 1969.

In the early years of demographic transition theory, the actual relationship between age of marriage and fertility (the average number of children a woman bore) was not clear to demographers and was quite vigorously debated. Coale and Edgar M. Hoover's highly influential 1958 book *Population Growth and Economic Development in Low-Income Countries: A Case Study of India's Prospects*, for instance, accepted that the age of marriage might be significant to differentials in fertility but does not argue that it could rise fast enough to "appreciably" lower fertility.[7] Coale and Hoover even worry that early pregnancy impaired reproductive ability, contributing ultimately to *smaller*, rather than larger, family sizes—early marriage, in other words, might not increase population. Their concern echoes the worries of Indian reformists in the 1920s: the argument in support of the 1929 CMRA was that early marriage led to maternal morbidity, infant mortality, and weak progeny.[8] In their understanding, delaying marriage would improve fertility. The economist Radhakamal Mukherjee, for instance, in his 1938 edited volume *Population Problem in India* declares that the *later* consummation of marriage among Muslims explains their higher birth rates.[9]

In 1961, however, Coale and C. Y. Tye made a dramatic move to incorporate age of marriage into population policy discourse. In a frequently cited paper published in the *Milbank Memorial Fund Quarterly* (a peer-reviewed journal focused on health care policy), Coale and Tye make a powerful case for delaying marriage as a means of stemming population growth.[10] They acknowledge that although no consistent relationship between age of marriage and family size had yet been found, demographers had been unduly focused on the wrong detail; even if the total number of children that each woman bore did not change depending on age of marriage, postponing marriage (and implicitly childbearing) would slow population growth, especially in high-fertility populations. Employing a mathematical model designed by Alfred Lotka to support their argument, Coale and Tye drew on empirical evidence comparing the population growth rates of two high-fertility populations that each had different age patterns for reproduction: the Chinese population in contrast to the Malay population in Singapore and the Hutterites in contrast to the Cocos Islanders. In both high-fertility populations, Coale and Tye demonstrate that the group with later patterns of childbearing experienced slower population growth. The authors conclude: "Our calculations suggest that postponement [of marriage] must be given serious consideration as a powerful supplementary component of population policy in the crucial decades ahead. Postponement would provide a substantial and immediate transitory reduction in the birth rates as well as a smaller permanent decline, and these would be in addition to, and perhaps even help to promote, further decline ultimately achieved through more prevalent and effective practice of contraception."[11] Other population and social scientists built upon Coale and Tye's work and broadened it to buttress modernization theory as it emerged in sociology and economics. Sociologist Norman B. Ryder, for instance, presented a paper at the annual meeting of the American Sociological Association in New York City on August 31, 1960, that begins, like Coale and Tye's, by recognizing that raising the age of marriage does not automatically lower "fecundity" but that "later marriage gives a young person a few premarital adult years in which to become committed to individual and societal rather than familial goals."[12] Early marriage, according to Ryder, "deters capital formation," and Western countries achieved high standards of living through "delayed gratification and prudential restraint."[13] Ryder's connection between marriage norms, population patterns, and economic growth expresses an idea that became a plank of modernization theory. In Britain, the Cambridge Group for the History of Population and Social Structure established in 1964 fostered scholarship by Peter Laslett and others that identifies the late age of marriage in European societies as an engine of capitalism.[14] J. W. Leasure, a demographer who focused on Spain and Eastern Europe, and economist J. J. Spengler, who studied the United States, affirm Malthus's advocacy of later marriage by applying it to parts of the world other than England.[15] These 1960s works mark a turning point after which raising the age of marriage became a significant topic within population science and policy circles.

Many demographers such as Coale went beyond academic journals to address policymaking circles. Along with Notestein, Coale actively sought a mandate within the United Nations for population control policies and activities. Coale served on a UN Association of the USA panel, which in 1969 produced a report recommending an expansion of the UNFPA and a multipronged interagency approach by the UN to stem population growth.[16] Wearing more than one hat, Coale produced scholarship on the age of marriage that turned it into an actionable policy item while also cementing receptivity within UN circles for a broader global population control agenda.

India's Place in Population Scholarship

Scholarship about India fueled this new emphasis in population control circles on the age of marriage. The focus on India was not in itself new: even Malthus had trained his sights squarely on India and its population; while teaching soldiers and administrators at the East India Company College in Hertford, England, from 1805 to 1834, he propounded the view that population growth caused famines in India.[17] Annie Besant, a vocal birth control advocate in Britain and later in India at the beginning of the twentieth century, also held up India as a problem site demonstrating the disasters of unchecked population growth, although she changed her views after moving to India.[18]

It was not just non-Indians who treated India as a problem site; Indian social reformers also viewed the birth rate in India with concern. Rahul Nair traces a specific turn that occurred in the 1920s among Indian intellectuals, especially economists and doctors, to focus on population as a core problem and attribute poverty to unchecked breeding.[19] In addition to being influenced by Malthusian ideas about the quantitative relationship between food supply and population growth, Indian social reformers were avid proponents of eugenics, or the improvement of racial or national populations through curtailing undesirable births—especially of the poor. As Sanjam Ahluwalia explains, there was a cohort of male Indian birth control advocates, many of whom were in conversation with US and UK figures, such as Sanger and Marie Stopes, who pursued eugenic ideas in the 1920s, 1930s, and 1940s.[20] Many early birth control activists were at first viewed as iconoclasts, such as mathematician R. D. Karve, who lost his university job for promoting contraception; he founded the first birth control clinic in India in 1921, and his Marathi magazine *Samaj*

Swasthya strongly advocated contraception. Another significant eugenicist sexologist was A. R. Pillay, who organized a "Wives' Clinic" in Sholapur.[21] They advocated contraception in the name of nationalism but often in opposition to social norms. By the 1940s, though, Nair argues, the imperative of controlling population was widely accepted among Indian nationalist intellectuals. The fact that the British colonial government tiptoed around the topic and did not disseminate birth control information, even though British public health officials widely espoused Malthusian views, is attributable to its reluctance to take on problems that it construed as cultural and social issues.[22]

Unlike the colonial government, leaders of the newly independent Indian government had fewer qualms about embracing birth control. Soon after the Indian independence in 1947, Prime Minister Jawaharlal Nehru undertook the project of curtailing population as part of the country's state-directed development agenda, articulated via Five-Year Plans. In December 1952 India became the world's first country to adopt a formal population policy. While Nehru was inspired by Soviet-style planning of time frames and targets, it was US demographers who shaped the content of Indian population policy: Nehru invited Notestein to consult with the Indian government under the auspices of the Ford Foundation.[23] The Ford Foundation gave the Indian government a $5 million grant in 1962 to intensify its population control efforts, and as Matthew Connelly documents, the size of the foundation's staff in its New Delhi office rivaled those of the US embassy in the city.[24] Other international organizations, such as the Rockefeller Foundation, also supported field-based studies in India, exploring contraception forms from the early 1950s.[25] The various state governments in India were open to trying a range of methods in these studies: in Tamil Nadu in 1956, the state government offered monetary incentives for undergoing sterilization.[26] The Ford Foundation's field offices around the world began to frequently draw on such India-based studies.[27] Coale and Hoover's pathbreaking *Population Growth and Economic Development in Low-Income Countries* featured India as its central case study.[28]

Raising the age of marriage as a population control measure grew popular through the results of key studies set in India in the early 1960s. In 1961 a novel study proposed by the Population Commission and carried out under joint UN and Government of India auspices in areas of Mysore (now Karnataka) is an important example. The Mysore Study, as it was called, used a household survey for collecting data on fertility-related matters, such as age of marriage and family planning methods; its results confirmed that women who had married later had, on average, a smaller number of children. This finding provided useful empirical ammunition to population strategists who sought policy change.[29] Another important study of the time was an effort funded by Ford and the US Agency for International Development (USAID) at the Gandhigram Institute in Tamil Nadu, where the population fell from "43 live births per 1000 people in 1959 to 28 per 1000 in 1968." Notably, scholars reviewing this change ascribed it to an increase in the marriage age.[30]

Given the importance of India as a research site, Indian demographers played a noticeable international role in emphasizing the age of marriage as a population control mechanism. A key example is Agarwala, who studied the age of marriage in India under Coale's supervision at the Office of Population Research at Princeton University in the late 1950s. S. N. Agarwala contributed to intergovernmental conversations as well as to the national planning agenda in India by predicting a steep fall in India's population if the age of marriage were raised. He published a widely cited article to this effect in the premier population studies journal *Population Index* in 1957 and in a 1962 book, *The Age at Marriage in India*.[31] In 1964 Agarwala's projections appeared in a journal, *Yojana* ("plan"), brought out by the Planning Commission of the Government of India.[32] He presented a paper at the 1965 World Population Conference in Belgrade that ratcheted up pressure on developing countries to raise the age of marriage, boldly projecting that increasing the female age at marriage in India to 20 would reduce the birth rate by 30 percent within one generation.[33] In 1966 he published a paper in the interdisciplinary Indian journal *Economic and Political Weekly*, arguing that raising the age of marriage would reduce population growth.[34]

Viewed by many in his field as an overestimate, Agarwala's calculations nonetheless provided the springboard for a new conversation among population scientists centered not on whether raising the age of marriage would support the goal of slowing population growth but rather on how quickly and to what extent. The *Eugenics Quarterly* (which changed its title to *Social Biology* in 1969) published several articles by demographers in the latter half of the 1960s reacting to Agarwala's projection; they each presented varying quantitative analyses of what an increase in the female age of marriage to 20 years would do. K. G. Basavarajappa, a demographer in Australia, and statistician M. I. Belvalgidad, of Lady Hardinge Medical College in New Delhi, were less enthusiastic about the potential impact of such a measure and projected a decline of not more than 10 percent in the birth rate.[35] Prem P. Talwar, a biostatistician at the University of North Carolina, suggested a higher immediate decline (around 25 percent) that would lessen over time (between 8 and 21 percent).[36] P. Krishnan, a doctoral candidate at the International Population Program at Cornell University, projected a 14 percent reduction within 28 to 29 years.[37] Agreeing with Talwar, statistician C. R. Malakar from the Indian Statistical Institute in Calcutta argued that smaller increases in age of marriage (up to 17 years) would not significantly impact birth rates.[38] Citing each other, as well as work by Coale and Tye from 1961 and Agarwala's Belgrade paper, these demographers and statisticians debated only the finer points of how to slow population growth by delaying marriage; they shared the premise that delaying marriage was good.

Following the 1965 Belgrade conference, population control more generally became a site of intensive investigation and commitment. By 1970 the topic of population emerged as a specialized area of UN activity with well-funded activism by the population lobby. The specific goal of raising the age of marriage became an established feature of population discourse at the UN. For example, a UN seminar on family planning held for the 1973 Economic Commission for Asia and the Far East (ECAFE) in Jakarta, Indonesia, recommended, "Governments which have not already done so ensure that the laws provide for a minimum age of marriage for women of not less than 16 years, for the registration of all marriages, and for the contracting of marriage only with the full and free consent of intending spouses."[39] The first UN intergovernmental conference on population held in Bucharest in 1974 concluded by recommending "[t]he establishment of an appropriate lower limit for age at marriage" with "lower" here meaning a minimum age of marriage.[40] Countries could demonstrate their political will to control population growth by raising their age of marriage. They recognized that an outward display of such intentions was necessary in order to garner international aid. International aid had become increasingly contingent upon a developing country's effort to take action about its "population problem." The US government under Lyndon B. Johnson not only pledged to combat the "population explosion" but prioritized spending foreign aid to control population growth over economic development.[41] It was therefore not surprising that India, which formally sought nonaligned status but still welcomed targeted development aid from the United States, followed this route. Although the delegation from India to the Bucharest conference joined a bloc of self-identified Third World countries that insisted that population concerns *not* be isolated from economic development, Indian policies during the 1970s actually belied that rhetoric: population control came to assume the stature of an end unto itself. The next section traces how, when the age of marriage was raised, it was disconnected from ongoing efforts to address women's well-being.

CHAPTER 5

Population Control Measures in India

In the 1960s projections by demographers such as Agarwala that delaying marriage would stem population growth made their way into policymaking publications such as *Yojana*. In 1974 they leaped to the front pages of the news. That year, the Indian Ministry of Health and Family Planning issued a mass announcement predicting that if the minimum age of marriage for females were raised to 18 years, a long-term reduction of 15 percent in the birth rate would take place; it predicted that if the age were raised to 20 years, a birth rate reduction of 19 percent would occur.[42] In the same year the *New York Times* reported another key development: "Prime Minister Indira Gandhi's government is considering laws to raise the legal age for marriage in India. The objective is to reduce the number of child mothers, whose babies are helping to increase the population by an estimated 13 million a year."[43] The timing of Gandhi's announcement—just a few days before the start of the UN World Population Conference in Bucharest—could not have been coincidental. Indeed, India's mere *intention* to do something about its population size signaled the country's acceptance and willingness to act on its "population problem." The transnational force of the idea of population control, as Connelly describes it, made it impossible to resist.[44] Raising the age of marriage as a simple amendment to the long-standing CMRA from 1929 provided relatively "safe" political ground from which India could be seen taking action on population control.

When this first legal proposal to raise the age of marriage appeared in August 1974, it was formulated and promoted entirely within the executive branch of the Indian government, with no explicit acknowledgment of parallel feminist engagement on the issue. The minister of state for the law simply announced in the upper house of Parliament that a government proposal to raise the age of marriage was in the works. After that, the issue reverted to central government bureaucracy until it reappeared in 1976 as part of a National Population Policy (NPP) statement.[45]

The 1976 NPP statement appeared in the midst of an infamous period in Indian history known as the Emergency: from June 1975 to March 1977, Gandhi's government suspended civil liberties and elections in response to growing criticism and, specifically, in reaction to a court case that convicted her of misusing state machinery. The NPP statement was part of a series of authoritarian rulings that planned to accelerate economic development. Karan Singh, the national minister of Health and Family Planning (and son of the last maharaja of Kashmir), authored the statement and included raising the age of marriage as one plank of a troublingly ambitious policy to reduce the population growth rate from 35 per thousand in 1974 to 25 per thousand in 1984. The statement identified population control as an end in itself, claiming that "waiting for education and economic development to bring about a drop in fertility" was not a "practical solution." Ironically, in Bucharest just two years earlier, Singh had famously created the slogan that "development is the best contraceptive" while rallying alongside other Third World countries against the very notion of population control as a discrete end detached from economic goals.[46] The 1976 NPP statement presents the benefits of raising the age of marriage thus:

> [It] will not only have the demonstrable demographic impact, but will also lead to more responsible parenting and help safeguard the health of the mother and child. It is well known that early pregnancy leads to high maternal and infant mortality. Also, if women of our country are to play their rightful role in its economic, social and intellectual life, the practice of early marriage will have to be severely discouraged. The present law has not been effectively or uniformly enforced. *It has, therefore, been decided that the minimum age of marriage should be raised to 18 for girls and 21 for boys, and suitable legislation to this effect will be passed. Offences under this law will be cognizable* by an officer not below the rank of a Sub-Divisional Magistrate. The question of making registration of marriages compulsory is under active consideration.[47]

Interestingly, raising the age of marriage is named in this document as the first concrete measure the government would take; other more controversial measures, such as sterilization using monetary compensation, group incentives for those who promote sterilization, and even compulsory sterilization, are mentioned in paragraphs 11 and 15 of Singh's NPP statement.[48] Such window dressing allowed the NPP statement to appear more benign than it actually was in its implementation; in the following year, population control rapidly became a monumental state program using aggressive methods, such as coercive sterilization.

The population control measures taken during Emergency rule have become the signature memory of that period. Sanjay Gandhi, Prime Minister Indira Gandhi's son, embarked on a notoriously zealous campaign to provide material incentives to rural men and women who underwent vasectomies and tubal ligations. The campaign, begun in April 1976, chalked up over 8 million sterilizations—6.2 million vasectomies and 2.05 million tubal ligations—up from 2.7 million sterilizations the previous year.[49] Sterilization had been encouraged in a variety of settings using mobile field hospitals since the early 1970s, but under the Emergency, states raised their sterilization targets, and coercion was explicitly promoted: In the state of Bihar, public food rations were withdrawn from couples with more than three children; in many parts of the country, men had to agree to be sterilized in order to obtain driver's licenses or be employable.[50] Field workers around the country were assigned quotas, which pushed them to force rural men and women to undergo sterilization in order to meet their own targets. These abuses provoked a severe backlash among observers and cast a shadow over all subsequent government efforts at population control. The policy of forced sterilizations contributed to the fall of Indira Gandhi's government—it was severely repudiated at the polls in March 1977 in what Connelly eloquently describes as one of "history's greatest political upsets."[51] The incoming Janata Party sought to overturn the previous government's practices by seeking less coercive population control measures. Family planning was renamed family welfare under a revised population policy in 1977. The new approach was much more heavily focused on education and motivation and spacing births.[52] Hence, the measure to raise the age of marriage to 18 for girls, proposed in the new lower house of Parliament (Lok Sabha), which was dominated by the Janata Party, had an important political significance at that historical juncture: it signified the Janata Party's commitment to a different kind of population policy.

On February 22, 1978, the *Times of India* reported that a bill to raise the age of marriage by amending the 1929 CMRA had been approved after a "lackadaisical debate" by India's lower house of Parliament. The proposed minimum age for marriage for girls and boys appears to have evoked little, if any, resistance. Raising the age of marriage provided Janata Party policymakers with a relatively safe issue—a benign measure in contrast to Sanjay Gandhi's coercive approach—from which to launch an incremental approach to reducing births. The debate in India's upper house of Parliament suggests that one aspect of the act—making child marriage a cognizable offense—encountered resistance from a few states.[53] Until this point, the law did not rule child marriage a cognizable offense, meaning that police could not investigate or arrest without a court-issued warrant those persons whom they found involved in arranging a child marriage. The reasoning used by lawmakers for keeping child marriage a noncognizable offense had been that the state wanted to prevent police harassment of individual citizens and also not interfere too deeply in the personal lives of citizens. However, as a result, the law against child marriage had been weakly enforced: marriages often took place well before police could secure a warrant and were then declared indissoluble; the accused parents were content to simply pay a fine or go to jail for a short period of time while the marriage remained valid. Only one state in the country had put in place the stricter measure of making child marriage a cognizable offense—Gujarat, where in 1964 a committee (called the Pushpaben Committee) established that child marriage was the cause of a high rate of suicides among girls. As a result, Gujarat had declared all offenses under CMRA to be cognizable.[54] The CMRA Amendment now made child marriage a cognizable offense in a limited sense under specific conditions; police could investigate complaints from the public and submit reports to magistrates but did not have the authority to arrest the offender or to stop the solemnization of marriages without obtaining permission from magistrates.

The passing of the CMRA Amendment in 1978, despite its new and dramatic age requirement of 18 years, was not widely hailed by population experts as a victory. It is worth recalling that even at the height of international advocacy to raise the age of marriage in order to reduce birth rates, proponents regarded it as a soft approach. Even Agarwala, outspoken on the issue of marriage age in the early 1960s along with Coale, his doctoral adviser, had moved steadily toward inciting a harder line and pushing for more intrusive, and invasive, measures. In 1966 working at a Demographic Research Centre in New Delhi, Agarwala had warned that too many reproductive-age people were having unprotected sex: "[O]nly 2.4% of reproductive age couples are contraceptive users, instead of the 65% who would have to use completely efficient contraceptive means in order to reduce the present birth rate of 40 per 1,000 to 25 per 1,000 by 1975: this indicates the vast size of the problem."[55] By the mid-1970s, while working as director of a World Bank Project in Lucknow, Agarwala was a proponent of sterilization: he evaluated with regret that the country's efforts to increase sterilization acceptors had fallen to "only 1.3 equivalent sterilizations" in 1973 and 1974 from 3.4 million in 1972.[56] Indeed, advances in contraception research and the emergence of the pill and the intrauterine device (IUD) during the 1960s, the passage of a liberal abortion law in India in 1971, as well as increased commitment by both the Indian and US governments to a population control agenda, changed the context of policymaking in one decade. The issue of age of marriage was subordinated to an array of family planning measures adjudged to be far more effective in reducing population growth. The success of these other measures is sometimes proven using statistical calculations: for example, the government's Department of Family Planning claimed that more than 20 million live births were averted between 1956 and 1975, with the annual birthrate falling from 42 per 1000 in 1960 and 1961 to 35 per 1000 in 1974 and 1975.[57] These figures, however, do not establish clear causality between the government's family planning measures and lowered fertility, because among other potential sources of the change was an increase in women's literacy and education—which also strongly correlated with lowered fertility.

CHAPTER 5

Feminist Responses to the CMRA Amendment of 1978

The most remarkable aspect of the 1978 passing of the CMRA is its low level of feminist participation. Feminist voices, which were increasingly a part of national political and academic conversations in this decade, were conspicuously quiet on this measure. To place this silence in context, it is worth rehearsing more general feminist conceptual trepidations about population control. Population control approaches have historically focused on meeting numerical targets and treating the control of women's fertility as a means to those ends. They also have, in a Malthusian vein, targeted the poor and used material incentives to garner compliance—in effect, placing coercive pressure on the poor to reproduce less. Feminist advocates, particularly in the latter part of the twentieth century, have called for approaches that treat women as ends in themselves and provide women resources to make healthy decisions—whether for or against childbearing.[58] As Ahluwalia details, some early twentieth-century feminists in India—as elsewhere—also participated in elitist eugenic thinking that treated birth control as imperative for poor women.[59] Nonetheless, feminist advocates of birth control leaned more strongly than population control advocates toward centering the well-being and agency of women.

When the field of demography turned its focus to specifying numerical targets for birth rates, some Indian feminists expressed their opposition. Malini Karkal, who served as senior research officer, Family Planning Unit, of the Demographic Training and Research Centre in Bombay, offered vociferous criticism of the priorities of other demographers in the late 1960s. Questioning the direct relationship between late marriages and low birth rates as theorized by Agarwala and others, Karkal interpreted the reduced birth rates in those areas of the world where age of marriage had increased to be a result of "changes in the outlook of the society towards the role of women and consequently the impact of the society on the women themselves."[60] While fully supporting raising the age of marriage as a "humane measure" to "protect girls from forced sex life," Karkal questioned raising the legal age of marriage for the sake of reducing births in India and argued the measure would not make a significant impact for that purpose "unless accompanied by change in the educational level and occupational status of women."[61] Karkal remained remarkably vigilant that feminist goals in reproductive health not be confused with the numbers-based logic of population control.[62]

Kumudini Dandekar, a demographer at the Gokhale Institute of Politics and Economics in Pune, raised a similar critique in 1974. Her lack of enthusiasm for the Indian Ministry of Health and Family Planning's efforts to pursue legislative change on age of marriage speaks volumes about the growing conflict between those who pursued a numbers-based population control agenda and those who centered the rights and needs of women. Underscoring that "in fact, there is no definite relationship between birth rate and age at marriage," Dandekar ambivalently comments, "There is nothing desirable or undesirable about present age at marriage, *per se*."[63] Like Karkal, Dandekar questioned the likelihood that legal measures to raise the age of marriage would, on their own and in the absence of other socioeconomic measures, substantively lower birth rates. She observes:

> It seems to us that further rise in the age at marriage can occur only with high motivation among women for a better life for themselves. This can lead to reduction in fertility. Such a motivation can come with better education, employment or general improvement in the level of living above a certain minimum.
>
> ... If education and employment could be made available for a majority of women and if marriage was not depended upon for sheer subsistence, there will be a society in India that could be called progressive, and it will control the age at marriage as directed by social circumstances.[64]

Karkal and Dandekar both refute the assumptions and lines of argumentation made by Agarwala and other demographers. Agarwala often touted the example of Ireland as a Catholic country that had achieved low birth rates by delaying marriage alone (presumably, without the assistance of contraception). Karkal countered the Irish example with the Indian state of Kerala, whose higher age of marriage did not correspond to lower rates of fertility. Dandekar, too, argued that the Irish example could not apply to the living and social conditions of India.

In the 1970s, as such feminist voices grew increasingly more vocal in official settings, these distinctions between instrumental approaches to women's bodies and advocacy on behalf of women became clearer. A useful site to explore Indian feminists' articulation of this issue is the historic 1974 report by the Committee on the Status of Women (henceforth Committee, to avoid confusion with the UN Commission on the Status of Women described in chapter 4) called *Towards Equality*, a comprehensive account of women's economic, social, political, and cultural status in India. This 353-page text has been frequently read as a landmark publication, a platform representing the positions of women's organizations and advocates of the time. It was authored by a group of prominent women academics, such as Lotika Sarkar, Vina Mazumdar, Leela Dube, and Urmila Haksar, among others, appointed in 1971 to form the Committee. Their goal over the next three years was to survey and make recommendations for improving the major indices of women's well-being in the country. The Committee carefully constructed a view distinct from more hard-line advocacy of population control. "Family planning is now the most heavily documented and evaluated among all major programmes of the Government of India," the Committee writes, even suggesting in a footnote that the government's preoccupation with family planning verges on excessive: "The importance attached by the Government to this kind of research is indicated by the fact that in spite of the heavy volume of research data available on family planning, this Committee was also asked to undertake case studies on family planning. The Committee, however, felt that this was not necessary."[65] The Committee refused to follow the causal logic used by the family planning movement that birth control improves women's status, arguing instead for attention to education and employment, in addition to age of marriage: "All recent studies seem to agree more on the *obverse* of the relationship, viz. that improved status of women, with rise in the age of marriage, education, employment, better living conditions and greater general awareness, have a direct impact on the adoption of family planning methods."[66] The report goes on to critique the Indian government's overwhelming support of family planning at the expense of other public health programs, the compulsory imposition of sterilization following abortion, and complications in the provision of birth control that harm, rather than improve, the health of women.[67] The combined recommendations in *Towards Equality* on birth control, sterilization, and abortion display a cautious stance toward the government's intensified approach to population control. The report points out the government's areas of potential conflict, rather than overlap, with feminist goals.

In keeping with such reservations about population control, the Committee's discussion of the age of marriage appears framed within the general context of the well-being of girls and women. The report notes important differences between rural and urban women. Among urban middle- and upper-class women, the Committee observes, the age of marriage of girls ranged between 16 and 24 years. But while the mean urban age of marriage was 19.2 years, in rural areas, it was 16.7 years.[68] Given that over 75 percent of the country lived in villages, it was likely that the majority of Indian girls in the years 1961 through 1971 were married below the age of 18. The Committee notes that among rural low-caste women, early marriage was often perceived as a social necessity because it served as a protection against "the lust of upper class men who wielded economic power over them."[69] The Committee recognizes the problem of low age of marriage in rural areas as being tied to social and economic pressures: "Early marriage and lack of education constitutes a vicious circle, affecting population growth and the health of the mother and the child and the status and education of girls."[70] This broadly worded statement shows that Indian feminists of this time articulated the needs of girls while also acknowledging a political context in which the benefits of curtailing "population growth" had primacy. They understood child marriage, perhaps like child labor, to be a symptom of economic deprivation—for which there were no simple legal punitive solutions.

If we analyze *Towards Equality* more closely on the question of raising the age of marriage, we see that the Committee finds that raising the age of marriage is desirable in order to remove the disparity with the legal age of discretion, the age at which a child can choose a guardian, and not for its potential impact on reducing population growth. As the Committee puts it:

> When the legal age of marriage in case of a female is below the age of discretion she cannot be expected to form an intelligent opinion about her partner in life. The policy or law which permits the marriage of a girl before she is physically and mentally mature is open to serious question. Child marriage is one of the significant factors leading to the high incidence of suicide among young married women in India. Therefore, increasing the marriage age of girls to eighteen years is desirable.[71]

Although the Committee phrases a legal change in age of marriage as "desirable," it does not explicitly recommend it as an urgent policy measure, and this is a striking omission given that the purpose of the report was to offer concrete recommendations. (Its only explicit recommendations relate to making offenses under the CMRA cognizable and to employ specially trained officers to enforce it.) In many ways, then, the 1978 CMRA Amendment was not connected to the demands of feminists, and it is not surprising that feminists offered little explicit support for the measure.

When reflecting on the 1978 amendment, the feminist legal scholar Jaya Sagade impugns legislators for not taking seriously "the social consequences of child marriage." She comments that "had education, employment, and personality development of young girls been the objects behind prohibiting child marriages along with concern for their reproductive health, *instead of fertility control*, the percentages of child marriages probably could have been reduced substantially." On the whole, she concludes, "women's experiences had no space in the area of law-making."[72] She views the 1978 amendment as a halfhearted effort that did not get to the core of the problem. In particular, she faults the measure for not declaring all child marriages void and for not declaring child marriage to be a cognizable offence under all circumstances, which would allow police to carry out arrests more easily.

Writing shortly after passage of the 1978 amendment, historian Geraldine Forbes contrasts the small number of feminist voices in the 1970s with the formidable activism in the 1920s of women's organizations toward passage of the 1929 CMRA. In the 1920s, as Forbes notes, several women's organizations, such as the WIA, the NCWI, and the AIWC, lobbied in support of the bill.[73] Compared to this moment, the level of agitation in the 1970s certainly appears weak. Sagade employs a similar contrast, surmising why women's groups supported the 1929 act and not the 1978 amendment. Although there were many elite social reformers with no understanding of patriarchal oppression who pushed for the 1929 CMRA, she notes that women's organizations recognized they had a stake in such a law and rallied to its support.[74] Widespread and open discussion on the issue likely left enough space for them to imagine the 1929 law as a means to gender justice, if not, at least, to improve the lives of young girls and women. In the late 1970s, on the other hand, the top-down nature of the introduction and passage of the CMRA Amendment provided limited opportunity for civic engagement. The Indian government expressed its intention in 1974 to change the law, and the issue had taken its course within governing and lawmaking circuits over the next four years. Because it was a policy measure primarily aimed at reducing population growth, women's organizations did not hold as great a stake in its passage.

Thus, even when feminist objectives to raise the age of marriage in the 1970s appeared on the surface to match those of the Indian government, the broader intentions behind those objectives did not. Feminists in 1970s India increasingly expressed skepticism toward the overzealous promotion of population control and the pursuit of feminist objectives within that frame. Their specific concerns played a large role in the feminist critiques of population control articulated within international feminist networks built during the following decade (such as in meetings of the International Women's Health Movement and of Development Alternatives with Women for a New Era. This critique of population control became firmly established in the 1980s through the advocacy of activists within India and beyond and in concert with movements for reproductive justice.

CMRA Shifts in Historical Perspective

When viewing the course of age of marriage legislation across twentieth-century India, a shift becomes clear: from concern about forced sex to a panic about population control. The earliest measures to regulate the age of marriage focused on the age at which girls were forced to cohabit with their husbands and, in effect, consummate their marriage.[75] In the 1890s, when social reformers participated in a public debate about child marriage, sex was at the center: they discussed the age at which girls were required to leave their natal homes to consummate their marriages. The public revulsion in this moment was focused on unwanted sexual encounters; the key protagonists, Rakhmabai in Bombay state (a 21-year-old who refused to join the husband to whom she had been betrothed at age 11) and Phulmoni in Bengal (an 11-year-old who died from vaginal hemorrhage after forced sex with her betrothed), were both figures who garnered considerable public sympathy for being trapped into early marriage. Social reformers at the time accomplished an increase in the age of consumation of marriage from 10 to 12 years as a means to protect "young girls from sexual abuse within the institution of marriage."[76] In the 1920s, legislative initiatives to restrain child marriages also aimed to prevent early sexual encounters. Sagade notes, "The major reason to prevent child marriages was to give protection to young wives who suffered enormously due to forcible sexual intercourse with them by their husbands.... These changes were aimed at treating women more humanely and were basically informed by a form of protectionism."[77]

By the 1970s population control interests that had supported research and development on contraception drove a stronger conceptual wedge between sexuality and fertility. It was fertility, in isolation, that preoccupied the Indian Planning Commission. The concern was no longer that early sexuality impeded fertility but that early fertility impeded development. Indeed, as seen from the phrasing of the 1976 NPP statement, population control became an end in itself that even superseded economic development. The decoupling of sexuality from fertility occurred as the age of marriage became less and less about the issue of girls' consent and more about their future procreative practices. The very reason that women's groups originally became vested in the issue receded significantly from view.

In some respects, all the same, the 1929 and 1978 measures to raise the age of marriage were similar: they were both successful because they mobilized the biopolitical logic of managing and counting life in order to ensure the health of the nation as a whole. The 1929 CMRA had to cite the health and future of a budding nation in order to secure the support of a range of legislators.[78] Eugenicist concerns were increasingly influential in that period: as described in chapter 3, the Age of Consent Committee advocating for the CMRA drew on medical arguments that early sexuality deteriorated the health of the mother. This committee's case for delaying marriage, then, was related in part to preserving the health of the incipient nation. The 1929 measure was broadly pronatalist in the way it conceptualized the role of young mothers, whereas by 1978, the fertility of young mothers was unreservedly viewed as a threat. Yet both antinatalist and pronatalist measures placed the needs of the nation, as imaginatively constructed, before the needs of the individual young female lives whose emotional, sexual, and reproductive lives were at stake.

Another respect in which both measures were similar is that they were oriented toward an audience beyond India—in particular, the prestigious realm of intergovernmental activity. As seen from analyses of the 1929 changes in chapter 3, all measures raising the age of sexual consent and marriage had an outward orientation; the goal was to demonstrate the country's "civilizational adequacy"—in the first case to the League of Nations and in the second case, to UN bodies focused on population control.

This chapter demonstrates how closely aligned Indian population control policies were with the intellectual positions of the international population control establishment. Indeed, Indian demographers and the Indian example contributed in vital ways to the treatment of the age of marriage as a technocratic measure aimed at reducing population growth, rather than a measure focused on expanding life chances and preventing forced sex for girls. A shift occurred from an overwhelming focus on potentially vulnerable girls to potentially overfertile girls who could be threats to the future of the nation. In the first case, the Indian state was called upon to protect vulnerable girls from harms related to forced sex and in the second to control their fertility. This episode is one more reminder of how the seemingly well-meaning focus on early marriage among girls is tethered to interests that have very little to do with girls themselves. The next chapter turns our focus squarely to girls as a conceptual category.

6

Investing in the Girl Child, 1989–2015

If raising the age of marriage in India to 18 happened without incident in the late 1970s, a consensus that 18 was a meaningful threshold also solidified around the globe in the late 1980s. The 1989 UN Convention on the Rights of the Child (UNCRC) established 18 as the age boundary between child and adult.[1] Although the League of Nations and the United Nations had coordinated two intergovernmental declarations on the rights of the child in 1924 and 1959, it was only in 1989 that the UNCRC specified an age marker distinguishing children from adults. This 1989 convention also goes down in history as the most widely ratified UN treaty in history, with 196 signatories—every UN member state except the United States.[2] The popularity of this convention points to a consensus that had emerged about protecting children, as well as agreement on how to define a child.

Curiously, though, the "child" remained scrupulously gender-neutral in the UNCRC. The treaty covers children's general rights to health, education, freedom from labor and sexual exploitation, and fair treatment before the law. Both masculine and feminine pronouns are used throughout the document in an effort to account for girls as well as boys. Yet, in the immediate wake of this treaty, a new discourse distinguishing the needs of girls from boys erupted in UN circles. The figure of the girl came to occupy center stage, and in particular, the "girl child" emerged as a key shorthand term in development and aid contexts. The focus of this chapter is on how this distinction emerged.

CHAPTER 6

The primary question explored is, When and why did concern crystallize around girls? I trace what I see as a discursive explosion: from a trickle of references in the early 1990s, girls and specifically the "girl child" came to occupy increasing attention in the mid-1990s and even greater institutional stature from the middle of the first decade of the twenty-first century into the second. The girl came to be articulated as an advocacy cause separate from women. To some extent, the girl even displaced the "Third World woman" as the archetypal target of international intervention by development, health, and antiviolence agencies. This chapter proposes possible reasons for the increasing attention to girls, such as discourses in development studies circles, nervousness about some feminist advocacy causes, as well as corporate interests. In particular, this chapter shows how the celebration of girlhood has enabled a specific kind of advocacy: a turn toward productive investment in girls.

A key contribution of this chapter is to show how intellectual influences traveled in multidirectional ways. The term "girl child" traveled, I argue, from Indian contexts to UN contexts. As also argued in chapter 5, India served as a site of both the problem and as a source of expertise—in this case, generating the discourse of the girl child. I offer an institutional genealogy traversing Indian demographic research, UN bureaucracies, NGO actions, and corporate campaigns, as well as Indian state-led development initiatives. The chapter begins by recounting the rise of interest in girls in India and then exploring how this interest moved to UN contexts. While a bulk of the chapter focuses on intergovernmental UN contexts, the last part of the chapter moves back to India, showing how the new orientation toward investing in girls has been taken up in programs initiated by states and the national government.

The "Girl Child": The Emergence of a Term

Enter "girl child" as a search term in UN electronic databases, and its first chronological appearance is in the title of a non-UN NGO conference on the human rights of the girl child held in New Delhi on December 11–14, 1989. Its next appearance is in 1990, as part of a UN International Children's Emergency Fund (UNICEF) document, "Focus on the Girl Child." Within just a few years, the term gained so much traction in UN conversations that a resolution was passed by the UN General Assembly on the girl child by all member states in 1995, followed by similar resolutions almost every single successive year until 2015. The "girl child" as a topic moved from being the specialization of agencies focused on children, such as UNICEF, to being the subject of annual reports by the secretary-general of the UN starting in 2006. In a culmination of this profusion of interest, the United Nations declared October 11 to be the

International Day of the Girl Child, beginning in 2012. In other words, from a trickle of references in the late 1980s, the girl child moved to become the focus of concerted action. The next four sections shed light on this process, covering the period from the late 1980s to 2015.

The term "girl child" first emerged in South Asia, where it was in circulation before it was used in UN contexts. It grew out of a base of South Asian research on this topic: feminist sociologists and economists in the worlds of development, health, and labor in South Asia were increasingly alert through the late 1980s to the deeper vulnerability of girls than boys to malnutrition, violence, and illiteracy.[3] Their campaigns had successfully led to policy shifts, such as the Maharashtra government's move in 1985 to make all education for girls free until the end of high school in public schools and state-aided private schools. By 1987 in New Delhi, a Campaign on the Rights of the Girl Child was underway, and a National Workshop on the Girl Child was held that year. By 1989 the term was familiar enough that it appeared in the title of an official report; the Government of India's Department of Women and Child Development produced *The Lesser Child: The Girl Child in India*, an accessible twenty-four-page well-researched and illustrated summary of the problems girls in India faced.

The increased interest in girls in India was primarily related to the problem of skewed sex ratios. For years, scholars had noticed that across swathes of northern and northwest India, boys and men far outnumbered girls and women, and the scholars attributed it to female malnutrition and infanticide.[4] Concerns came to a head in the mid-1980s as prenatal sex-selection tests became available and were used to prevent the birth of girl children. Women's groups began to agitate against sex-selective abortions: in 1986 the Bombay-based group of feminists and scientists Forum against Sex Pre-Determination and Sex Pre-Selection began a campaign to outlaw sex-determination tests in prenatal diagnostic technology. The compounded effect of female feticide, female infanticide, and female malnourishment was a sex ratio deeply skewed against females. This problem was most famously crystallized in the phrase "missing women" popularized by Indian economist Amartya Sen; in a 1990 article in the *New York Review of Books*, he estimated that over a hundred million girls/women were missing as a result of such practices.[5]

The growing concern about girls' impoverished life chances led to national and regional commitments: the South Asian Association for Regional Cooperation (SAARC) declared 1990 the Year of the Girl Child. This regional association, founded in 1985, was primarily focused on economic integration and forming a trade bloc, but it facilitated cooperation on other fronts, such as health and population. At a June 1990 meeting of South Asian ministers responsible for women and development in Islamabad, Pakistan, the ministers recommended that the entire decade 1991–2000 be called the Decade of the Girl Child. In November 1990 at the Maldives meeting, all the South Asian heads of state endorsed that declaration.[6]

This South Asian academic and advocacy focus on the girl child traveled via the research of experts to intergovernmental organizations and multilateral financial institutions. UNICEF was a key agent in popularizing this term. In 1990 its executive board approved placing a priority focus on the girl child. The report of an April 1990 UNICEF meeting mentions that there was a "stress" on "the importance of women in development" with "particular attention [given] to improving the situation of the girl child." It attributes this emphasis to South Asian members, noting that SAARC countries "referred to their declaration of 1990 as the 'Year of the Girl Child.'"[7] The 1991 UNICEF booklet *The Girl Child: An Investment in the Future* also draws heavily on research from India: the front matter of this booklet states that it was prepared by Agnes Aidoo, the senior adviser of the Development Programme for Women, who served as the UNICEF representative to Tanzania, and that it was based on an initial report by Neera Sohoni, an Indian economist who worked for UNICEF in New Delhi and New York, who published a 1995 study, *The Burden of Girlhood*.[8] Much of the research cited in the 1991 UNICEF booklet is the work of scholars in India. Among the few authors cited more than once in the booklet are those who focus on India: an article by Sundari Ravindran on child health in India, a book by Meera Chatterjee on the status of female children in India, and a pediatric journal article by Shanti Ghosh about the girl child in SAARC countries.[9] The booklet also devotes a section to highlighting the ongoing efforts to promote the girl child in South Asia under the auspices of SAARC. These details confirm that the UNICEF emphasis on the girl child emerged out of the contributions of Indian scholars and concern about the conditions that girls face in South Asia.

From Women's to Girls' Issues in the UN

The UN interest in the girl child in the 1990s was an outgrowth of the general receptivity within the UN to women's issues in this period. Agencies made forceful interventions on the issues of violence against women, HIV prevention, and trafficking prevention: The UN Commission on Human Rights instituted a position of a special rapporteur on violence against women in 1994; the General Assembly passed resolutions on trafficking of women starting in 1993; and there were reports on the effects of traditional practices, specifically female circumcision/genital mutilation. The "girl" appeared in conjunction with "women" in the titles of documents on each of these topics.

A critical ferment appears to have occurred around 1990 in UN settings, leading to the formation of separate institutional bodies and resolutions focused specifically on the girl child. This ferment is evident at the surface level when examining the classifications found in UN document indexes. The UNDOC Current Subject Index, a series of print volumes that annually classified all the reports, letters, and miscellaneous publications by UN bodies, is a meaningful source for assessing the relative importance given to a topic.[10] When a topic is found in the subject index, this indicates institutional attention to it; at the very least, it indicates the existence of documents specifically focused on that topic. The first instance of "girl" appearing in the subject index is in 1985; the subject indexes before this date contain no such category. A count of the number of entries under the category "girl" following its first appearance can be instructive. The increasing number of documents with titles specifically focused on girls in the 1990s, especially in the mid-1990s, is a clear sign of an explosion of attention to this topic. The following table lists the number of entries found between 1985 and 2007, when the index was discontinued.

Table 6.1. Number of entries under "girl" in UNDOC Current Subject Index, 1985 through 2007

Year	No. of entries
1985	1
1986	5
1987	2
1988	4
1989	1
1990	4
1991	10
1992	9
1993	9
1994	10
1995	45
1996	76
1997	—
1998	73
1999	35
2000	33
2001	46
2002	62
2003	55
2004	13
2005	46
2006	29
2007	41

CHAPTER 6

Until the 1990s, the subject category "girl" had a scant few documents listed under it; the index entry for the category begins by referring readers to search instead under "adolescents," "female circumcision," and "women." In 1985 and 1989, for instance, only one entry is under "girl"; in 1987 there are two. As points of comparison, the subject categories "children" and "women" in these years have at least thirty entries in addition to subcategories, such as "women's advancement" and "women's development" or "child labor" and "child health." In 1991, however, there is a sudden change for the category "girl": ten entries are listed under it, reflecting the higher activity focused on this issue in the prior year. In 1992 and 1993, there are nine entries, and then an even more dramatic rush of attention in the mid-1990s, with forty-five and seventy-six entries in 1995 and 1996, respectively; the number of entries drops a little after the mid-nineties but stays steadily high throughout the 2000s. The jump in 1996 can be attributed to the 1995 Beijing Fourth World Conference on Women, which facilitated the increased attention to girls; the jump can also be a result of the first General Assembly Resolution on the Girl Child in 1995. Many of the entries listed are titles of reports focused on continuing topics of research and action, such as trafficking in women and girls, and female circumcision/genital mutilation. But some are specifically focused on the girl child, particularly after 1995.

As mentioned earlier, no entries used the term "girl child" until 1990. It was neither a subject category of its own nor in the title of any listed documents until that point. "Girl child" appears for the first time in 1990 in the UNDOC index in the title of a UNICEF document, "Focus on the Girl Child: Implementation of UNICEF Policy." A 1985 entry under "children" indicates that the term "girl child" was not yet popular then in UN circles: there was an NGO forum on the *Female Child Today* (italics mine); the more grammatically correct "female child" was used for the conference on the topic of girls. A quick look at another UN indexing source called the UN yearbooks, which summarize key activities by all UN agencies, also corroborates this observation: the subject index of the UN Yearbooks shows no entries under either "girl" or "girl child" until 1990, when there are three page references for the term "girl child," which seems quite definitely to have been inaugurated in UN circles in, or just before, 1990.[11]

The tautology in the term "girl child" is interesting: girls are, a priori, children—but using the word "child" confers and confirms vulnerability. Perhaps "child" is used because the word "girl" has ambiguous age referents: women in their twenties and thirties continue to be called girls, long after using the word "boy" is inappropriate for men of the same age. "Child," then, reminds readers of the young age of the girls in question. The French term used in UN documents, *"la petite fille"* (the little girl), is again interesting for its connotation of a young child, even though much of the activism focuses on girls who are adolescents.

The term "girl child" is also clearly an attempt to clarify that the needs of girl children are separate from those of boys. As the UNICEF booklet *The Girl Child* explains, the term "girl child" prevents us from erasing the specific needs of girls, which can occur when using the androcentric category "child." The 2007 secretary-general's report on the girl child also clarifies this problem in a forceful way: "The specific situation of girls [is] often being concealed behind generic concepts such as 'women and girls,' 'boys and girls' or 'children' in general." The report lists several problems as specific to girls: "son preference, prenatal sex selection, female genital mutilation, early and forced marriage, early pregnancy and honor crimes."[12]

Presenting "girl child" as a category separate from "women" also underlines the point that girls have specific needs that are not identical to those of women. Until the 1990s UN concerns associated with girls typically fell under the umbrella of women's issues. For instance, many of the sponsors of the efforts to formulate the Convention on the Rights of the Child (CRC) included groups committed to the Convention on the Elimination of Discrimination against Women (CEDAW) in the late 1970s and 1980s. The same NGOs had consultative status for both conventions on women and children.[13] Indeed, all children's issues as a category tended to be yoked to those of women. A rather literal expression of this fusing of women and children can be again seen in UNDOC indexes. Documents listed under the category "woman" were frequently cross-referenced under "children." For instance, a document titled "State of the World's Women" is referenced under "child health" in 1985, and another titled "Advancement of Women" is listed under the subject category "children" in 1988. In a parallel fusing of concerns, the UN Children's Fund executive director's report is listed under "women" in 1985. The items listed under "girl" prior to 1990 also seem generically fused with documents pertaining to women. For example, in 1987, the two items listed under "girls" were about the UN Decade for Women; in 1989, the single entry is about refugee and displaced women.

Although the issues concerning women and children were conflated, it was women's groups who played crucial roles in taking up the issue of children's rights. Protecting children was a key plank of many women's movements in various parts of the world, especially on topics such as nutrition, health, antitrafficking, and marriage. This porosity in the boundary between women's issues and children's issues in social movement history is related to ideologies of maternalism shaping women's movements; women frequently took on children's issues as an extension of their normative social roles as mothers. The "women in development" (WID) and the "women and development approaches" (WAD) of the 1970s and 1980s were able to successfully prioritize attention to women in development circles because of their shared argument that it was women who, as primary caregivers in households, secured the well-being of children—and thereby the future workforce. It is also the case that women's advocacy garnered wider political power when it cited women's responsibility for future generations. Apart from maternalism, the fact that all women (except the transidentified) had themselves once experienced girlhood made such fluid identification across the age categories "woman" and "girl" possible.

It is certainly true that women's campaigning on behalf of girls has been important because girls typically have fewer opportunities for public expression and activism than women. Yet the conflation of "women and girls" and "women and children" has also created a dilemma: it contributes to women's infantilization. Such infantilization of women can be seen in protection-oriented laws against night work and trafficking that conflate women and children, hampering women's ability to obtain work. The most recent text of the CRC also frequently mentions women, confusing women's and children's issues. Such a yoking of women to children, especially to girls, inscribes women as primarily vulnerable figures. For many reasons, then, the untethering of "girl" from both "children" and "women" and its independent articulation as "girl child" in UN and NGO language in 1990 was a significant development. Both the discursive consolidation of the girl and the increasing importance of girls as targets of attention have implications for how we understand women's movements.

Dissecting UNICEF's Role

The 1990 through 1992 period was pivotal in highlighting girls' issues across many intergovernmental and multilateral agencies. For instance, in 1990, the World Bank published a report *Educating Girls and Women: Investing in Development*, an initial salvo in its effort to mainstream gender into its reporting mechanisms. Most striking was the role of UNICEF, which moved speedily after 1990 to focus on the girl child; executive director James P. Grant and its NGO committee took the lead in promoting girls' access to education. The UN Yearbook for 1990 mentions UNICEF's groundbreaking World Summit for Children held at the UN headquarters, with unprecedented attendance levels—159 governments participating and 71 heads of state present and 45 NGOs. Its culmination was the World Declaration and Plan of Action for the Survival, Protection, and

Development of Children. The summit's ten-point plan of action mentions focusing on the "girl child" as a means to ensure the well-being of mothers: "Efforts for the enhancement of women's status had to begin with the girl child. Equal opportunity should be provided for the girl child to benefit from health, nutrition, education and other basic services to enable her to grow to her full potential."[14] Among the World Summit for Children's sectoral goals for the 1990s decade were women's health and education. Under this section, we see "special attention to the health and nutrition of the female child" as the first item and "universal access to primary education with special emphasis for girls" as the last.[15] Such formulations that fuse girls' interests with those of women present an interesting reversal of the logic that had conventionally been used to promote women's status: that women assured the well-being of children. Instead, here we see the girl child articulated as a woman-in-the-making, whose health secured that of future women, who, in turn, secured all children's futures. This formulation of the girl as a *key* to unlocking the problem of massive development deficits was the preamble to the later, more corporate-driven, urge to invest in girls' potential, described later in this chapter.

Yet the focus on girls was not solely driven by instrumental development logics. There was certainly cause for greater attention to girls; their needs were simply not being met in any way commensurate with those of boys. The UNICEF booklet *The Girl Child* lays out clearly why girls deserved to be studied as a distinct category: It points out that girl children did not enjoy the same benefits and rights as boy children, and there was a lack of gender-specific information about girls. It describes how girls around the world unevenly bore the brunt of poverty, getting less food, education, and health care. It places these educational, economic, and health problems that girls face on the same continuum as problems women face, pointing out that just like women, girls' domestic work is rendered invisible, and their illiteracy and malnutrition ignored. It calls for investment in girls as a means to assure better futures for adult women, detailing policy recommendations on health, nutrition, workload, and education.[16]

Grant emphasized the language of justice by coining the phrase "the apartheid of gender."[17] Under his leadership, UNICEF organized Education for All Girls: A Human Right—A Social Gain, a conference in New York in April 1992, attended by nearly three hundred participant NGOs, governments, and donor agencies. The conference resulted in a call for action to governments and NGOs to eliminate the discrimination that girls faced, which Grant declared would not end "without educating girls."[18] That same year, the World Bank's chief economist, Larry Summers, delivered a keynote lecture in Islamabad, explaining the economic benefits of educating girls and, principally, how education lowered fertility.[19]

In its progress report issued in 1992 about implementing UNICEF policy on women in development, UNICEF also devoted a specific section to the "progress made in the situation of the girl child," which was requested by the UNICEF executive board. The report presents a snapshot of how policymakers perceived challenges facing girl children and defines "girls" as females from birth to age 18, specifying that the age cohorts 0–5, 5–10, 11–15, and 16–18 years are meaningful for particular issues. In paying special attention to the latter two cohorts, it indicates the emphasis on girls' puberty and adolescence. It also offers a general justification for the focus on girls in demographic terms: it notes that in Africa, girls form a large proportion of the female population because nearly 55 percent of the population is under 20 years of age. For South Asia and China, the report notes a different demographic reason: boys seriously outnumber girls in these regions, an excess of historic proportions. It singles out India, where because of amniocentesis and ultrasound technology, an "estimated 78,000 female fetuses were aborted between 1978 and 1983."[20] The report goes on to mention the irony that women are often the "principal inculcators" of son preference.

From this report, we glean a sense of why girls' rights were articulated as a matter separate from women's rights. Three advocacy topics facilitated the detaching of girls from women, female feticide and infanticide, female genital mutilation (also termed "female genital cutting" by many feminist activists), and HIV among street children. In the first two types of practices, adult women were the principal perpetrators, even if the driving ideologies were rooted in male dominance. Female feticide as a problem was directly linked to abortion, which women's advocates historically had struggled to legalize. Opponents of abortion could now point to widespread female feticide as one of the reasons for obstructing abortion; this issue distinguished, in literal terms, girls' rights from a long-standing women's rights plank. Genital cutting, too, singled out girls as specific victims distinct from women, because it was women—female community elders or midwives—who carried out the ritual procedure. Although women were certainly victims of misogynistic thinking in both these contexts, they were also its functionaries. In the third category, HIV among street children, children were identified as a separate constituency from women principally because mothers and other household managers were absent.[21] The increasing attention to these three issues in the early 1990s, which this report reflects, can explain why advocacy for the girl could be detached from women's issues in this moment.

The most visibly distinct UNICEF institution focused on girls in this period was the Working Group on the Girl Child, which was formed in 1993.[22] This separate working group in Geneva was formed with the goal of raising the visibility of girls' rights for inclusion in the Platform for Action for the historic 1995 Beijing conference on women. According to the co-chair of the Working Group, Mary Purcell, the idea for a separate section in the platform came up at a meeting in Dakar. African delegates convinced others that the original position of treating girls as an afterthought to women's issues was "conservative" and that girls deserved separate consideration. In 1994 the Working Group called for an official separate section to the Beijing Platform, which finally took shape in 1998 as section L: The Girl Child.

UN Momentum

Around 1995 the awareness of the girl child as a distinct topic emerged beyond UNICEF circles. A CRC report stresses the plight and specific needs of the girl child, and a report on its 209th meeting in January 1995 notes the occurrence of a "general debate on the girl child." The debate concluded that national and international legal and social measures were needed to protect girl children, in particular, through standardizing an age of marriage and gathering gender-specific statistics.[23]

In 1995 the UN General Assembly passed its first Resolution on the Girl Child, the first of at least sixteen such resolutions to date. These resolutions were signed by all the member states annually at the December UN plenary meetings. The resolutions have a broadly parallel structure: they open by recalling relevant UN conventions or commitments; note with pleasure any recent developments, such as summits on specific issues; express concern about specific issues; and offer collective-action items phrased as "calls" to all members states to enact specific measures.[24]

The action items in these resolutions between 1995 and 2015 follow a generally consistent emphasis on the prevention of discrimination and violence against girls and promoting education and health services for girls. Up close, one can see variation in topics and, at times, the naming of specific concerns such as "high levels of obstetric fistula and maternal mortality and morbidity."[25] Taken together, the resolutions indicate the shifts in topics associated with girls. Although early marriage, genital mutilation, and nutrition are consistently important across all the years, trafficking, pornography, and HIV become especially significant around 1999 to 2003; access to schooling assumes greater importance early in the first decade of the twenty-first century; the rise of child-headed households gets attention in 2005; and child labor as a problem is parsed in greater detail after 2007.

As is sometimes typical in bureaucratic practice, there is repetition in content across years. Resolutions for the few key years of 1995, 1996, 2005, and 2007 set the tone and became the blueprint for successive years. The first UN General Assembly Resolution on the Girl Child in December 1995 emerged in the wake of several landmark conferences, namely, the 1989 Vienna Declaration on Human Rights, the 1990 World Summit on Children, the 1995 Fourth World Conference on Women in Beijing, and the 1995 Copenhagen Summit on Social Development. The 1995 resolution urges all states to, first of all, "eliminate all forms of discrimination against the girl child and to eliminate the violation of the human rights of all children, paying particular attention to the obstacles faced by the girl child," to implement "gender-sensitive strategies," and to "increase awareness of the potential of the girl child and to promote the participation of girls." It also called on major agencies of the UN, such as FAO, UNICEF, UN Educational, Scientific, and Cultural Organization (UNESCO), and WHO to "take into account the rights and the particular needs of the girl child."[26]

The resolution of December 21, 1995, served as a prototype from which successive resolutions drew their formats and content. Each successive year's resolution added tweaks to this blueprint, bringing into increasingly sharp focus a range of issues, from education to early marriage to trafficking to HIV prevention. The 1996 resolution specifies what were seen as girls' distinct issues. Apart from education, this resolution lists different kinds of violence and discrimination: sexual exploitation, incest, early marriage, female infanticide, prenatal sex selection, and female genital mutilation. The resolution also is noteworthy for its emphasis on legal changes, specifically calling for "the enforcement of laws on the minimum legal age for marriage." It again repeats this point about preventing child marriage when it urges states "to enact and strictly enforce laws to ensure that marriage is entered into only with the free and full consent of the intending spouses, to enact and strictly enforce laws concerning the minimum legal age of consent and the minimum age for marriage where necessary."[27] The emphasis on preventing child marriage remains a constant feature of the resolutions thereafter, becoming the top priority in the years after 2007.

Even though the term "girl child" might have emphasized girls who were infants or under 10 years of age, it is clear from the second resolution (1996) that adolescent girls were squarely at the center of UN conversations. The third item in the 1996 resolution's calls for action is to give attention to the rights and needs of adolescent girls, which call for special action for their protection from sexual exploitation and abuse, harmful cultural practices, teenage pregnancy and vulnerability to sexually transmitted diseases and human immunodeficiency virus / acquired immunodeficiency syndrome and for the development of life skills and self-esteem, reaffirming that the advancement and empowerment of women throughout the life cycle must begin with the girl child at all ages.[28]

In moving swiftly from issues affecting female infants to those affecting female teens, the UN discourse effectively compressed the age of girls. In treating feticide, malnutrition, schooling, incest, marriage, and sexual slavery in one frame, we see the consolidation of the girl child as a highly vulnerable figure and across a large age range.

Around 2005 the General Assembly resolutions shifted in tone from raising awareness of problems to becoming more action-oriented. The number of action items listed in the UN General Assembly resolutions also grew considerably higher: from 1995 to 2004, the average is 10 to 20 items; 2005, 32; 2006, 25; and 2007, 32. After 2007 the number grows even larger: 2009, 43; 2011, 50; and 2013, 48. The increases are likely related to the growing information gathered from various UN agencies in the secretary-general's reports on the girl child. Many of these items repeat others in their substance, and this, perhaps, reflects the bureaucratic imperatives of the process: new items and emphases are tacked onto lists even when they echo earlier ones, perhaps at the insistence of specific UN actors.

More generally, however, the increasing action orientation in the UN General Assembly may be related to a new urgency generated by the UN's CSW, which successfully argued that ten years beyond the signing of the 1995 Beijing Platform for Action, not enough had been done for girls.[29] The Resolution on the Girl Child, signed at the sixty-fourth plenary meeting in December 2005, stands out for its call to have the secretary-general not only ensure that all UN bodies take into account the needs of girl children but also to submit a report to the General Assembly on its implementation.[30] From 2006 onward, the secretary-general compiled reports that presented thoughtful overviews of all the work done by UN agencies in the name of girls.

The emergence of annual special reports by the secretary-general on the girl child after 2006 is also an indication of the elevation of this topic under the stewardship, starting in 2007, of a new secretary-general: Korean diplomat Ban Ki-Moon, who took over after Ghanaian diplomat Kofi Annan (1997 to 2006).[31] That Ban's office took on the role of compiling these reports is a sign of the urgency and seriousness with which the girl child was viewed within the UN system, as well as the power of the CSW to pressure the system to focus on girls. The secretary-general's reports, compiled in 2006, 2007, 2009, 2011, and 2013, are fifteen-to-twenty-page documents that summarize the actions taken on a variety of fronts: human rights and antiviolence, health, and education. The reports present a compelling portrait of the consolidation of institutional interest in girls. Each takes distinct angles, but all are striking in their citing of studies from a range of institutions: from scholarly journals, such as *Lancet* and *Journal of Child Psychology and Psychiatry*, to reports by UNICEF, WHO, the International Labor Organization (ILO), and the Joint UN Programme on HIV/AIDS (UNAIDS). The reports are also noteworthy in their clear-eyed naming of gender-blind research and male dominance as underlying problems. For example, the first secretary-general's report (2006) notes that "official statistics tend to focus on the more visible forms of child labour where more boys are found, while undercounting the informal sector where girls are concentrated."[32] It lists issues important to girls such as the need for "safe spaces" that are girl-friendly support networks, and the problems of violence in educational settings, armed conflicts, and prostitution. In 2007 the secretary-general also produced a separate report on forced marriage of the girl child.[33] This nineteen-page special report connects forced marriage and child marriages as a problem and reviewed the many reasons for such practices, noting in particular that they occur in places where pervasive economic insecurity combines with embedded beliefs about protecting girl's sexual honor and virginity. The report also calls for consolidating 18 years as the common universal standard for age of marriage around the world.[34]

Ban's tenure also coincides with the more general effort to publicize action on the girl child through the UNFPA's creation in 2007 of an Inter-Agency Task Force on Adolescent Girls. This task force was created with the express goal of facilitating communication among the key UN bodies UNICEF, ILO, UNAIDS, UNESCO, and WHO in devising country plans that focused on the needs of adolescent girls. As the UNESCO webpage describes, this task force "supports collaboration at the country level—with government ministries, NGOs and women's and girls' networks—to identify marginalized adolescent girls in selected communities and to implement programmes aimed at ending their marginalization." The Inter-Agency Task Force for Adolescent Girls turned its attention explicitly to child marriage, producing a report in 2011 stating that one hundred million girls could be married within the next decade if concerted prevention efforts were not undertaken,[35] and the 2011 secretary-general's report offers a detailed look at child marriage, reviewing commitments to enforce minimum marriage-age laws. It is clear that there was a confluence of attention to child marriage, and when the General Assembly adopted a resolution in December 2011 declaring October 11 the International Day of Girl Child, it drew specific attention to child marriage.

Girls as a Site of Investment

The 2007 UN Task Force on Adolescent Girls described above consolidated not only an interest in girls but also a particular orientation toward them: its mandate was to "invest" in girls. The idea that focusing on girls' education yielded valuable downstream social effects was not in itself new—it was of a piece with two decades of development discourse orthodoxy explaining why focusing on women was important to development agendas: women as caregivers could transmit and extend the effects of aid rather than consume it themselves. But with respect to girls, a specifically future-oriented financialized discourse took root around 2005 in UN circles that directly adopted the language of investing. In the 2004 UNICEF State of the World's Children Report, for instance, a section, "Multiplier Effect," proclaims that "girls' education is the most effective means of combating many of the profound challenges to human development."[36] The simplicity of this idea (with its inherent simplifications) contributed to its popularity. This term "invest" became pervasive very quickly and was featured even on the masthead banner of the UN Foundation's webpage about adolescent girls: "What We Do: Investing in Adolescent Girls."[37]

The use of the term "invest" was also related to a striking turn in the UN's modus operandi—growing partnerships with private-sector corporations. In 2005 the UN paired with the Nike Foundation to form the Coalition for Adolescent Girls, which grew into the Girl Effect network launched in 2008, consolidating funding from a wide range of sources, such as the Bill and Melinda Gates Foundation, the Bangladesh-based development organization BRAC, the US-based Novo Foundation, and UK Aid. In the 2013 secretary-general's report, the trend toward public-private partnerships is especially clear; this report cites organizations such as the Together for Girls Initiative (which combines the forces of UN agencies, the US government, and private-sector members); the Global Partnership for Education, a World Bank initiative; and the UN Girls Education Initiative, which also works across public and private sectors.

Corporate campaigns, such as the Girl Effect, specifically centered adolescents in their call for investing in girls. The campaigns generated a blitz of banners with various versions of the idea that adolescent girls were the key to "ending poverty for themselves and the world" and that it was specifically 12-year-old girls who would spark this revolution and "raise the standard of

CHAPTER 6

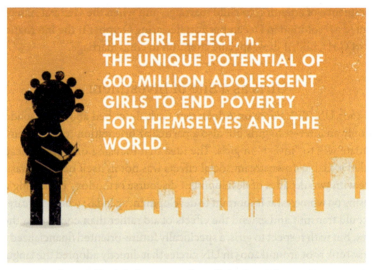

Figure 6.1. Definition of the Girl Effect. Source: The Girl Effect, http://fawg.org.fj/wp-content/uploads/2011/08/girl1.jpg, accessed September 12, 2018.

living in the developing world."[38] The UN Foundation's Girl Up campaign also adopted a similar focus on investing, with the word "investment" in its homepage description of its mission.[39]

The profusion of campaigns featuring the word "girl" and an investment orientation signals how this became a consensus across development agencies, corporate charity campaigns, national legislators, and intergovernmental agencies alike. The UN secretary-general, at an event launching the 2013 film *Girl*

Figure 6.2. The Revolution Will Be Led by a 12-Year-Old Girl. Source: The Girl Effect, http://shapingyouth.org/wp-content/uploads/2008/12/revolution.jpg, accessed September 12, 2018.

Figure 6.3. Girl Up logo. Source: Girl Up, UN Foundation. https://www.girlup.org/wp-content/themes/-wp-min/css/img/girl-up-logo.svg, accessed January 4, 2019.

Rising, declared, "The greatest return comes from investing in girls and women. When they are educated, they drive development in their families, communities and nations."[40] Melinda Gates, wife of billionaire Bill Gates, comments in a 2015 interview with *Fortune* magazine that "if you want to make life better for a community, you should start by investing in its women and girls."[41] Ellen Johnson Sirleaf, former president of Liberia, echoes this sentiment in a CNN opinion editorial in August 2015 that Africa is not really "rising . . . unless we invest more in girls."[42]

What explains the turn toward the vocabulary of *investing* in girls, rather than, say, assistance, development, aid, welfare, or even nurture and protection? To invest implies, as mentioned earlier, a financialization of the target. The expectation is that the money spent will grow or, in this case, yield benefits for those beyond the target herself.[43] At its core, it takes an instrumental approach to girls, viewing the girl not so much as an end in herself but as a means to other ends. It is easy to locate this language of investment as part of a general neoliberal climate that celebrates individuated subjects. More specifically, though, it points to the entry of corporate funding into charitable development efforts. Corporate funding imbues it with distinct vocabularies: to "invest" suggests actions that are more than charity. Rather than giving away money, investments are instead calculated strategies to create wealth that grows. And the girl is a much more fruitful target of investment than the woman: there are more future years to reap dividends for social spending. This calculus rests also on the presumption that girls are inevitably future reproducers.[44]

The orientation toward investing in girls also coincided with the growing culture of corporate social responsibility. In the latter part of the twenty-first century's first decade, it became a widespread imperative for megacorporations—such as Nike or Microsoft—to demonstrate their largesse via dramatic social-responsibility actions. The emergence of girls as a target coincided with this trend. Importantly, girls formed the ranks of both potential consumers and workers for such corporations. Teenage girls, for example, are both potential future consumers and workers for Nike. And more tellingly, Nike's treatment of young female workers in its factories had been a target of activist concern and campaigns since the 1990s—the company features prominently in literature on women workers in export processing zones.[45] In light of this controversial history, Nike sought to recuperate its image by representing a positive relationship to young women and girls. Quite felicitously, its focus on not just girls but also encouraging *sports* as a means to girls' empowerment expanded the base of consumers for its shoes.[46] Deferring marriage (which the Nike-sponsored Girl Effect campaign promotes) produces a pool of available workers. Nike's campaign exemplifies how the "girl" then conveniently collated corporate interests, state priorities, and protective UN goals. The next section traces a similar confluence of discourses of investment and protection in India, where they find an especially dramatic expression.

State Initiatives in India: Policy Changes

The emerging NGO consensus about investing in girls around 2008 had an important literal corollary in state actions in India: several state (provincial) governments began programs that channeled money directly into the hands of families where girls were born, rather than into institutions focused on girls' welfare. These striking programs, called conditional cash transfer (CCT) schemes, provided monetary incentives to impoverished families with newborn girls in order to improve the girls' life chances. Cash is transferred to families in installments when a series of conditions is met: when families immunize, educate, and then delay a girl's marriage past age 18. In effect, such state interventions seek to discriminate positively in favor of girls.

The earliest version of CCTs focused on delaying marriage aimed to curtail female infanticide and feticide. These were all linked problems, since the high cost of dowry shaped parent decisions to kill female fetuses and/or neglect infants. In 1994 the Indian state of Haryana pioneered a government program that subsidized parents who gave birth to a girl child: under a program called Apni Beti Apna Dhan ("one's girl is one's wealth"), the state government transferred cash over an eighteen-year period to parents below the poverty line after the birth of a daughter, on the condition that they educate the child and do not marry her off before she turned 18.[47]

This form of direct state investment in girls is a conceptual innovation. It holds that by linking the birth and well-being of a girl child with cash inflow, subtle changes will occur in how families value girls and lead to the erosion of son preference. CCTs have been widely used in Latin America to improve child and maternal health, but an explicit focus on girls is a distinct feature of Indian programs. Such programs are no longer restricted to individual states, such as the Apni Beti Apna Dhan program in Haryana. From 2007 to 2010, several new programs were inaugurated covering various states, so that in 2015 fifteen different programs crossed multiple states of India, each with different names and stipulations. This spike in CCT programs oriented toward girls is consistent with the more general climate of promoting investment in girls. Dhanalakshmi, the 2008 program of the central government's Ministry of Women and Child Development established in seven states, provides staggered cash at various milestones: at each immunization of infant girls and then every year of school until eighth grade. States such as Madhya Pradesh, Karnataka, Bihar, and Gujarat have their own independent programs with similar features.[48] While many of these programs are designed to serve girls from birth until they turn 18, other programs hone in on the adolescent phase: the Kishori Shakti Yojana (Female Youth's Strength Scheme) was inaugurated in 2001, echoed by a national Nutrition Programme for Adolescent Girls (NPAG) in 2002 and 2003. In 2011 the Rajiv Gandhi Scheme for Empowerment of Adolescent Girls (also known as Sabla) consolidated many of these programs focused on adolescent girls.[49] And in 2013, recognizing the complex environment in which NGOs, private-sector initiatives, and media shape attention to child marriage, the central government's Ministry of Women and Child Development authored a National Strategy Document on Prevention of Child Marriage to offer broad guidance to states and other stakeholders and to specifically assist children who were married early.[50]

Because many of these programs are less than a decade old, their success is still being evaluated. Some studies indicate problems with implementation: the large number of conditions that such programs stipulate (with cash transfers made at multiple microsteps, such as after each immunization or after each grade in school) generate opportunities for corruption and bureaucratic delays.[51] However, a 2015 longitudinal study of the oldest program, the Apni Beti Apna Dhan, found clear results that families receiving cash transfers delayed the marriage of girls until they were past 18; it shows that this policy of investing in girls can undercut the practice of child marriage.[52] Another study of the same program confirms its positive effect on the sex ratio and immunization of girls.

At the same time, both studies note that many families spend the cash transferred at age 18 on the girl's *marriage* in the following year, showing that government money is being used as a way to reduce the burden of marriage costs, rather than imagine futures beyond marriage for girls. By delineating 18 as the age at which the cash transfers end, CCT programs very frequently underline attention to the legal age of marriage for girls, giving it an unprecedented solidity. Paradoxically, naming this age boundary can also appear to encourage families to release girls for marriage immediately after they turn 19, undermining the spirit of the state intervention, which is to promote changes in attitudes toward girls—to promote viewing them less as liabilities and more as assets.

An important conclusion to be drawn from Indian state interventions in the first two decades of the 2000s is that there is political cachet to be gained from policies focused on girls. The United Progressive Alliance (UPA) government in power in India from 2005 to 2014 initiated several CCTs and also renamed preexisting programs; the Sabla scheme consolidated other adolescent programs begun earlier. Apni Beti Apna Dhan was renamed Ladli in this period. Such jockeying to take credit for policies means that clear electoral gains are to be made from investing in girls. The direct cash transfers from governments can deepen already problematic patronage relationships in electoral politics; parties and elected officials can be perceived as distributors of largesse and seek to buy votes through such mechanisms. Nurturing girls, in other words, is not necessarily an end in itself but rather a means by which political victories can be secured.

The CCTs' problematic reliance on families as the conduit of investment in girls or protection of girls does not increase power and autonomy for girls, because parents are often the locus of the problem. If cash is transferred not to parents but instead to girls at age 18 as savings deposits that only the girls can access, it will be an improvement. Similarly, if the law were to allow children to petition independently against a marriage, it might open up more avenues for challenging child marriages.

* * *

This chapter relays a genealogy since the early 1990s of the current intergovernmental, corporate, and state interest in the girl. The transnational account of the travels of the terms "girl" and "girl child" starts with their origins in India, moving from Indian academic reports to the discourses of specific UN bodies, such as UNICEF. The chapter shows how interest in girls moved from a vaguely formulated concern to a set of highly detailed calls to action adopted by the UN General Assembly at regular annual intervals and even more urgently voiced in reports of the chief official of the UN, the secretary-general. Changes in India in the recent past were related to this intensified commitment to girls.

This is not just an argument about changing nomenclature and a superficial preference for the word "girl"; important shifts in tenor have occurred. The girl child is not only a site of negative affective attention—a tragic figure in need of urgent protection—but also a site of positive productive investment. If the discourse of population control in the 1960s and 1970s shaped policy measures pertaining to girls' sexual practices, in the decades that followed this discourse was supplemented, and in some ways even supplanted, by an emphasis on investing in their education. From a biopolitical standpoint, there is a pivot in emphasis from curtailing life (through population control) to fostering life (through investing in girls). This new tenor has come about in the context of a range of institutions—corporations, intergovernmental foundations, and state governments—calling for direct and indirect investment in girls. The most striking examples of investing in girls can be found in the conditional cash transfer programs initiated in Indian states, described in the final section.

Without a doubt, the concerted international attention to girls has meant increasing legitimacy for girl-friendly policies within countries and even pressure for greater action. These shifts, though well intentioned, frequently miss the mark of according greater autonomy to girls. As this chapter shows, girls continue to be viewed as indices of something else and a means to other goals— the development stature of the nation, the progressive social-responsibility credentials of a corporation, or the political cachet of a new party in power.

7

Curtailing Parents?

Marriage and Consent Laws, 2004–2018

If, at the start of the twentieth century, India had one of the lowest legal ages of marriage in the world, 12, in the early twenty-first century, the age of marriage and age of consent, 18, have come under challenge as being unduly high. Since around 2006, sexual consent has again become a legal flashpoint in India, albeit with a new configuration of the relationship between feminism and the law. Feminists are now, unusually, arguing for lowering the age of consent after nearly a century of calling to raise it.

The feminist debates in the 2010s are taking place amidst a new activist environment. Unlike in the 1970s, when the CMRA was amended, by the twenty-first century, a robust network of well-funded NGOs was advocating for girls and for child welfare. Alongside the monetary schemes to ward off early marriage described in the previous chapter, legal measures have come under new scrutiny in the first two decades of the twenty-first century. The range of new entities—NGOs, UN-funded international organizations, and state-aligned legal hotlines—as well as more performance-driven government ministries have resulted in a more concerted effort to raise the age at which girls get married.

This chapter tracks the legal and activist efforts under way in India since 2006 to curtail child marriage and address sexual consent. The history offered in previous chapters is used to dissect the complexities of recent laws prohibiting child marriage and altering the age of consent. The first section of this chapter describes the changes to laws affecting child marriage, explaining the context of law enforcement and its challenges. The second section focuses on feminist dilemmas about how to understand consent. Both sections note how curbing parental control over children's marriage practices has become a much more central focus of activism and lawmaking.

Child Marriage: A Shifting Landscape

During the many decades that the 1929 CMRA was in effect, the incidence of child marriage in India dropped—but not in dramatic ways. The mean age of marriage for girls in India went up from 15.9 years in 1961 to 19.3 years in 1991, but this higher mean age obscured wide internal variation: 11.8 percent of girls were married before they turned 13 years, the 1991 National Family Health Survey (NFHS) showed.[1] Two-thirds of the women surveyed did not know what the legal age of marriage was.[2] NFHS figures for 1998 and 1999 also reveal a continuing high incidence of early marriage: 61 percent of all women in the age group 20 to 49 were married before they turned 18.[3] The 2005 and 2006 NFHS reveals that nearly half the women (47.4 percent) in the age range 20 to 24 had been married before they turned 18. States in north and northwest India were the most common sites of early marriage.[4]

These figures showed how weak the enforcement of the child marriage law was. Early marriage is attributable to several forces—dowry, parental control over choice of mates, building caste and kinship alliances, fear of sexual predation, poverty, and a premium on virginity—but blame can also be placed on flaws in the CMRA itself for not signaling greater social opposition to this practice.[5] Even after its amendment in 1978 (described in chapter 5), the CMRA did not name child marriage a cognizable offense, which would have empowered police officials to arrest parents without warrant. The CMRA required independent parties—neither belonging to the groom's nor bride's family—to report the marriage to authorities. Only motivated police officials would obtain an arrest warrant from a judge and be willing to carry out arrests in the face of possible opposition from families and even an entire community. The revoking of a marriage could mean embarrassment and an unclear future status for the bride. Furthermore, not all child marriages by definition were declared void. The CMRA only allowed child marriages that had lasted less than a year to be prosecuted—so a person had only one year after the marriage to petition to dissolve it; after one year, that marriage was decriminalized. The punishment for arranging a child marriage, which was three months of imprisonment and a fine of up to one thousand rupees, was also fairly mild.[6] (In 2006, 1,000 INR would have been around $22.14 USD.)

CHAPTER 7

A new law passed in 2006 sought to address these challenges. The Prohibition of Child Marriage Act (PCMA) purports to offer better possibilities for enforcement than the CMRA. In a deft rhetorical swipe, it replaced the term "restraint" with "prohibition," although, as explained below, the new law comprises mostly amendments to the CMRA. The bill was introduced in November 2004 after the UPA alliance between the Congress Party and Left Front took power in the Indian central government in April 2004. The bill was referred to a parliamentary standing committee of members of different political parties in the Parliament, such as E. M. Sudarsana Natchiappan (Congress Party), Ram Jethmalani (Bharatiya Janata Party), and P. C. Alexander (Congress Party). The report of this committee, presented to Parliament in November 2005, offers justifications for the new law drawn from UN discourses and feminist scholarship. Its first sentence cites a UNICEF publication declaring child marriage to be a violation of human rights.[7] The committee report also cites the work of legal scholar Jaya Sagade,[8] the Delhi-based activist lawyer collective called Human Rights Law Network, the government-funded National Human Rights Commission, and the UN's CEDAW. Documents produced in this period by the Ministry of Women and Child Development also indicate an awareness of UN norms: the ministry's national report on "A World Fit for Children," the consensus document produced by the UN General Assembly of 2002, announces the government's commitment to end child marriage as part of its intention to meet the UN's target goals of the children's program.[9]

The publicity for the PCMA also bears all the marks of the new environment in which UN agencies, government ministries, and NGOs coordinate efforts to shape and enforce the law. The *Handbook on the Prohibition of the Child Marriage Act, 2006*, which explains the provisions of the act in "user-friendly language," is jointly authored by the Ministry of Women and Child Development, UNICEF, and HAQ, a New Delhi–based NGO focused on child rights.[10] Information about this law is abundantly found in the webpages of NGO campaigns, such as Breakthrough's Nation against Early Marriage (www.breakthrough.tv), GirlsNotBrides.org, and independent legal assistance websites, such as IndianKanoon.org (meaning "Indian justice"). This arena of action is vastly different from the 1978 context of the amendment of the CMRA, when activist organizations offered barely any input or assistance.

The PCMA addresses commonly mentioned gaps in the CMRA and seeks to give teeth to the law in the following ways:

- declares all child marriages automatically "void" if obtained by trafficking or abduction and "voidable" if any party to the marriage petitioned against them;

- allows for the children involved—male or female—to file a petition themselves to void their marriage after their own legal age of marriage (18 for girls, 21 for boys);
- directs courts to require that after the marriage was dissolved, the family of the male contracting party provide a maintenance sum to the female contracting party until her remarriage;
- increases the punishment for child marriage to up to two years of imprisonment and pronounces a heftier fine for the groom's family and for anyone involved in solemnizing the marriage; calls for setting up public servants named child marriage prohibition officers with powers equivalent to a police officer and who are responsible for preventing child marriage in their jurisdiction by approaching courts for an injunction, collecting evidence, raising awareness, and furnishing statistics.[11]

The last point, the creation of child marriage prohibition officers, provides greater legitimacy and support to grassroots workers who advocate against child marriage. Such official support is important in view of widespread community intolerance for whistleblowers.[12] The fact that courts can direct families of the groom to pay the bride maintenance also means greater economic security for girls who want to dispute or dissolve their early marriage. Despite these improvements, the Law Commission of India proposed to amend the 2006 law almost immediately because of lingering inadequacies. The major concerns were that the distinction between voided and voidable marriages created confusion and that the difference in the minimum age of marriage—18 for girls and 21 for boys—maintained an unnecessary double standard. Also, the law still requires any minor to petition via a guardian (parent or adult well-wisher) to annul the marriage; such a guardian can be difficult to find if the marriage in question has strong support of the family and community.[13] These points of friction have slowly been addressed at the state level: In October 2017, the legislature of the southern state of Karnataka took the lead in declaring all child marriages automatically void under the PCMA, thereby eliminating the category of voidable marriages, and its move was lauded by the Indian Supreme Court.[14]

There are signs that the PCMA has increased the reporting of child marriage. In 2001 only 85 cases were registered under the CMRA, at a time when surveys show that at least a third of all girls were married before they turned 18. In 2012, after the PCMA had been in effect for five years, the number of registered cases doubled to 169.[15] The National Crime Records Bureau indicates that in 2014, 2015, and 2016, the number of registered cases continued to increase: to 280, 293, and 326 cases, respectively.[16] The number of registered cases is barely a fraction, of course, of the thousands of unreported underage marriages. The primary importance of these cases lies in conferring publicity to the problem. Perhaps the more encouraging figure comes from the 2015 and 2016 NFHS. This survey finds that the actual incidence of marriage below 18 years has dropped over the last decade: the percentage of women aged 20 to 24 years who were married before they turned 18 dropped from 47.4 percent in 2005 and 2006 to 26.8 percent in 2015 and 2016. In other words, while nearly half of Indian women in this age group in 2005 and 2006 were married before they turned 18, only slightly over a quarter of women in this age group ten years later were married before turning 18.[17] This shift is a more dramatic one than those described under the CMRA at the start of this chapter and suggests that there is an important change underway.

Feminist Misgivings

If child marriage was framed primarily as a fertility and demographic problem in the context of population control efforts described in chapter 5, the 2010s have brought the focus back on girl's sexual practices. And this time, unlike in the 1970s, feminists in India have found themselves in the thick of the conversation. After nearly a century of calling to raise the legal age of marriage and sexual consent, feminists are taking the seemingly contradictory position of arguing against, rather than for, raising the age. This contradiction arises primarily because of two different ways that child marriage law is being used: to prosecute parents who marry off their children too young or by parents who use the law to prevent their children getting married against their wishes. In many cases relating to child marriage law, parents of daughters have often been prosecutors rather than defendants. This is because they use the law to protest elopements: they harass the person who married their daughter against their wishes. Parents have declared "void" the marriages that they refuse to accept—often marriages that are intercaste or interreligious.[18] If one takes into account how frequently elopement cases are prosecuted under the CMRA, raising the age of consent and the age of marriage can often end up benefiting parents more than the teenagers involved. The feminist lawyer Flavia Agnes, who heads the Bombay NGO Forum against Oppression of Women, notes that the law against child marriage has frequently become "a weapon to control the expression of sexuality, and curb voluntary marriages, and is used to augment parental power."[19] Agnes has strenuously argued *not* to raise the age of statutory rape from 16 to

18 and has led the charge, shared by other women's groups, that raising this age of consent would, in fact, curtail, rather than extend, young women's freedoms.

It is not just child marriage that is the focus of present controversies; the age of sexual consent is also under deliberation. In May 2012 child-welfare advocates pushed for the passage of the Protection of Children from Sexual Offences Act, which defines all those below 18 years as children. This law defines punishments for a range of sexual offenses involving children from assault and harassment to viewing pornography with a child. It is the first of its kind in India specifically focused on child victims and draws its force from including male child victims. It primarily imagines perpetrators to be adults and victims to be children when it raised the age of consent to 18. However, this new age of consent has implications for how cases of consensual teenage sexual activity are understood because it potentially treats all sex below 18 as criminal. This matter did not attract much attention at the time the law was passed.[20] But if we take the long perspective that this book offers on the historical disjunctures between ages of consent to marriage, prostitution, and sexual activity in India, it is a startling development.

Soon after the law came into force in November 2012, a gruesome event precipitated a closer look at the age of consent: the sexual assault and murder of Jyoti Singh Pandey in December 2012. This gang rape followed by murder incited a national conversation on legal measures to curb rape. With unusual alacrity, the government assembled a committee to prepare a report and recommendations. This was followed by two successive legal interventions: first, an immediate executive-led response called the Criminal Law Amendment Ordinance passed in February 2013, followed by a more formal measure debated in legislative circles; the Criminal Law Amendment Bill, March 2013; and the final Criminal Law Amendment Act, passed in April 2013. The general spirit of these legal interventions was to expand protective measures in response to rape, such as increasing the number of special cells with women police officers trained to deal with rape and increasing criminal penalties for gang rape. Some legislators also called to increase the age of statutory rape to 18. The first measure in response to the Pandey rape and murder, the Criminal Law Amendment Ordinance of February 2013, increased the age of consent to 18 years.

Feminist groups were paying close attention in the wake of the gang rape and murder and strenuously resisted this measure. They called to reduce the age of consent in the Criminal Law Amendment Bill, discussed in March 2013.[21] However, several political parties who sought to present themselves as protectors of women came to characterize this debate as a battle about Indian values and cast feminists as being anti-Indian; in media reports, the fact that feminists supported *lowering* the age of consent became fodder for pitting feminist groups against child rights groups, an unusual storyline.[22] The final Criminal Law Amendment Act raised the age of consent to 18, making India one of the countries with the highest age of consent in the world.[23] As of early 2019 the feminist effort to again lower the age of consent to 16 continues.[24]

The feminist position asking to lower the age of consent makes greater sense when one understands the distinct stakes that parents have in the concept of sexual consent in India. Parents' interests can be deeply at odds with those of their children. Whether we are discussing cases of parents arranging marriages early or refusing to accept their teenager's elopement, the institution at stake is arranged marriage. Parents' reasons for arranging early marriage are varied: most typically, poverty shapes their decision because it is burdensome to financially support a daughter who will likely not contribute to future household income because she will join another household after her marriage and also because she has less access to paid formal work than a son. Parent decisions also stem from protectiveness and fear that the daughter will lose her virginity to the "wrong" person. In environments of great physical insecurity, parents' concerns include fear of rape.

For elite or high-status parents, arranging matches within the bounds of kinship networks ensures the orderly transmission of property. The distinct link between marriage and sex is important to consider here, as well. In contexts where virginity is held at a premium, marriage is deemed as a prerequisite for sex. Marriage is so much the norm that courts and parents in India have insisted on girls and women marrying their rapists as a means to avoid shame and to restore their own respectable status, because rape victims are otherwise deemed defiled or unmarriageable.[25]

The system of parents arranging children's marriages is routinely justified in paternalist terms—that parents will protect their young daughters from predatorial or deceptive strangers, or that the social ties cemented by two families in the process of arranging betrothals protects marriages from dissolution, or that the ties prevent the daughter from feeling alienation when away from her natal family. In a caste-riven society, however, arranged marriages are also a lynchpin in preserving social order, and the power and legacy of caste identities are the most important reasons why parental roles in arranging marriages have been so resilient in India.

India is far from being the only country with this entrenched practice. Wherever lineage has been a key principle at stake, parental involvement in marriage alliances has been deep. As Holly Brewer reflects on early marriage in the colonial United States and seventeenth-century England, "Young marriages ... have everything to do with lineage, maintaining inherited status, and the ideologies underlying social stability, order, monarchy.... Controlling marriage was important to stabilizing a patriarchal system of allocating power by making sure lineage was not corrupted and that social relations remained consistent and boundaries between ranks respected."[26] In any such context, the obvious feminist goal is to support the ability of young women and girls to make marital choices that can potentially defy the wishes of their parents.

One important path toward this feminist goal would be to reframe marriages based on voluntary choice as the norm rather than the exception. In much of South Asia, an individual's partner choice has been a priori framed in legal and cultural terms as outside the norm, with terms such as "love marriages" and "elopement marriages." A shift in framing might be on the horizon given that in urban environments in India, the principle of an individual's partner choice is becoming more and more common.[27] Sexual activity is, concurrently, also occurring early. An analysis of the 2005–6 NFHS found that the mean age of sexual debut was 16.98 years.[28] Doctors have reported an alarming rise in cases of misuse by young people of emergency contraceptive pills as their birth control of recourse.[29]

It is in this changing context that feminist groups underscore how raising the age of sexual consent would empower parents: they could intervene in their children's sexual activity and choices in coercive ways, such as taking their children's partners to court for engaging in sex that parents disapprove of. Under the law, until the children turn 18, parents can prevent children from having sex that they consider unsavory. An unfortunate resonance is between what the law intends—preventing rape and early marriage before 18—and facilitating parental control. There is also a growing fissure between this desire of parents to control children's sexual choices and the actual sexual experiences of teenagers in contemporary India. Realistically acknowledging early sexual activity and addressing its health and emotional implications are the call of the hour.

The conversation around early sexual activity raises fundamental questions about how we imagine the life-cycle stage of adolescence. For decades, psychologists and activists have called to nurture and protect adolescents from labor and responsibility—of both the productive and reproductive kind. While we have imagined the state as the agent of protection, and rapacious strangers and/ or economic necessity as the problems, what has not been specified is the role that parents play. The context of India brings into focus how parents frequently determine the sexual freedom of adolescents. Feminists in India are asserting the capacity of adolescents to make independent sexual choices. As parents and feminists (as well as feminist parents) in India respond to the prospect of early sexual activity among young people, it is striking that the collective political response is a legal effort to lengthen the category of childhood by pushing out its boundaries until age 18. If early twentieth-century psychologists imagined preparation for adulthood as a long process, what seems to be taking place in contemporary India is a kind of legal wishing-into-being, at an institutional level, of a longer childhood.

Conclusion

Child marriage is a sobering challenge around the world in the twenty-first century. According to UN data, roughly 15 million girls are married every year before they turn 18, and a total of 700 million women and girls alive in the late 2010s were married before they turned 18.[1] Given such numbers, it is not surprising that the problem garners the attention of both national governments and NGOs: The US government channels considerable funding into reporting and altering child marriages around the world, and several UN and NGO initiatives aimed at eradicating child marriage have been initiated in the first two decades of the twenty-first century, as detailed in the previous chapters.[2] India is the focal point of such advocacy against child marriage. UNICEF's website on child marriage features a woman in a sari. The UN's webpage about its initiative on adolescent girls features a South Asian face. The International Center for Research on Women, which worked with the US Congress as it passed an act funding global efforts to combat child marriage, focuses its projects on India and Nepal. In such a context, what does looking at the history of sexual maturity laws in India teach us about how to think about the problem of child marriage?

A standard response to a policy problem such as child marriage is to consider the instruments available at the state's disposal—typically, laws and policies. But this book reminds us that legal measures, such as raising the age of marriage, and policies, such as conditional cash transfers, are brought about through political processes that frequently serve interests *other* than those of girls. Each chapter in this book demonstrates how laws ostensibly focused on protecting girls were simultaneously aligned with other forces, such as national prestige, colonial ideologies, economic development priorities, and parental anxieties about respectable reproduction. Nationalist concerns and parental anxieties shaped efforts to raise the age of marriage in 1920s India; as chapter 3 describes, the raised ages of consent secured parental control over girls' sexual mobility. Chapter 5 tracks how population control discourses had goals other than the well-being of girls in raising the legal age of marriage in the 1970s. Chapter 6 traces how NGO and corporate interests are at play in publicizing the girl as a site of investment in the 2010s. In chapter 7, parental anxieties, again, figure in the efforts to maintain a high age of consent for marriage and sexual activity.

Imperial ideologies have also been strengthened via the expansion of vulnerable girlhood. Both the League of Nations conferences on trafficking and UN debates on marriage age underscore how sexual age standards served as an index for hierarchically ordering societies. The scientific understanding of puberty delineated in chapter 1 as well as the early psychological scholarship on adolescence described in chapter 2 both embedded racial distinctions between peoples and nations. Taken together, all the chapters elucidate a variety of peripheral interests served even when the ostensible focus rests on girls.

The girl is never a transparently meaningful category. This book reminds us of the importance of attending to not just laws but how legal categories, or subjects of the law, come into being. The very idea of girlhood expanded over the twentieth century, as puberty no longer defined girls' readiness for sex, marriage, and childbearing. This lengthened sense of maturity has revised sexual maturity laws. A comparison between the League of Nations conversations described in chapter 1 and the UN debate about marriage age described in chapter 4 demonstrates this shift: in the League of Nations context, the age of puberty was the primary focus when discussing age of consent. By the 1950s, when UN delegates first proposed an international treaty on marriage age, several delegates argued for higher age standards that allowed for emotional maturation and opportunities for education beyond puberty.

The shifts in political orientations toward girlhood across the twentieth and twenty-first centuries are also striking. In the 1920s Indian women's movement advocates adopted a strongly protective stance toward girls, arguing to raise the age of marriage for girls well above the legal age of 12 in order to prevent the strain of early sexual activity and childbearing. In the 1920s and 1950s protecting girls was also a plank of intergovernmental action on a common minimum age of marriage and prostitution. In the 1960s Indian demographers began to

CONCLUSION

advocate a more instrumental line of reasoning: raising the age of marriage as a means to curb population growth. In 1978 legislators raised the age of marriage drastically to 18 years, framing the potential fertility of girls as a problem. In the 1990s concern about "missing" girls began to circulate as part of a global shift toward improving the life chances of girls. In global development discourse, this came to be articulated as an investment in national economic futures. The first two decades of the twenty-first century witnessed new ways to prevent early marriage, including cash incentives for holding off until turning 18. What becomes clear from this history is a shift from protecting girls from forced sex to seeing their potential fertility as a population threat, to then seeing girls as targets of investment. In other words, what was meant by the girl—the subject of laws—changed significantly.

Another lesson this book offers is to recognize that old legal discourses shaping age standards do not always fit new needs. If in the early twentieth century it seemed imperative to reformers that the phase of girlhood be chronologically expanded, this change also led to increased levels of parental oversight. The protective orientation shaping the expansion of legal girlhood has not always served girls well. As chapter 7 shows, the legal changes in the 1970s aimed at protecting girls facilitated parental infringements on girls' autonomy. Those advocating for raising the age of marriage sought to ensure that parents did not arrange marriages early; but a raised age of marriage has enabled parents to dictate girls' sexual practices for longer and even harass girls about any relationships they embark on without parental approval. In effect, raising the age of marriage and sexual consent has frequently decreased girls' control over their sexual lives.

Both chapters 3 and 7 show that the expansion of girlhood as a sheltered life phase has been accompanied by the gathering force of protectionist sexual control. This book seeks to make clear the distinction between these two impulses and guard against the latter. Whereas the principle of sheltering girls means preventing girls from being forced into domestic work, marriage, and motherhood, protectionist sexual control prevents girls from pursuing sexual decisions independent of parental and community wishes.

The reason these two impulses have been so frequently confused is that the definitions of girlhood have centered girls' vulnerability. At various moments detailed in this book, the girl has alternately signaled fertility, economic potential, and sexual transgression—but vulnerability is a constant feature in this shifting constellation. Because the figure of the vulnerable girl has such great emotive charge, it is easily trafficked toward multiple ends. The varying imperatives shaping sexual age standards—whether imperial racism, conservative nationalism, or parental control—have obstructed our ability to ask with clarity what girls' interests might be.

Looking ahead, it is perhaps most urgent to maintain a vigilance about the celebration of girlhood in humanitarian discourses. In the current intellectual infrastructure of development and global aid, the "empowered girl" is a much more common mascot than the "suffering Third World woman." Yet the emphasis on resilience in this current iteration of the girl is also a turn toward greater responsibilization of the girl. The recent campaigns chapter 6 describes stress the deferral of marriage, but they do not question the inevitability of a reproductive future. The girl celebrated is not playful and experimentative; she is obedient, hardworking, and serves her community. The coordinated and concerted action against child marriage in the 2010s is unprecedented, and there is, in these first decades of the twenty-first century, a special affective commitment to girlhood itself. But as this book shows, we need to pay attention to which qualities of adolescence for girls are celebrated.

* * *

In drawing this book to a close, it is worth noting its limits. While the book is broadly chronological, the chapters are not watertight in the shifts they describe; ideas in one historical moment lingered and affected others. For example, the discourse of population control, described in the chapter about the 1960s and 1970s, continues to influence later eras. And the imperative of parental control described in chapter 3 continues to play a role in the emerging present, as described in chapter 7. My purpose has been to make analytical delineations, but the boundaries between eras are, of course, messier; neither events nor currents of thought were bound by decadal markers.

Also, regions vary tremendously within India. Much of the book's focus has been on what "India" represents in conversations about sexual age standards. The enormous social complexity across the geographic territory of India—from class and caste divides to religious and urban-rural differences—means that any declarations about Indian girlhood are, at best, loose generalizations. One line of research that was beyond the scope of this book is to explore differences between rural and urban India in how girlhood is understood; this remains, perhaps, the most salient divide. As explained in chapter 5, differences have been persistent between rural and urban societies in the age of marriage and access to education.

The genealogies here offer examples, in a transnational feminist vein, of multidirectional flows of knowledge. Examples of classic diffusion include the

CONCLUSION

centrifugal flow of Eurocentric knowledge from Anglo-US expert discourses to India, in the context of both colonialism and the Cold War. But we also see ideas flowing in the opposite direction, from India to UN circles, particularly, via Indian experts shaping research on demography and population control as well as in the travels of the term "girl child." Indeed, one of the book's claims is that the contemporary celebration of the "girl" in international development circles is in no small measure an outgrowth of South Asian exigencies and Indian knowledge production.

But this interest in illuminating Indian contributions is by no means nationalist. In keeping with a transnational feminist orientation, this book critiques both British colonial functionaries and Indian national elites. For instance, it shows that Anglo imperial discourses were not the only sites depicting Indian girls as abject targets of rescue; Indian population theorists also framed Indian girls as manipulable objects. When it came to depictions of puberty, both European and American race science and conservative Indian legislators upheld the narrative that puberty arrived early in India, whether due to climate or custom. The global opprobrium that India and Indians received for child marriage was cited by Indian reformists to propel changes in Indian law, but it also led to defensive Indian postures abroad. In United Nations settings, delegates of newly independent India defended arranged marriage, claiming cultural sovereignty, and sought to derail efforts at harmonizing a common age of marriage. This book thus offers a critical account of both spurious civilizational hierarchies and nationalist pride.

Given how compelling the figure of the girl is and given how it is harnessed to so many interests, we would do well to keep our eyes more keenly trained on the itineraries of girlhood. This book traverses the varied worlds of bureaucracies, legal debates, medical textbooks, social science journals, women's magazines, and NGO reports to show how various iterations of the adolescent girl condensed over time. In mapping the interests and logics informing changes in laws and policies, it demonstrates how girls have shifted from being a subject of protection to a biopolitical target. Even as the girl appears in our time as a figure laden with capacity and shining with potential, this book shows how sexual disciplining and national reputation are the driving forces behind its emergence and elevation.

Notes

Introduction

1. By the term "biopolitical states," I mean states that derive power from managing the health and life of their populations. Michel Foucault briefly formulated the concept of biopolitics in part 5, vol. 1, *History of Sexuality* (London: Vintage, 1979); his lectures at the College de France (published in 2004, 2007) develop it further.

2. Ashwini Tambe, *Codes of Misconduct: Regulating Prostitution in Late Colonial Bombay* (Minneapolis: University of Minnesota Press, 2009).

3. UNICEF's 2009 report *State of the World's Children* finds that 46 percent of the world's child brides (girls married under 18) live in India. See also the website for the campaign Girls Not Brides, which reiterates that India has the world's largest number of child brides, http://www.girlsnotbrides.org/child-marriage/india/, accessed December 12, 2015.

4. Matthew Connelly, *Fatal Misconception: The Struggle to Control World Population* (Cambridge, MA: Belknap, 2008), 11.

5. Ibid.

6. For a rich account of how child marriage in India became a "global" scandal, see Mrinalini Sinha, *Specters of Mother India: The Global Restructuring of an Empire* (Durham, NC: Duke University Press, 2006).

7. For clarifications about the difference between transnational and international feminism approaches, see Ashwini Tambe, "Transnational Feminist History: A Brief Sketch," *New Global Studies* 4, no. 1 (2010): art. 7.

8. Eileen Boris and Jennifer Fish account for the increasing influence of nongovernmental organizations in shaping UN conventions in "'Slaves No More': Making Global Labor Standards for Domestic Workers," *Feminist Studies* 40, no. 2 (2014): 441–43.

NOTES TO INTRODUCTION

9. Most accounts of global women's movements, such as those by Amrita Basu, Myra Marx Ferree and Aili Mari Tripp, and Nancy Naples and Manisha Desai, begin with the UN Decade for Women. See Basu, *The Challenge of Local Feminisms* (Boulder: Westview, 1995); Marx Ferree and Tripp, eds., *Global Feminisms: Transnational Women's Organizing and Human Rights* (New York: New York University Press, 2006); Naples and Desai, *Women's Activism and Globalization: Linking Local Struggles and Transnational Politics* (New York: Routledge, 2002).

10. Following pathbreaking works such as Howard Chudacoff, *How Old Are You? Age Consciousness in American Culture* (Princeton, NJ: Princeton University Press, 1989), scholarship that takes age seriously as a category of analysis has burgeoned in the first two decades of the twenty-first century. See, for instance, the inaugural forum of the *Journal of the History of Childhood and Youth* 1, no. 1 (2008): 89–124, featuring reflections by Steven Mintz, Leslie Paris, Mary Jo Maynes, and Laura Lovett. See also Corinne T. Field and Nicholas L. Syrett's edited volume *Age in America: The Colonial Era to the Present* (New York: New York University Press, 2015).

11. Philippe Ariès, *Centuries of Childhood: A Social History of Family Life* (New York: Knopf, 1962). For examples of research on childhood provoked by Ariès across multiple continents, see Holly Brewer, *By Birth or Consent: Children, Law, and the Anglo-American Revolution in Authority* (Chapel Hill: University of North Carolina Press, 2005); Vern Bullough, "The Age of Consent: A Historical Overview," in *Adolescence, Sexuality, and the Criminal Law*, ed. Helmut Graupner and Bullough (New York: Haworth Press, 2004), 25–42; Hugh Cunningham, *Children and Childhood in Western Society since 1500* (New York: Pearson, 2005); Lloyd DeMause, ed., *The History of Childhood* (New York: Psychohistory Press, 1974); Jacques Donzelot, *The Policing of Families* (London: Hutchinson, 1980); Anna Mae Duane, ed., *The Children's Table: Childhood Studies and the Humanities* (Athens: University of Georgia Press, 2013); Beverly Grier, *Invisible Hands: Child Labor and the State in Colonial Zimbabwe* (Portsmouth, NH: Heinemann, 2006); Karen Sanchez-Eppler, *Dependent States: The Child's Part in 19th Century American Culture* (Chicago: University of Chicago Press, 2005); John C. Sommerville, *The Discovery of Childhood in Puritan England* (Athens: University of Georgia Press, 1992); Peter N. Stearns, *Childhood in World History* (New York: Routledge, 2006); Matthew Waites, *The Age of Consent: Young People, Sexuality, and Citizenship* (Basingstoke, UK: Palgrave, 2005).

12. For scholarship on child labor in India, see Asha Bajpai, *Child Rights in India: Law, Policy, and Practice* (New Delhi: Oxford University Press, 2003), and Myron Weiner, *The Child and the State in India: Child Labor and Education Policy Comparative Perspective* (Princeton, NJ: Princeton University Press, 1991). For scholarship on son preference in India, see Mita Bhadra, *Girl Child in Indian Society* (Jaipur: Rawat, 1999); Jean Dreze and Amartya Sen, *Hunger and Public Action* (Oxford: Oxford University Press, 1989); and Jaya Sagade, *Child Marriage in India* (New Delhi: Oxford University Press, 2005).

13. Satadru Sen, *Colonial Childhoods: The Juvenile Periphery of India, 1850–1945* (London: Anthem, 2005).

NOTES TO INTRODUCTION

14. See, for instance, Catherine Driscoll's forceful claims in *Girls: Feminine Adolescence in Popular Culture and Cultural Theory* (New York: Columbia University Press, 2002). Crista DeLuzio also notes the challenges in reconciling notions of femininity and adolescence in *Female Adolescence in American Scientific Thought, 1830–1930* (Baltimore: Johns Hopkins University Press, 2007). See also LaKisha Simmons, *Crescent City Girls: The Lives of Young Black Women in Segregated New Orleans* (Chapel Hill: University of North Carolina Press, 2015), on how black girls experienced childhood differently from black boys in the Jim Crow South.

15. Ariès, *Centuries of Childhood*, 58.

16. See Stearns, *Childhood in World History*, on this point.

17. For narratives about girls' sexual maturation in India, see Jyoti Puri, *Woman, Body, Desire in Post-Colonial India: Narratives of Gender and Sexuality* (New York: Routledge, 1999). For more general scholarship on girlhood, see Jennifer Helgren and Colleen Vasconcellos, eds., *Girlhood: A Global History* (New Brunswick, NJ: Rutgers University Press, 2010).

18. Simmons, *Crescent City Girls*.

19. DeLuzio, *Female Adolescence*.

20. Driscoll, *Girls*, 7.

21. Modern Girl around the World Project, *The Modern Girl around the World: Consumption, Modernity, and Globalization* (Durham, NC: Duke University Press, 2009). See also Helgren and Vasconcellos, *Girlhood*.

22. While discussions about scriptural authorization of child marriage are complicated by the range of views available (as discussed in chapters 1 and 3), a number of nineteenth-century texts about child marriage cite the ancient sage Parashara's recommendation that marriage occur before puberty. Parashara is viewed as a source of the earliest Purana and several verses in the Rig Veda and lived possibly around 1500 BCE. (The Rig Veda also contains countervailing views on child marriage, such as the views of Sushrut, who advised waiting until after puberty, as mentioned in chapter 2.) The exhortation to marry girls before puberty was codified in the Manu Smriti, authored around 300 BCE. An example of a nineteenth-century text citing Parashara and Manu is Trailokyanath Mitra, *The Law Relating to the Hindu Widow* (Bombay: Thacker, 1881). For a longer discussion of this point, see Brian Hatcher, "The Evils of Child Marriage: Ishwar Chandra Vidyasagar," trans., *Critical Asian Studies* 25, no. 3 (2003): 476–84. See also P. Krishnan, "Age at Marriage in a Nineteenth Century Indian Parish," *Annales de Démographie Historique* (1977): 271–84.

23. This point is also made by Ruby Lal, who explores how playfulness and girlhood were articulated in nineteenth-century literary texts in *Coming of Age in Nineteenth Century India: The Girl Child and the Art of Playfulness* (Cambridge: Cambridge University Press, 2013).

24. Examples of research on the 1891 debates include Padma Anagol-McGinn, "The Age of Consent Act (1891) Reconsidered: Women's Perspectives and Participation in

NOTES TO INTRODUCTION

the Child-Marriage Controversy in India," *South Asia Research* 12, no. 2 (1992): 100–118; Uma Chakravarti, *Rewriting History: The Life and Times of Pandita Ramabai* (New Delhi: Kali for Women, 1998); Dagmar Engels, "The Age of Consent Act of 1891: Colonial Ideology in Bengal," *South Asia Research* 3 (1983): 107; Tanika Sarkar, "Rhetoric against Age of Consent: Resisting Colonial Reason and the Death of a Child-Wife," *Economic and Political Weekly* 28, no. 36 (1993): 1869–79; Mrinalini Sinha, "The Lineage of the 'Indian' Modern: Rhetoric, Agency, and the Sarda Act in Late Colonial India," in *Gender, Sexuality, and Colonial Modernities*, ed. Antoinette Burton (London: Routledge, 1999), 207–21, and *Specters of Mother India*; Judith Whitehead, "Modernising the Motherhood Archetype: Public Health Models and the Child Marriage Restraint Act of 1929," *Social Reform, Sexuality, and the State*, ed. Patricia Uberoi (New Delhi: Sage, 1996), 187–209.

25. Stephen Robertson, "Age of Consent Laws," Children and Youth in History, item 230, *Center for History and New Media*, http://chnm.gmu.edu/cyh/case-studies/230, accessed October 25, 2017. See also Stephen Robertson, *Crimes against Children: Sexual Violence and Legal Culture in New York City, 1880–1960* (Chapel Hill: University of North Carolina Press, 2005). Jessica Pliley analyzes how panics about "white slavery" raised the age of consent in "Protecting the Young and the Innocent: Age and Consent in the Enforcement of the White Slave Traffic Act," in *Child Slavery before Emancipation: An Argument for Child-Centered Slavery Studies*, ed. A. M. Duane (Cambridge: Cambridge University Press, 2017): 156–76.

26. For examples of postcolonial feminist legal scholarship on this point, see Rajeswari Sunder Rajan, *The Scandal of the State: Women, Law, and Citizenship in Postcolonial India* (Durham, NC: Duke University Press, 2003); Ratna Kapur, *Erotic Justice: Law and the New Politics of Postcolonialism* (London: Taylor and Francis, 2005).

27. Michael Grossberg, "Guarding the Altar: Physiological Restraints and the Rise of State Intervention in Matrimony," *American Journal of Legal History* 26, no. 3 (1982): 197–226.

28. Ann Higonnet, *Pictures of Innocence: The History and Crisis of Ideal Childhood* (New York: Thames and Hudson, 1998).

29. Kathryn Bond Stockton, *The Queer Child, or Growing Sideways in the Twentieth Century* (Durham, NC: Duke University Press, 2009), 12.

30. The connection between progress-oriented narratives of childhood growth and linear notions of time have been analyzed fruitfully by Lee Edelman, *No Future: Queer Theory and the Death Drive* (Durham, NC: Duke University Press, 2004); and Jack Halberstam, *In a Queer Time and Place: Transgender Bodies, Subcultural Lives* (New York: New York University Press, 2005), who critically note that queer desire among children is rarely made visible. They develop the notion of queer temporalities that do not orient themselves toward the goal of future reproduction; Stockton names this orientation "growing sideways."

31. See Stearns, *Childhood*.

32. See, in particular, chapter 2 of Nazera Sadiq Wright, *Black Girlhood in the Nineteenth Century* (Urbana: University of Illinois Press, 2016).

NOTES TO INTRODUCTION AND CHAPTER 1

33. Even though such infantilization was meant to diminish the status of adult women, Anna Mae Duane's point is that infantilization becomes insulting only when childhood means inferiority or powerlessness; these are not inherent qualities of childhood. See Anna Mae Duane, "When Is a Child a Slave?" in Duane, *Child Slavery*, 1–22.

34. Sophia Amoruso, *#GirlBoss* (New York: Penguin, 2014); Megan Seely, *Fight like a Girl: How to Be a Fearless Feminist* (New York: New York University Press, 2007); Lena Dunham, *Not That Kind of Girl: A Young Woman Tells You What She's Learned* (New York: Random, 2014); Gwendolyn Pough, Elaine Richardson, and Aisha Durham, eds., *Home Girls Make Some Noise* (Mira Loma, CA: Parker, 2007).

35. The exception I have in mind here is transgender women who may not have lived their childhoods as girls.

36. For more on the Girl Effect, see Kathryn Moeller, "Searching for Adolescent Girls in Brazil: The Transnational Politics of Poverty in 'The Girl Effect,'" *Feminist Studies* 40, no. 3 (2014): 575–600.

37. For a critique of how a logic of exceptionality shapes how Malala functions as a cultural figure, see Wendy Hesford, "The Malala Effect," *JAC Online: Journal of Rhetoric, Culture and Politics* 34, no. 1–2 (2014): 139–64.

38. Barack Obama, "Remarks by the President to the Clinton Global Initiative," September 25, 2012, https://www.whitehouse.gov/the-press-office/2012/09/25/remarks-president-clinton-global-initiative.

39. For more on this point, see Michelle Murphy, "The Girl: Mergers of Feminism and Finance in Neoliberal Times," *S&F Online* 11, nos. 1–2 (2012–13), http://sfonline.barnard.edu/gender-justice-and-neoliberal-transformations/the-girl-mergers-of-feminism-and-finance-in-neoliberal-times/.

40. For a representative example, see Miriam Forman-Brunell and Leslie Paris, eds., *The Girls' History and Culture Reader: The Twentieth Century* (Urbana: University of Illinois Press, 2011).

Chapter 1. Tropical Exceptions

1. The Union for the Protection of Girls (also called Union Internationale des Amies de la Jeune Fille), which in 1921 was a forty-five-year-old organization based in Switzerland, had a membership of over 16,500 and held a conference in Neuchatel in the month prior to the League of Nations conference. It submitted its formal proposal via the Swiss delegate to the conference. I use the terms "prostitution" and "prostitute" in order to be consistent with the discourse of the era discussed.

2. Proposal of Ernest Béguin (Switzerland), proposal, Sixth Plenary Meeting, Records of the International Conference on Traffic in Women and Children, July 1921 (C.484.M.339.1921. IV) 15, League of Nations Documents Archive, Robarts Library, University of Toronto. The records for all League of Nations antitrafficking conferences identified in subsequent notes are available at the University of Toronto, except when specified otherwise.

3. S. M. Edwardes, Legislative Assembly, memo, 19, Judicial 58/22, Home Department 1922, National Archives of India, Government of India, New Delhi.

NOTES TO CHAPTER 1

4. The notion of "puberty" in this context reduced various kinds of maturation that cisgirls typically experience down to a single threshold event, menarche.

5. The imperial association between sexual appetite and civilizational backwardness has been critically explored in several histories of colonial sexuality. See, for instance, Anne McClintock, *Imperial Leather: Race, Gender, and Sexuality in the Colonial Context* (New York: Routledge, 1995); Mrinalini Sinha, *Colonial Masculinity: The Manly Englishman and the Effeminate Bengali* (New Delhi: Kali for Women, 1995); Ann Stoler, *Carnal Knowledge and Imperial Power: Race and the Intimate in Colonial Rule* (Berkeley: University of California Press, 2002); and Philippa Levine, "Sovereignty and Sexuality: Transnational Perspectives on Colonial Age of Consent Legislation," in *Beyond Sovereignty: Britain, Empire, and Transnationalism, c. 1880–1950*, ed. Kevin Grant, Philippa Levine, and Frank Trentmann (Basingstoke, UK: Palgrave, 2007), 16–33.

6. Partha Chatterjee, *The Nation and Its Fragments: Colonial and Postcolonial Histories* (Princeton, NJ: Princeton University Press, 1993).

7. This problem has been thoroughly examined and debated in feminist human rights literature. While Martha Nussbaum's 1999 *Sex and Social Justice* (New York: Oxford University Press) stands as a resounding critique of using culture and national sovereignty as grounds in refusing human rights, more nuanced accounts of this problem can be found in Isabelle Gunning, "Arrogant Perception, World-Travelling, and Multicultural Feminism: The Case of Female Genital Surgeries," *Columbia Human Rights Law Review* 23 (1991): 189–248; and Uma Narayan, *Dislocating Cultures: Identities, Traditions, and Third World Feminisms* (New York: Routledge, 1997).

8. For more on imperial "arrogance" in human rights settings, see Gunning, "Arrogant Perception."

9. Nitza Berkovitch, *From Motherhood to Citizenship: Women's Rights and International Organizations* (Baltimore, MD: Johns Hopkins University Press, 1999). See Barbara Metzger, "Towards International Human Rights Regime during the Inter-War Years: The League of Nations' Combat of Traffic in Women and Children," in Grant, Levine, and Trentmann, *Beyond Sovereignty*, 54–79.

10. Susan Pedersen, *The Guardians: The League of Nations and the Crisis of Empire* (Oxford: Oxford University Press, 2015).

11. Lauren Benton, *Law and Colonial Cultures: Legal Regimes in World History, 1400–1900*. (Cambridge: Cambridge University Press, 2002), 3. See also her more recent work with Lisa Ford, *Rage for Order: The British Empire and the Origins of International Law, 1800–1850* (Cambridge, MA: Harvard University Press, 2016).

12. The Maharaja of Bikaner, Ganga Singh, who commanded a camel corps in Egypt, was instrumental in the inclusion of India in the League of Nations; he persuaded delegates at the Versailles Peace Conference of 1919 to do so. See Hugh Purcell, *The Maharaja of Bikaner* (London: Haus, 2010).

13. Abolitionism, the Anglo-American progressive movement to eradicate prostitution and venereal disease in the early twentieth century, had stimulated the rise of many such well-knit international organizations signaled by the terms "moral" and/or "social 'hygiene.'" For

NOTES TO CHAPTER 1

detailed studies, see Daniel Gorman, "Empire, Internationalism, and the Campaign against the Traffic in Women and Children in the 1920s," *Twentieth Century British History* 19, no. 2 (2008): 186–216; Metzger, "Towards an International Human Rights Regime," 54–79.

14. One of the earliest tasks that the League of Nations secretary-general assumed in December 1920 was to send a questionnaire to member countries asking them to list measures taken against trafficking. The Indian response to the questionnaire pointed out that sections of the Indian Penal Code dealing with kidnapping for illicit purposes (section 366) and with the sale of girls into prostitution (section 372) both set down 16 as an age of consent. See "Answers to Questionnaire," file no. 21–31–19, Judicial 58/22, Home Department 1922, National Archives of India, Government of India, New Delhi.

15. "League of Nations: International Conference on Traffic in Women and Children," Judicial 58/22, Home Department 1922, National Archives of India, Government of India, New Delhi, 11. See also pp. 30–38 of "Report on the International Conference on the Traffic in Women and Children, held at Geneva on 30th June 1921, by Edwardes, ICS (retired) and Delegate for the Government of India," Judicial 58/22, Home Department 1922, National Archives of India, Government of India, New Delhi.

16. For a critique of antitrafficking efforts in this era, see Tambe, *Codes of Misconduct*.

17. The broader goal of antitrafficking activists even in contemporary settings has been to nullify the notion of women and girls consenting to prostitution. For a detailed exploration of this point, see Pamela Haag, *Consent: Sexual Rights and the Transformation of American Liberalism* (Ithaca, NY: Cornell University Press, 1999).

18. Proposal of Ernest Beguin (Switzerland), Sixth Plenary Meeting of International Conference on Traffic in Women and Children, July 1921 (C.484.M.339.1921.IV), 15, League of Nations Documents Archive.

19. Stephen Meredyth Edwardes, *Bombay City Police: A Historical Sketch* (London: Oxford University Press, 1923). See also Edwardes, *Crime in British India* (New Delhi: ABC, 1924/1983). Both books were published after he retired from service in 1918.

20. For details about Edwardes's role in Bombay's sex trade, see chapter 3 in Tambe, *Codes of Misconduct*.

21. S. M. Edwardes quoted in the memo From Legislative Assembly, Judicial 58/22, Home Department 1922, National Archives of India, Government of India, New Delhi, 19.

22. For a fuller account of this feminist historical argument, see Ashwini Tambe, "Colluding Patriarchies: The Colonial Reform of Sexual Relations in India," *Feminist Studies* 26, no. 3 (2000): 586–600.

23. S. M. Edwardes quoted in the memo From Legislative Assembly, Judicial 58/22, Home Department 1922, National Archives of India, Government of India, New Delhi, 19.

24. See remarks of Stanislas Posner (Poland), in Advisory Committee for the Protection of the Welfare of Children and Young People, Third Meeting, March 26, 1926 (C.264.M.103.1926.IV), League of Nations Documents Archive, 12. For an account of conditions in Poland that were shaping prostitution, see Keely Stauter-Halsted, *The Devil's Chain: Prostitution and Social Control in Partitioned Poland* (Ithaca, NY: Cornell University Press, 2015).

NOTES TO CHAPTER 1

25. See remarks of Gaston Bourgois (France), in Advisory Commission for the Protection of the Welfare of Children and Young People, Third Meeting, March 26, 1926 (C.264.M.103.1926.IV), League of Nations Documents Archive, 13. The French and Polish delegates drew attention to issues of climatic difference for differing reasons. French delegates had, from the start of the conference, articulated the view that age of consent was a delicate matter and that France did not seek to lay down the law in its colonies. The Polish delegate sought to distance the context of Poland, where the age of consent was low, from those of countries of the East, or Asia.

26. See remarks of Count Carton de Wiart (Belgium), Advisory Commission for the Protection and Welfare of Children, and Young People, Joint Meeting of the Traffic in Women and Children Committee and the Child Welfare Committee, April 30, 1927 (C.338.M.113.1927.IV), League of Nations Documents Archive, 60.

27. See remarks of M. Martin (France), ibid., 62.

28. See remarks of Henri Rollet, Joint Meetings of the Traffic in Women and Children Committee and the Child Welfare Committee, First Meeting, March 19, 1928 (C.195.M.63.1928.IV), League of Nations Documents Archive, 48.

29. See remarks of Professor Conti (Italy), Ninth Session of the Traffic in Women and Children Committee, April 2–9, 1930, Geneva (C.246.M.121.1930.IV), League of Nations Documents Archive, 37.

30. I should clarify that this view is not restricted to the 1920s. A recent review of childhood in world history also uncritically states that tropical heat causes "early" puberty. See Stearns, *Childhood in World History*.

31. Ann Stoler, "Racial Histories and Their Regimes of Truth," *Political Power and Social Theory* 11 (1997): 183–206.

32. Warwick Anderson explores the decline of climate as a category in "Climates of Opinion: Acclimatization in Nineteenth-Century France and England," *Victorian Studies* 35, no. 2 (1992): 152.

33. David Arnold, *The Tropics and the Traveling Gaze: India, Landscape, and Science, 1800–1856* (Seattle: University of Washington Press, 2006), 113.

34. Levine, "Sovereignty and Sexuality," 20.

35. See Anderson, "Climates of Opinion"; and W. Scheidt, "The Concept of Race in Anthropology and the Divisions into Human Races, from Linnaeous to Deniker," in *This Is Race: An Anthology Selected from the International Literature on the Races of Man*, ed. Earl W. Count (New York: Schuman, 1950).

36. *Oeuvres Completes De Montesquieu* (Paris: Nagel, 1748/1950).

37. Albrecht von Haller, *First Lines of Physiology* (New York: Johnson, 1786/1966), 190.

38. John Roberton, "On the Alleged Influence of Climate on Female Puberty in Greece," *Edinburgh Medical and Surgical Journal* 62, no. 160 (1844): 1–11.

39. Audrey Smedley, *Race in North America: Origin and Evolution of a Worldview*, 3rd ed. (Boulder, CO: Westview, 2007), 2.

40. Edward Tilt, *On Uterine and Ovarian Inflammation: On the Physiology and Diseases of Menstruation* (London: John Churchill, 1862), 41.

NOTES TO CHAPTER 1

41. See Paul Rabinow, *French Modern: Norms and Forms of the Social Environment* (Cambridge, MA: MIT Press, 1989); and Eric Jennings, *Curing the Colonizers: Hydrotherapy, Climatology, and French Colonialists* (Durham, NC: Duke University Press, 2006), 34.

42. See Jennings, *Curing the Colonizers*.

43. Ivan Bloch, *Anthropological Studies on the Strange Sexual Practices of All Races and All Ages* (New York: AMS Press, 1930), 26.

44. H. S. Crossen and R. J. Crossen, *Diseases of Women* (St. Louis, MO: Mosby, 1930), 828.

45. Ibid.

46. John Whitridge Williams, *Obstetrics* (New York: Appleton, 1903), 83.

47. Howard Kelly, *Medical Gynecology* (New York: Appleton, 1908), 83.

48. George Engelmann, "Age of First Menstruation on the North American Continent," *Transactions of the American Gynecological Society* 26 (1901): 87.

49. See K. A. Shah, "The Age of Menarche in Gujarati College-Girls," *Journal of the Indian Medical Association* 11 (June 1–30, 1958): 347–51.

50. H. Peters and S. M. Shrikhande, "Age at Menarche in Indian Women," in *Fertility and Sterility*, vol. 8, ed. M. Edward Davis (Baltimore, MD: Harper and Row, 1957).

51. On this point, see R. S. Goyal, "Dimensions of Adolescent Motherhood in India," *Social Biology* 41, no. 1–2 (1994): 130; and S. Bharati and P. Bharati, "Relationship between Menarcheal Age and Nutritional Anthropometry in Urban Girls of the Howdah District, West Bengal, India," *Anthropologischer Anzeiger* 56, no. 1 (1997): 57.

52. A. H. Slyper, "The Pubertal Timing Controversy in the USA, and a Review of Possible Causative Factors for the Advance in Timing of Onset of Puberty," *Clinical Endocrinology* 65, no. 1 (2006): 1–8.

53. Carla Rice, "The Spectacle of the Child Woman: Troubling Girls in/and the Science of Early Puberty," *Feminist Studies* 44, no. 3 (2018): 535–66.

54. For a biographical account of Rathbone's vast political range, see Susan Pedersen, *Eleanor Rathbone and the Politics of Conscience* (New Haven, CT: Yale University Press, 2004).

55. See, for example, Rathbone, Joint Meetings of the Traffic in Women and Children Committee and the Child Welfare Committee, First Meeting, March 19, 1928 (C.195.M.63.1928.IV), League of Nations Documents Archive, 49–51. See also Minutes of Third Meeting of the Advisory Commission for the Protection of Children and Young People, March 26, 1926 (C.264.M.103.1926.IV), League of Nations Documents Archive, 14–15.

56. Rathbone, First Meeting (C.195.M.63.1928.IV), League of Nations Documents Archive, 49.

57. Ibid.

58. See remarks of M. Maxwell (British Empire), Third Meeting (C.264.M.103.1926.IV), League of Nations Documents Archive, 14.

59. Rathbone, First Meeting, 49, 50.

60. Wall, ibid., 50.

61. Bernard, ibid., 51.

NOTES TO CHAPTER 1

62. In *Birth of Biopolitics*, Michel Foucault unfolds the argument that the category of the "natural" is a major discursive element of modern governmentality. He notes that political economists since the middle of the eighteenth century have drawn on the notion of "laws of nature" to depict ideas about economic phenomena, such as labor and capital mobility, and political phenomena, such as rights. Individuals and states were also characterized as being endowed with natural traits and rights. The individual was seen to be born with natural rights, and states were presumed to bear a natural sovereignty and right to self-determination. Foucault, *The Birth of Biopolitics: Lectures at the College de France 1978–1979*, trans. Graham Burchell (New York: Macmillan, 2008).

63. Anthony Anghie, *Imperialism, Sovereignty, and the Making of International Law* (Cambridge: Cambridge University Press, 2004), 264.

64. Stephen Legg, "Of Scales, Networks, and Assemblages: The League of Nations Apparatus and the Scalar Sovereignty of the Government of India," *Transactions of the Institute of British Geographers*, n.s., 34 (2009): 234–53.

65. Berkovitch, *From Motherhood to Citizenship*, 75–76.

66. Enquiry into Measures of Rehabilitation of Prostitutes, Advisory Committee on Social Questions, 1938, introduction (C.218.M.120.1938.IV), League of Nations Documents Archive, 7.

67. Ibid.

68. M. Sugimura, Minutes of Meeting of the Advisory Commission for the Protection and Welfare of Children and Young People, March 26, 1926 (C.264.M.103.1926.IV), League of Nations Documents Archive. 14.

69. Bourgois, ibid.

70. Rathbone, ibid.

71. Estrid Hein, ibid.

72. Wall, First Meeting, March 19, 1928 (C.195.M.63.1928.IV), League of Nations Documents Archive, 50.

73. See remarks by S. W. Harris (Great Britain), Ninth Session of the Traffic in Women and Children Committee, April 2–9, 1930, Geneva (C.246.M.121.1930.IV), League of Nations Documents Archive, 35.

74. See the section "Replies from Governments," Eleventh Session of the Traffic in Women and Children Committee, April 4–9, 1932, Amendments to the Conventions of 1910 and 1921: Elimination of Age Limit (C.503. M.244 1932.IV), League of Nations Documents Archive, 3.

75. Traffic in Women and Children, July 1, 1938 (C.218.M.120.1938.IV), League of Nations Documents Archive. This is a lengthy report on the rehabilitation of prostitutes, with respect to their early lives, together with a questionnaire on the circumstances in which women enter into a life of prostitution and the replies by various governments and organizations.

76. Although the league's membership was at one point as high as sixty-three states and included colonies, European imperial states or "great powers" formed the core council and

directed its policies. The league's bipartite assembly-and-council structure was echoed by the United Nations, which has a General Assembly and Security Council.

77. M. D. Callahan, *A Sacred Trust: The League of Nations and Africa 1929–1946* (Brighton, UK: Sussex Academic Press, 2004).

78. A few key early examples include Andrew Parker, Mary Russo, Doris Sommer, and Patricia Yaegar, eds., *Nationalisms and Sexualities* (New York: Routledge, 1992); M. Sinha, *Colonial Masculinity*; McClintock, *Imperial Leather*; Stoler, *Carnal Knowledge and Imperial Power*; Philippa Levine, "Sexuality, Gender, and Empire," in *Gender and Empire*, ed. Levine (New York: Oxford University Press, 2002), 134–55; and Antoinette Burton and Tony Ballantyne, eds. *Bodies in Contact: Rethinking Colonial Encounters in World History* (Durham, NC: Duke University Press, 2005).

Chapter 2. Adolescence as a Traveling Concept

1. Harris, Ninth Session of the Traffic in Women and Children Committee (C.246.M .121.1930.IV), League of Nations Documents Archive, 35.

2. Driscoll, *Girls*, 51–53.

3. DeLuzio, *Female Adolescence*.

4. Ibid., 51–89.

5. G. Stanley Hall, *Adolescence: Its Psychology and Its Relations to Physiology, Anthropology, Sociology, Sex, Crime, Religion, and Education*, vol. 1 (New York: Appleton, 1905).

6. Joseph F. Kett, "Reflections on the History of Adolescence in America," *History of Family* 8 (2003): 358.

7. Howard Chudacoff traces the rise of chronological age consciousness in connection to time consciousness in US culture, relating it to the mass production of clocks and the advent of railroads and streetcars operating on schedules. Chudacoff asserts the importance of Hall's work in "intensifying" the use of age norms. *How Old Are You?*, 66.

8. Kett, "Reflections."

9. Chudacoff, *How Old Are You?*, 34–38.

10. G. Stanley Hall, "Psychic Arrests in Adolescence," *Journal of the Proceedings and Addresses of the Forty-Second Annual Meeting of the National Education Association Held at Boston, Massachusetts, July 6–10* (Chicago: University of Chicago Press, 1903), 811.

11. DeLuzio, *Female Adolescence*, 94.

12. See Leslie Paris, "The Adventures of Peanut and Bo: Summer Camps and Early-Twentieth-Century American Girlhood," in Miriam Fornell-Brunell and Leslie Paris, eds., *The Girls' History and Culture Reader: The Twentieth Century* (Urbana: University of Illinois Press, 2011), 89; Driscoll, *Girls*, 7.

13. DeLuzio, *Female Adolescence*; Simmons, *Crescent City Girls*.

14. DeLuzio, *Female Adolescence*, 93.

15. Ibid., 13.

16. Margaret Mead, *Coming of Age in Samoa* (New York: William Morrow, 1928).

17. Jeffrey Jensen Arnett, "G. Stanley Hall's Adolescence: Brilliance and Nonsense," *History of Psychology* 9, no. 3 (2006): 186–97.

18. Hall, *Adolescence*, xvi.

19. Nancy Lesko, *Act Your Age: The Cultural Construction of Adolescence* (New York: Routledge, 2001), 46.

20. Hall, *Adolescence*, 2:649.

21. The most prominent advocate of recapitulation theory was German biologist Ernst Haeckel, who in the 1890s drew a parallel between embryonic development and species evolution and expressed his ideas in the condensed phrase "ontogeny recapitulates phylogeny." For more on Hall's use of recapitulation theory, see Gail Bederman, *Manliness and Civilization: A Cultural History of Gender and Race in the United States, 1880–1917* (Chicago: University of Chicago Press, 1995).

22. Baljit Kaur, Shailaja Menon, and Rajani Konantambigi, "Child and Adolescent Development Research," in *Psychology in India Revisited*, ed. Janak Pandey (New Delhi: Sage, 2001), 2:206.

23. Sagade, *Child Marriage*, xxvii.

24. The lone Indian woman on the committee was Rameshwari Nehru, editor of the Allahabad women's journal *Stri-Darpan* and later president of the All India Women's Conference. For more details, see Sanjam Ahluwalia, *Reproductive Restraints: History of Birth Control in India, 1877–1947* (Urbana: University of Illinois Press, 2008), 119.

25. Age of Consent Committee, *Report of the Age of Consent Committee, 1928–1929* (Calcutta: Government of India Central Publication Branch, 1929), 169.

26. Ibid., 187.

27. Ibid., 170.

28. Ibid., 171.

29. Ibid., 189, 160.

30. Ibid., 160.

31. See the 1930 report of the National Christian Council, for example, which mentions that the convener of the Committee on Social Hygiene, B. C. Oliver, traveled for eight months in 1929 to the United States and the United Kingdom to seek "valuable help and advice." *Proceedings of the Fourth National Christian Council* (Nagpur, India: Office of the National Christian Council, 1930), 28, Library of the Yale Divinity School, New Haven, Connecticut.

32. J. Krishnan, *Sex Education for Children in India* (Madras, India: Christian Literature Society of India, 1930), 12.

33. "Announcement about Marriage Hygiene," *Nature* 3 (August 1935): 175–76.

34. For more on Pillay and his experiences as editor of the journal, see Ahluwalia, *Reproductive Restraints*, 63–65.

35. G. S. Ghurye, "The Age at Marriage," *Marriage Hygiene* 1, no. 1 (1934): 264–70.

36. Victor Frankl, "Erotic Problems of Modern Youth," *Marriage Hygiene* 3, no. 3 (1937): 232–35.

37. Lester Kirkendall, "Sex Problems of Adolescents," *Marriage Hygiene*, 2nd ser., 1, no. 4 (1948): 205–8.

NOTES TO CHAPTER 2

38. For an account of how racialized assumptions shape knowledge about puberty, see Carla Rice, *Becoming Women: The Embodied Self in Image Culture* (Toronto: University of Toronto Press, 2014).

39. See Radhakamal Mukerjee and N. N. Sen Gupta, "The Evolution of Sex in the Individual," *Marriage Hygiene* 2, no. 1 (1935): 27.

40. *Proceedings of the Fourth National Christian Council*, 30.

41. Moni John Mukerjea, *A Study of the Problem of Adolescence in India* (Lucknow, India: T. C. E. Journals, 1945), 30.

42. See, for example, Association for Moral and Social Hygiene in India, *The Seventh All-India Conference on Moral and Social Hygiene* (New Delhi: AMSH, 1959); and "Understanding the Adolescents: A Report of the Discussion Series Held at the Indian Social Institute," *Social Health* 6, no. 2 (1968): 14–19.

43. Shakuntla Lall, "A Seminar on Teen-Agers," *Social Health* 2, no. 3 (1963), 17.

44. Ibid., 18.

45. B. K. Baksht, "Discussion Series of Family Life Education: A Short Report," *Social Health* 3, no. 4 (1965): 10–18.

46. The speakers were P. Pasricha, research officer, US Educational Foundation in India; P. Mehta, director, Central Bureau of Educational and Vocational Guidance; W. Mathur, convener, health committee of the Association for Moral and Social Hygiene (AMSH) in India and faculty at the Delhi School of Social Work; B. K. Rao, sexologist and psychoanalytic consultant; and B. D. Bhatia, a director of a child guidance clinic, who then moved to the United States.

47. Baksht, "Discussion Series," 12, 14, 17, 12.

48. "Understanding the Adolescents," *Social Health* 6, no. 2 (1968): 15.

49. Ibid., 18.

50. Armaily Desai, "Bearing of Sex Education and Student Counseling Programme on V.D. Control," *Social Health* 2, no. 2 (1963): 4–7.

51. Anthony D'Souza, "Sex Education of Today: Responsibilities of Home and School," *Social Health* 7, no. 2 (1969): 9.

52. Maharashtra, one of twenty-eight states in India, lies on the western side of the country and at 120,000 square miles is about the size of the US state of New Mexico. Over sixty million people speak the language Marathi. Mumbai (Bombay) is the capital of the state.

53. For work on women's magazines in other Indian languages in this period, see Mytheli Sreenivas, "Emotion, Identity, and the Female Subject: Tamil Women's Magazines in Colonial India, 1890–1940," *Journal of Women's History* 14, no. 4 (2003): 59–82; Himani Banerjee, "Fashioning a Self: Educational Proposals for and by Women in Popular Magazines in Colonial Bengal," *Economic and Political Weekly* 26 (1991): 50–62; and Shobhana Nijhawan, *Women and Girls in the Hindi Public Sphere: Periodical Literature in Colonial North India* (New Delhi: Oxford University Press, 2012).

54. Vidya Bal, interview by author, July 15, 2008, Pune, India.

55. See, for instance, Sumathi Ramaswamy and Martin Jay, *Empires of Vision: A Reader* (Durham, NC: Duke University Press, 2015).

56. Ariès, *Centuries of Childhood*.
57. Higonnet, *Pictures of Innocence*.
58. Duane, *Children's Table*.
59. Jean-Jacques Rousseau, *Emile, or On Education*, trans. Alan Bloom (New York: Basic Books, 1762/1979).
60. For more on the visual elaboration of romantic childhood, see Higonnet, *Pictures of Innocence*.
61. Y. B. Mathur, *Women's Education in India (1813–1966)* (New Delhi: University of New Delhi Press, 1973).
62. V. C. Sinha, *Elements of Demography* (New Delhi: Allied, 2009), 321.
63. John C. Caldwell, Pat Caldwell, and Bruce K. Caldwell, "The Construction of Adolescence in a Changing World," *Studies in Family Planning* 29, no. 2 (1998): 149.

Chapter 3. Legislating Nonmarital Sex in India, 1911–1929

1. See page 27 of Legislative Assembly Debates, February 27, 1924, vol. 4, no. 19, Judicial 58/II/22, Home Department 1922, National Archives of India, Government of India, New Delhi.
2. Tek Chand and H. L. Sarin, *The Child Marriage Restraint Act* (Calcutta: Eastern Law House, 1951), 48.
3. Feminist historians have insightfully cast the debates on child marriage as a staging of political hostilities between reformists and religious revivalists that ultimately also subordinated girls' sexual agency. The contest between revivalists and reformists in the 1891 debates on child marriage is detailed in Anagol-McGinn, "Age of Consent Act"; Uma Chakravarti, *Rewriting History*; Engels, "Age of Consent Act"; and Meera Kosambi, "Gender, Reform, and Competing State Controls over Women: The Rukhmabai Case (1884–1888)," *Contributions to Indian Sociology* 29, nos. 1–2 (1995): 265–90. Mrinalini Sinha presents an incisive reading of competing masculinities in the 1891 debate in *Colonial Masculinity*. Tanika Sarkar explains how the Age of Consent controversy figured in the formation of nationalists' worldview in "Rhetoric against Age of Consent." Himani Banerjee explores the construction of the passive, young female body in the discourse on child marriage in "Age of Consent and Hegemonic Social Reform," *Gender and Imperialism*, ed. Claire Midgeley (Manchester, UK: Manchester University Press, 1998), 21–44.
4. As explained in chapter 1, I intentionally use the terms "prostitute" and "prostitution" to remain faithful to the historical discourse examined even though the terms "sex worker" and "commercial sex" are preferred today.
5. See Carolyn Cocca's account of the raising of the age of consent in the United States in the late nineteenth century in *Jailbait: The Politics of Statutory Rape Laws in the United States* (Albany: State University Press of New York Press, 2004). She finds that male legislators who resisted the raising of the age of consent in the United States in 1890s codified the requirement that female victims of underage sex be of previously chaste character. For an analysis of variations in the age of consent between regions of the world, see Waites,

Age of Consent, who notes that most laws specify the seduction of minors as a problem. For a table comparing the age of consent across countries in the 1920s, see also the *Report*, appendix X-A.

6. Cocca, *Jailbait*; Waites, *Age of Consent*.

7. Gayle Pheterson uses the term "whore stigma" to describe the common hostility directed toward sex workers based on the dichotomous construction of "good" and "bad" women in *The Prostitution Prism* (Amsterdam: Amsterdam University Press, 1996). To illustrate how public attention was far more focused on issues affecting "respectable" women, compare the outcry over the age of consent and widow remarriage in the 1880s and 1890s (Chakravarti, *Rewriting History*) with the relatively muted reception in India to the Contagious Diseases Acts enforcing compulsory medical checks on prostitutes in the 1880s. On this point, see Tambe, *Codes of Misconduct*, and Sumanta Banerjee, *Dangerous Outcasts: The Prostitute in Nineteenth Century Bengal* (Calcutta: Seagull Books, 1998).

8. Scholarship in colonial history has seen important shifts toward transnational frameworks, but many studies of gender reforms have remained focused on the dyad of British-Indian relations. Among the few exceptions are Mrinalini Sinha's rich work on feminist internationalism in *Specters of Mother India*, esp. 1–62; Barbara Ramusack's study of the age of marriage reforms in "Women's Organizations and Social Change: The Age-of-Marriage Issue in India," in *Women and World Changes*, ed. Naomi Black and Ann Baker Cottrell (Beverly Hills, CA: Sage, 1981), 198–216; and Sanjam Ahluwalia's account of American and British birth control activists' encounters with India in *Reproductive Restraints*. The journal *Gender and History* devoted volume 10, no. 3, in 1998 to exploring the long history of feminist internationalism. I continue in this vein by showing how Indian reformists responded to the "imperial internationalism" of antitrafficking efforts.

9. Upendra Baxi, "The 'State's Emissary': The Place of Law in Subaltern Studies," in *Subaltern Studies 7: Writings on South Asian History and Society* (Delhi: Oxford University Press, 1993), 250.

10. The declared policy of the colonial state both under the East India Company and of the formal raj, was "not to disturb people's law formations" (Baxi, "State's Emissary," 253). The policy was formalized under Queen Victoria's 1858 pronouncement of noninterference with religious practices.

11. Several Indian feminist historians have analyzed the implications of the creation of a sphere of personal law. See Lata Mani, "Contentious Traditions: The Debate on *Sati* in Colonial India," in *Recasting Women: Essays in Colonial History*, ed. K. Sangari and S. Vaid (New Delhi: Kali for Women, 1989), 88–126; Janaki Nair, *Women and the Law in Colonial India: A Social History* (New Delhi: Kali for Women, 1996); Tanika Sarkar, *Hindu Wife, Hindu Nation: Community, Religion, and Cultural Nationalism* (Bloomington: Indiana University Press, 2001); M. Sinha, *Specters of Mother India*; Mytheli Sreenivas, *Wives, Widows, and Concubines: The Conjugal Family Ideal in Colonial India* (Bloomington: Indiana University Press, 2008); and Sunder Rajan, *Scandal of the State*. They concur that despite British officials' avowed noninterference with local customs, the colonial state exerted influence in arenas of gender reform whenever it was politically expedient. The

state realigned family forms to a model based on male heads of households and chaste wives.

12. On this point, see Nair, *Women and the Law*; and Sreenivas, *Wives, Widows, and Concubines*. For a complex account of the relationship between nuclear and extended family forms, see Rochona Majumdar, *Marriage and Modernity: Family Values in Colonial Bengal* (Durham, NC: Duke University Press, 2009).

13. The needs and voices of actual women were often of secondary interest to men who were legislators (Nair, *Women and the Law*; Mani, "Contentious Traditions"). The scandals that prompted legislation enabled much political posturing by male legislators, as Sarkar (*Hindu Wife*) and Sunder Rajan (*Scandal of the State*) show. At the same time, as Mrinalini Sinha's intricate analysis of women's associational politics in the 1920s argues, women activists also used such scandals as opportunities to articulate their political subjectivities (*Specters of Mother India*).

14. M. Sinha, *Specters of Mother India*.

15. For more on this well-established point in South Asian history, see Mani, "Contentious Traditions."

16. Reformist legislators drew on preexisting social evolutionary narratives linking gender reform to civilizational status. The framing of women's advancement in civilizational terms was widespread in suffrage struggles in Britain. See Antoinette Burton, *Burdens of History* (Chapel Hill: University of North Carolina Press, 1994).

17. Chakravarti, *Rewriting History*; Sarkar, *Hindu Wife*; M. Sinha, *Colonial Masculinities*.

18. Archana Parasher, *Women and Family Law Reform in India: Uniform Civil Code and Gender Equality* (New Delhi: Sage, 1992); David Washbrook, "Law, State, and Agrarian Society in Colonial India," *Modern Asian Studies* 15, no. 3 (1981): 649–721.

19. Existing hierarchies of caste, the joint family, and land ownership were consolidated through property laws in order to facilitate the colonial state's revenue collection. See Washbrook ("Law, State, and Agrarian Society") on the importance of joint family structures to revenue collection of the colonial state. Nair (*Women and the Law*) explores how inheritance practices of temple dancers and matrilineal Nayars were standardized to meet patrilineal norms. For an excellent study of the implications of widow remarriage for property relations, see Chakravarti, *Pandita Ramabai*.

20. The association between Indian promiscuity and cultural inferiority emerges in varied historical eras. An influential early example is the traveler Abbé Jean-Antoine Dubois's impressions in 1815: "Most of the religious and civil institutions of India were only invented for the purpose of awakening and exciting passions towards which they have already such a strong natural tendency." As examples, he lists "the shameless stories about their deities . . . the public and private buildings bearing on their walls some disgusting obscenity, the many religious services in which the principal part is played by prostitutes, who often make even the temples the scene of their abominable debauchery." Dubois, *Hindu Manners, Customs, and Ceremonies*, trans. Henry Beauchamp (Oxford: Clarendon, 1905/1968), 308. For details on the implications of later Victorian standards on regulating prostitution in the nineteenth century, see Kenneth Ballhatchet, *Race, Sex, and Class*

under the Raj: Imperial Attitudes and Policies and Their Critics, 1793–1905 (New York: St. Martin's, 1980). Katherine Mayo's "Mother India" is a broad indictment of Indian sexual promiscuity from the 1920s, as Mrinalini Sinha notes in her introduction to *Specters of Mother India*.

21. This is the core of Francis Hutchins's argument in *The Illusion of Permanence: British Imperialism in India* (Princeton, NJ: Princeton University Press, 1967). He argues that the longer the colonial presence in India, the more autocratic and conservative its policy. Local traditions were selectively preserved toward this end.

22. I draw here on Hutchins's discussion of the changing understandings of Indian traits. Ibid., 65–71.

23. Two well-publicized court cases in Bengal and Maharashtra were the provocation for the 1891 Age of Consent bill. In Bengal, an 1890 case of an 11-year-old child bride, Phulmoni, who died as a result of brutal sexual intercourse with her 35-year-old husband raised much indignation. Her husband was not, however, charged with rape, as sexual intercourse with a wife over 10 years of age could not be classified thus, according to the 1860 Indian Penal Code. In Maharashtra, in the case of Rukhmabai, a girl who, upon puberty, refused to move to the house of the man she was betrothed to as a child, the appeals court ruled that Rukhmabai was obliged to live with him or face imprisonment. For details, see Chakravarti, *Rewriting History*; Kosambi, "Gender Reform and Competing State Controls over Women"; Sarkar, "Rhetoric against Age of Consent"; and H. Banerjee, "Age of Consent."

24. This change took place via an amendment of section 373 of the Indian Penal Code. For details, see Sen's insightful study of childhood and juvenile-reform institutions in *Colonial Childhoods*, 119–21. Sen has analyzed this episode in the context of the creation of the category of the native delinquent; he also examines how delinquency among native girls was constructed through this episode.

25. Ibid., 120–21.

26. For more on this history, see Tambe, *Codes of Misconduct*. For an account of conditions in Europe that drove women into prostitution, see Stauter-Halsted, *Devil's Chain*. Stauter-Halsted also notes the widespread consternation in the early 1900s around cases of girls aged 11 or 12 entering prostitution, a contrast to the relatively sanguine attitude toward children who were hereditary prostitutes in India. *Devil's Chain*, 42.

27. For the early history of the conventions against white slave traffic, see League of Nations, *Prevention of Prostitution: A Study of Measures Adopted or under Consideration Particularly with Regard to Minors* (Geneva: League of Nations, 1943), 7–13.

28. The 1910 convention specified that anyone who "procured, enticed, or led away, even with her consent, a woman or girl under age, for immoral purposes, [would] be punished, notwithstanding that the various acts constituting the offense may have been committed in different countries." For those over age 20, trafficking was a crime if it involved "fraud . . . violence, threats . . . [or] abuse of authority." See International Convention for the Suppression of the White Slave Traffic. Judicial 58/22, Home Department 1922, National Archives of India, Government of India, New Delhi, 35.

29. The Government of India did, however, belatedly accede to a 1904 convention on trafficking, which called for coordinated action against procurers crossing borders. Sections 372 and 373 of the Indian Penal Code, dealing with the sale and purchase of girls into prostitution, laid down 16 as the victim's age of consent.

30. For a summary of the bill's clauses and the legislative department's response, see Judicial A, July, Home Department 1913, National Archives of India, Government of India, New Delhi, 273–89. The bill literally reproduces parts of the text of the 1910 convention and proposes to make criminal the dedication of girls to temples, procuration of girls, and defilement of girls under 16; guardianship of children by prostitutes; transferring of wives; mock marriages; and concubinage of girls under 16. It is perhaps not surprising that Dadabhoy, a Parsi, proposed this bill: the Parsis were a relatively prosperous Zoroastrian community originally from Iran; they were committed to philanthropy, social reform, and the advancement of women.

31. The "fraudulent means" included "false pretenses, by administering to, or causing to be taken by her, any drugs, matter or thing with intent to excite sexual desire." See page 162 of the file "A Bill to Make Further Provision for Protection of Women and Girls and Purposes" in Judicial A, November, 131–50, Home Department 1912, National Archives of India, Government of India, New Delhi.

32. The English enactment was 8 Edw VII, ch. 67, as stated in the section "Statement of Objects and Reasons," ibid., 177. There had been steady efforts in Britain to raise the age of consent in order to combat prostitution—the Criminal Law Amendment of 1885 raised the age of consent from 13 to 16 in an effort to prevent the sale of children into prostitution.

33. In combining distinct offenses such as rape and adultery under one category, "immoral sexual intercourse," the Dadabhoy bill erased the differences in girls' capacities for consent and agency. Adultery, unlike rape, connoted sex that was illegitimate in the eyes of the law; however, unlike rape, it was not forced on the girl. A girl could have willingly engaged in adultery. Even as the violence of rape is minimized by such a construction, a woman's capacity for agency is denied by casting her adultery as rape.

34. See Parker for the history of judicial definitions of "unchastity" from 1800 to 1914; he describes how the polyvalent use of the term "prostitute" assisted in entrenching marriage. Kunal Parker, "A Corporation of Superior Prostitutes: Anglo-Indian Legal Conceptions of Temple Dancing Girls, 1800–1914," *Modern Asian Studies* 32, no. 3 (1998): 559–633.

35. V. C. Sinha, *Elements of Demography*, 321.

36. See page 25 of "Proposed Legislation to Check Immorality" in Judicial A, November, 131–50, Home Department 1912, National Archives of India, Government of India, New Delhi.

37. William H. Vincent, note, August 1, 1912, ibid., 22.

38. Secretaries of the Society for the Protection of Children in Western India to the Judicial Department of Bombay, memo, June 3, 1910, ibid., 109.

39. N. B. Divatia, note, August 5, 1910, ibid., 132.

40. Henry Wheeler to Legislative Department, memo, September 4, 1912, ibid., 28.

NOTES TO CHAPTER 3

41. G. M. Bhurgri to Judicial Department, ibid., 133.

42. Secretaries of the Society for the Protection of Children in Western India to the Judicial Department of Bombay, memo, June 3, 1910, ibid., 109.

43. This point has been discussed in depth by H. Banerjee, "Age of Consent," 25–26.

44. For more on legal definitions of concubinage, see Sreenivas, *Wives, Widows, and Concubines*.

45. Vishnu Raghunath Natu quoted in Legislative Department memorandum, May 27, 1912, Judicial A, November, 131–50, Home Department 1912, National Archives of India, Government of India, New Delhi, 13.

46. Rao Bahadur A. B. Desai, ibid., 13.

47. G. V. Joshi, ibid., 123.

48. Government of Bombay to Home Department, memo 3325, April 30, 1912, ibid., 3.

49. Judicial Department to Marquess of Crewe, memo 30 of 1913, July 24, 1913, in Judicial A, July, Home Department 1913, National Archives of India, Government of India, New Delhi, 273–89, 219.

50. The 1885 act was passed in the midst of a strong campaign against white slavery led by the Ladies National Association and Josephine Butler. It made nonmarital intercourse with a girl under 16 an offense, while all sex with a girl below the age of 13 was classified as rape. See Stephen Cretney, *Family Law in the Twentieth Century: A History* (Oxford: Oxford University Press, 2003).

51. Judicial Department to Marquess of Crewe, 216.

52. M. Sinha, *Specters of Mother India*. The Women's Indian Association, founded in Madras in 1917, was envisioned as a secular multiethnic association of women across India. Among its stated goals were raising the age of marriage, female suffrage, and expanding education for girls and women. Its journal *Stri Dharma* regularly provided updates on branch meetings in its campaign against child marriage.

53. "Answers to Questionnaire," file no. 21–31–19, Judicial 58/22, Home Department 1922, National Archives of India, Government of India, New Delhi.

54. Edwardes had been appointed Indian representative to the League of Nations Conference at the last minute by the government in Britain.

55. See p. 3 of Legislative Assembly Debates, vol. 2, No. 29, February 7, 1922, Judicial-B 58/22, Home Department 1922, National Archives of India, Government of India, New Delhi.

56. Ibid., 2.

57. Ibid.

58. In his responses to Pyari Lal and J. Chaudhuri, Vincent inflated the implications of the bill, warning that "the Convention does not deal only with prostitutes. It goes very much further than that. It prohibits the procuring of any girl for a single act of intercourse." Ibid., 8. Vincent was, at this point, almost reaching retirement and on his way out of India.

59. Ibid., 10.

60. Ibid., 13.

NOTES TO CHAPTER 3

61. Ibid., 8.

62. Ibid., 9–10.

63. Ibid., 11.

64. Ibid., 14.

65. M. Sinha, *Specters of Mother India*.

66. League of Nations International Conference on Traffic in Women and Children, in Judicial 58/22, Home Department 1922, National Archives of India, Government of India, New Delhi, 15.

67. Joshi proposed Act 20 of 1923 to raise the age of consent from 16 to 18 in section 366 of the Indian Penal Code. See pp. 1 and 2 of File 63-III of 1924, Judicial 58/II/22, Home Department 1922, National Archives of India, Government of India, New Delhi, 1.

68. Ibid., 1–2.

69. When the bill was circulated among the provincial governments, it drew vastly different responses: governments of the United Provinces, Bombay, and Assam strongly supported it, while governments of Bihar and Orissa warned of agitation and discontent if it were passed. *Report*, 11.

70. See pages 7–9 of Indian Penal Code Amendment Act, 1924 (Act V of 1924) Legislative Assembly Debates 4, no. 19, February 27, 1924, Judicial 58/II/1922, Home Department 1922, National Archives of India, Government of India, New Delhi. Madan Mohan Malaviya, as mentioned earlier, was a veteran Indian National Congress member from Allahabad, elected president of the party in 1909, 1918, 1932, and 1933. He was also the founder of the right-wing Hindu Mahasabha. Mohammed Ali Jinnah, commonly hailed as the founder of Pakistan and head of the Muslim League, was at this time the Muhammadan Urban delegate from Bombay City in the Legislative Assembly.

71. The discussion about *Indian Penal Code*, sec. 361, takes place on page 8 of Legislative Assembly Debates, 4, no. 19, February 27, 1924, Judicial B, 58/II/1922, Home Department 1922, National Archives of India, Government of India, New Delhi.

72. Ibid., 8–9.

73. For details on Jinnah's marriage to Ruttenbai, see Hector Bolitho, *Jinnah: Creator of Pakistan* (London: John Murray, 1954), 74–75.

74. See John Cell, *Hailey: A Study in British Imperialism* (Cambridge: Cambridge University Press, 2002), 30.

75. *Indian Penal Code*, secs. 366, 372, 373.

76. In 1922 Gour proposed a law prohibiting the dedication of girls to temples as temple dancers, or *devadasis*. Gour's position conveyed the sexual puritanism associated with nationalist social reformists: he viewed devadasis as prostitutes whose presence had to be curbed in the name of "moral hygiene." Prominent women activists, such as Muthulakshmi Reddi of the Women's Indian Association, shared his position. For details, see Kay Jordan, "Devadasi Reform: Driving the Priestess or the Prostitutes Out of Hindu Temples?" *Religion and Laws in Independent India*, ed. Robert Baird (Delhi: Manohar, 1993), 262.

77. M. Sinha, *Specters of Mother India*. The National Council of Women in India (NCWI), founded in 1925 to federate provincial women's councils and to build links

NOTES TO CHAPTER 3

with international women's movements, also emphasized the need to transform social practices surrounding child marriage.

78. Ibid.

79. An account of the 1925 debate is provided in the *Report*.

80. The All India Women's Conference, founded in 1927, which went on to become the most comprehensive women's organization in the country, lobbied aggressively for raising the age of marriage on the assumption that this would promote women's education.

81. The role of women's organizations in lobbying for a raised age of marriage in the 1920s has been carefully traced by Geraldine Forbes, "Women and Modernity: The Issue of Child Marriage in India," *Women's Studies International Quarterly* 2, no. 4 (1979): 407–19; Ramusack, "Women's Organizations"; Jana Matson Everett, *Women and Social Change in India* (New York: St. Martin's, 1979); M. Sinha, *Specters of Mother India* and "Lineage of the 'Indian' Modern," 207–21; and Judith Whitehead, "Community Honor/Sexual Boundaries: A Discursive Analysis of *Devadasi* Criminalization in Madras, India, 1920–1947," in *Prostitution: Whores, Hustlers, and Johns*, ed. James Elias et al. (New York: Prometheus, 1998), 91–106. Forbes and Ramusack profile the work of individual women's organizations, the WIA, NCWI, and AIWC, on the age of marriage; Everett places these efforts within the broader history of women's activism in the late colonial period. M. Sinha notes the internationalist strains in women's activism on the age of marriage, particularly in response to the charges made in Katherine Mayo's *Mother India*, and Whitehead examines the eugenicist underpinnings of marriage reform in this period. For details of the origins of AIWC, see Aparna Basu and Bharati Ray, *Women's Struggle: A History of the All India Women's Conference 1927–1990* (New Delhi: Manohar, 1990). For an early retrospective look at the work of WIA, AIWC, and NWCI, see Amrit Kaur, "Women's Movement in India," *Stri Dharma* 16, no. 4 (1933): 177–238.

82. M. Sinha, *Specters of Mother India*.

83. For an excellent articulation of this ideal construct of the female citizen, see Kaur, "Women's Movement." It confirms aspects of Partha Chatterjee's well-known argument that Indian womanhood was configured as a site of spirituality. See Partha Chatterjee, "The Nationalist Resolution of the Women's Question," *Recasting Women: Essays in Colonial History*, ed. K. Sangari and S. Vaid (New Brunswick, NJ: Rutgers University Press, 1990), 233–53. See also M. Sinha's influential analysis in *Specters of Mother India* of how the woman question was framed in Indian nationalist discourse in the 1920s.

84. M. Sinha, introduction, *Specters of Mother India*.

85. Although women had been granted the franchise in some provinces and were elected members of provincial councils, they had not been nominated to the Central Legislative Assembly; they hence relied on bills proposed by nationalist legislators, such as Hari Singh Gour and Harbilas Sarda. When Gour introduced a bill to curb child marriage in the 1927 Central Legislative Assembly, women's organizations used it as an occasion to launch a widespread campaign. The AIWC sent a three-hundred-member delegation to the assembly to monitor the debates on the bill and sent deputations to the viceroy and to the Age of Consent Committee, which reviewed Gour's bill. The committee, which also had a women's activist as a member, Rameshwari Nehru, unequivocally recommended a new law raising the age of marriage.

86. Chand and Sarin, *Child Marriage Restraint Act*, 48.

87. Only two women were members of this committee, British physician M. O'Brien Beardon and Nehru.

88. See *Report*, chap. 10, esp. 187, 189, 191, 192, 193, 195. These pages list types of offenses for which the age of consent should be 18.

89. Ibid., 189.

90. Ibid.

91. Radha Kumar, *The History of Doing: An Illustrated Account of Movements for Women's Rights and Feminism in India, 1880–1990* (New Delhi: Kali for Women, 1994); and Radha Kumar, "Factory Life: Women Workers in the Bombay Cotton Textile Industry, 1919–1939," in *Dignity and Daily Bread: New Forms of Economic Organizing among Poor Women in the Third World and First*, ed. Sheila Rowbotham and Swasti Mitter (London: Routledge, 1994), 53.

92. For a history of women factory workers in Bombay in this period, see Priyanka Srivastava, "Creating a Healthy and 'Decent' Industrial Labor Force: Health, Sanitation, and Welfare in Colonial Bombay" (PhD diss., University of Cincinnati, 2004).

93. For an analysis of women textile workers' labor militancy in Bombay, see Kumar, *History of Doing*. Ramusack provides a review of expanding economic opportunities for women in this period in "Women in South Asia," in *Women in Asia: Restoring Women to History*, ed. Barbara Ramusack and Sharon Sievers (Bloomington: Indiana University Press, 1999), 54–55.

94. For details about educational institutions for girls, see Mathur, *Women's Education*; Azra Asghar Ali, *The Emergence of Feminism among Indian Muslim Women, 1920–1947* (Delhi: Oxford University Press, 1999); Ramusack, "Women in South Asia."

95. Mathur (*Women's Education*) and Asghar Ali (*Emergence of Feminism*) attribute the rising demand for female education in the 1920s principally to its value on the marriage market, but they also note education's appeal for poorer parents. Mathur writes that the progress in women's education was possible "because more and more women were now getting respectable jobs" (*Women's Education*, 74). Schooling for girls also flourished because of the policy of active government financial support for female education—in Madras, all girls were admitted to schools at half the standard fees, although after 1927, it was necessary to produce a poverty certificate to qualify (Mathur, *Women's Education*, 85). George Noronha offers a critique of the slow spread of women's education in "Backgrounds in the Education of Indian Girls" (PhD diss., Catholic University of America, 1939).

96. *Report*, 187–88.

97. Ibid., 157, 171.

98. Ibid., 114, 187, 189, 187. Italics mine.

99. Ibid., 187, 186.

100. Ibid., 169.

101. Ibid., 160.

102. Several studies of marriage and reproduction in early twentieth-century India have argued that the ideology of eugenics underlay the goals of many social reformists.

Whitehead traces the rise of a new archetype of motherhood based on goals of furthering the physical strength of the "race" in "Modernising the Motherhood Archetype: Public Health Models, Mothering, and the Child Marriage Restraint Act of 1929," *Contributions to Indian Sociology* 29, nos. 1–2 (1995): 186–209. Both Ahluwalia and Sarah Hodges in their analyses of birth control and reproductive health elaborate the instrumental understanding of mothers as vehicles of racial vigor. See Sarah Hodges, "Indian Eugenics in an Age of Reform," in *Reproductive Health in India: History, Politics, Controversies*, ed. Hodges (New Delhi: Orient Longman, 2006); Ahluwalia, *Reproductive Restraints*. The remarks in the *Report* illustrate this strain of eugenics: "Towards the end of the last decade, public attention began to be increasingly directed towards the improvement of the physique of the nation. The great European war had proved the need for a more healthy and sturdy race . . . child marriage is sapping the vitality of the people" (*Report*, 10). Katherine Mayo's widely read locating of Indian civilization's defects in its practice of child marriage also contributed to such currents of thought (M. Sinha, *Specters of Mother India*).

103. *Report*, 157.
104. Ibid., 170.
105. Ibid.
106. Ibid., 189, 190.
107. Several feminist theorists of the state, such as Wendy Brown and Sunder Rajan, use the construct of the state as a Janus-faced entity. See Wendy Brown, *States of Injury* (Princeton, NJ: Princeton University Press, 1995); Sunder Rajan, *Scandal of the State*. M. Sinha also implicitly recognizes this dual stance of the colonial state in her discussion of the Mayo controversy in *Specters of Mother India*.
108. Age of Consent Committee, *Report*, 340–41.
109. A typical example of this comparative framework is Kiran Bose, "Women's Position in the World and Indian Women," *Stri Dharma* 17, no. 10 (1934), which summarizes the "position of women" in the United States and parts of the British empire in order to set up a discussion of women in India.
110. Waites, *Age of Consent*, 40–59.
111. M. Sinha, *Specters of Mother India*.
112. Cretney, *Family Law*, 61.
113. Ibid., 190.
114. For examples of similar controversies over social reform, see Mani, "Contentious Traditions," on the debate over sati; and Chakravarti, *Rewriting History*, on the status of widows.

Chapter 4. Early Marriage as Slavery

1. Even though the bulk of its substance is focused on preventing forced marriage, the 1962 convention also affirms the right to marry and has assumed renewed importance in contemporary times. Article 16 of the 1948 Declaration of Human Rights was the first UN statement articulating marriage as a human right, and the 1962 convention opens with a preamble quoting this article, going on to elaborate some of its aspects. This convention

NOTES TO CHAPTER 4

on marriage has recently been cited as enshrining the right to marry in numerous news and opinion pieces about same-sex marriage. See, for example, "Same-Sex Unions and Intermarriage: Against as a Jew, for as a Citizen," *Times of Israel*, May 15, 2012, http://blogs.timesofisrael.com.

2. See, for instance, Boutros Boutros-Ghali, introduction to *The United Nations and the Advancement of Women 1945–1965*, Blue Book Series, vol. 6, rev. ed. (New York: United Nations, 1996). See also Devaki Jain, *Women, Development, and the UN: A Sixty Year Quest for Equality and Justice* (Bloomington: Indiana University Press, 2005).

3. Boutros-Ghali, introduction.

4. The following nongovernmental organizations served on the CSW's Liaison Committee of Women's Organizations: the International Council of Women, International Alliance of Women for Equal Rights and Responsibilities, World's Women's Christian Temperance Union, St. Joan's International Social and Political Alliance, International Federation of Business and Professional Women, Soroptimist International Association, Pan-Pacific and South East Asia Women's Association, and International Council of Social Democratic Women. Some of these groups, such as the International Alliance of Women and St. Joan's Alliance, emerged in the early twentieth century out of histories of struggle for suffrage in their home countries of the United States and United Kingdom, respectively, while other groups relied on networks of internationalist socialist agitation, such as the International Council of Social Democratic Women. The International Council of Women represents one of the oldest efforts to link advocacy for women with the agendas of intergovernmental organizations, such as the League of Nations and the UN.

5. Egon Schwelb, "Marriage and Human Rights," *American Journal of Comparative Law* 12, no. 3 (1963): 338.

6. Boutros-Ghali, introduction, 21.

7. Ibid., 22.

8. Jain, *Women, Development*, 27.

9. Ibid.

10. UN Conference of Plenipotentiaries on a Supplementary Convention of the Abolition of Slavery, the Slave Trade, and Institutions and Practices Similar to Slavery, *Preparation of the Convention: Note by the Secretary-General*, June 8, 1956, 24/3, 2, microfiche, UN Economic and Social Council Collection, Library of Congress, Washington, DC. (The UN Economic and Social Council Collection is hereafter referred to as ECOSOC.)

11. Ibid., 3.

12. Jain, *Women, Development*, 28.

13. Schwelb, "Marriage and Human Rights," 337.

14. Ibid., 4.

15. *Recommendation Addressed by the Council of the UN Conference of Plenipotentiaries on a Supplementary Convention on the Abolition of Slavery, the Slave Trade, and Institutions and Practices Similar to Slavery, Note by the Secretary-General*, November 12, 1956, 2934, ECOSOC.

NOTES TO CHAPTER 4

16. UN Conference of Plenipotentiaries... Practices Similar to Slavery, *Text of Articles of Supplementary Convention adopted on First Reading*, August 30, 1956, E/CONF./24/14, ECOSOC, 2.

17. Muslim marriages are a striking exception, since they are traditionally conceived as a contract that includes the right to divorce.

18. I thank Laura Rosenthal for reminding me of this example.

19. Rokeya Sakhawat Hossain, *Sultana's Dream*, trans. Barnita Bagchi (New Delhi: Penguin, 2005).

20. See chap. 3 of Angela Y. Davis, *Women, Race, and Class* (New York: Random, 1981).

21. Anna Mae Duane, *Child Slavery before and after Emancipation: An Argument for Child Centered Slavery Studies* (Cambridge: Cambridge University Press, 2017), 3.

22. I thank Claire Moses for her helpful comments on this point.

23. UN Conference of Plenipotentiaries... Practices Similar to Slavery, *Preparation*, E/CONF./24/3, ECOSOC, 6.

24. Ibid., 5.

25. For details on the widespread incidence of child marriage in Britain, see Holly Brewer, "Marriages 'Under the Age of Consent': The Perils of Demography and the Power of Ideology," unpublished paper.

26. Schwelb eloquently recounts the many comments by African delegates in favor of granting women and girls greater freedom in marriage in "Marriage and Human Rights," 349–50.

27. Benton and Ford, *Rage for Order*.

28. Schwelb, "Marriage and Human Rights," 8.

29. Ibid., 5.

30. UN Conference of Plenipotentiaries... Practices Similar to Slavery, *Resolutions Adopted by the Conference, 3 and 4 September 1956*, E/CONF./24/21, ECOSOC.

31. The first members of the CSW were Jessie Mary Grey Street, Australia; Evdokia Uralova, Byelorussian Soviet Socialist Republic; Way-Sung New, People's Republic of China; Graciela Morales F. de Echeverria, Costa Rica; Bodil Begtrup, Denmark; Marie-Hélène Lefaucheux, France; Sara Basterrechea Ramirez, Guatemala; Shareefah Hamid Ali, India; Amalia González Caballero de Castillo Ledón, Mexico; Alice Kandalft Cosma, Syria; Mihri Pektas, Turkey; Elizavieta Alekseevna Popova, Union of Soviet Socialist Republics; Mary Sutherland, United Kingdom; Dorothy Kenyon, United States; and Isabel de Urdaneta, Venezuela. See the online background note in "Short History of the Commission on the Status of Women," 2006, http://www.un.org/womenwatch/daw/CSW60YRS/CSWbriefhistory.pdf, accessed June 28, 2015.

32. CSW, *Consent to Marriage and Age of Marriage: Report by the Secretary-General*, January 20, 1958, 6/317, ECOSOC.

33. Ibid., 4.

34. Jain, *Women, Development*.

35. CSW, *Questionnaire on Consent to Marriage, Age of Marriage, and Registration of Marriage*, September 24, 1958, 6/335, ECOSOC.

NOTES TO CHAPTER 4

36. CSW, *Statement Submitted by St. Joan's International Social and Political Alliance, a Non-governmental Organization on the Register of the Secretary-General*, March 11, 1958, 6/NGO/48, ECOSOC, 1.

37. CSW, *Statement Submitted by the Antislavery Society for the Protection of Human Rights, a Non-governmental Organization in Category B*, October 20, 1959, 6/NGO/72, ECOSOC, 2.

38. Ibid., 3.

39. CSW, *Statement . . . Antislavery Society*, 3. For a history of the practice of parents arranging children's marriages in Britain and colonial America, see Brewer, *By Birth or Consent* and "Marriages."

40. CSW, *Statement Submitted by the International Alliance of Women, a Non-governmental Organization in Category B*, March 6, 1961. /NGO/110, ECOSOC, 2.

41. CSW, *Statement Submitted by . . . St. Joan's*, 3.

42. Ibid.

43. CSW, *Statement Submitted by the International Federation of Women Lawyers, a Non-governmental Organization in Category B Consultative Status*, March 19, 1958, 6/NGO/56, ECOSOC, 1.

44. *Report Prepared by the Secretary-General in Accordance with ECOSOC Resolution 722B (28)*, Draft Convention and Draft Recommendation on the Age of Marriage, Consent to Marriage, and Registration of Marriages, November 23, 1959, annex A, 6/353, ECOSOC, 2.

45. Draft Convention and Draft Recommendation . . . Marriages, *India: Amendment to the Text of the Draft Convention*, A/4844, annex 1, October 5, 1961, A/C.3/L.910, 1. Unfortunately, no name is provided for the Indian delegate in this record.

46. Schwelb, "Marriage and Human Rights," 373. Italics mine. Kasliwal was an advocate from Jaipur who was an elected Congress party member of the Indian lower house of Parliament. For details about this episode, see Schwelb, "Marriage and Human Rights."

47. Ibid., 337.

48. *Memorandum by the Secretary-General*, Draft Recommendation . . . Marriages, January 23, 1963, E/CN.6/414, ECOSOC, 1.

49. Ibid., 2.

50. Alison Bashford tracks the important role U Thant played in enshrining reproductive rights as part of human rights in *Global Population: History, Geopolitics, and Life on Earth* (New York: Columbia University Press, 2014).

51. CSW, Seventeenth Session. *Summary Record of the Four Hundred and Eighth Meeting*, June 26, 1963. 6/SR.408, ECOSOC, 3, 12, 6.

52. Srini Sitaraman, *State Participation in International Treaty Regimes* (London: Ashgate, 2009).

53. Quoted in B. Sivaramayya, "Convention on Consent to Marriage, Minimum Age for Marriage, and Registration of Marriages 1962, with Special Reference to India," *Journal of the Indian Law Institute* 8, no. 3 (1966): 406.

54. For a recent criticism of India's position, see Jyostna Jha, *Reducing Child Marriage in India: A Model to Scale Up Results* (New Delhi: Centre for Budget and Policy Studies, 2016).

Chapter 5. Population Control and Marriage Age in India, 1960–1978

1. In a small minority of cases called "special marriages," or those not involving religious approval, the age of marriage was raised to 18 for girls and 21 for boys in 1954, via the Special Marriage Act. As Pervez Mody notes, however, such marriages were not only few but stigmatized—they were viewed as "unholy," unlike the dominant form of arranged marriages, which secured the approval of family, extended kin, community, and religion. Pervez Mody, "Love and the Law: Love-Marriage in Delhi," *Modern Asian Studies* 36, no. 1 (2002): 225. The higher age of marriage for special marriages is not surprising given that the marriages in question were typically those cases carried out against the wishes of parents and community. Not only was it easier and less controversial to raise the age for this practice but it also actually served the interests of parents to set the legal age high, since parents could more easily treat marriage matches that they did not arrange as illegal, as explained in chapter 3.

2. The exceptions are Geraldine Forbes, "Women and Modernity: The Issue of Child Marriage in India," *Women's Studies International Quarterly* 2, no. 4 (1979): 407–19; Sagade, *Child Marriage*; and Asha Bajpai, *Child Rights in India*.

3. See Ahluwalia, *Reproductive Restraints*.

4. Ibid.

5. I acknowledge the invaluable research assistance of Rajani Bhatia in this section on demographic transition theory.

6. See Frank W. Notestein and Frederick Osborn, "Reminiscences: The Role of Foundations, the Population Association of America, Princeton University, and the United Nations in Fostering American Interest in Population Problems," *Milbank Memorial Fund Quarterly* 49, no. 4 (1971): 67–85; Frank W. Notestein, "Demography in the United State: A Partial Account of the Development of the Field," *Population and Development Review* 8, no. 4 (1982): 651–87.

7. See Ansley J. Coale and Edgar M. Hoover, *Population Growth and Economic Development in Low-Income Countries: A Case Study of India's Prospects* (Princeton, NJ: Princeton University Press, 1958). The claims in Coale and Hoover's book that population reduction spurred economic growth laid the groundwork for decades of World Bank policy. Coale and Hoover's research was supported by the International Bank for Reconstruction and Development, the Milbank Memorial Fund, and the Rockefeller Foundation.

8. Age of Consent Committee, *Report*, 164, 168.

9. Radhakamal Mukherjee, ed., *Population Problem in India* (Mylapore, India: Madras Law Journal Office, 1938), 139. For a careful discussion of this text, see Ahluwalia, *Reproductive Restraints*.

10. Ansley Coale and C. Y. Tye, "The Significance of Age-Patterns of Fertility in High Fertility Populations," *Milbank Memorial Fund Quarterly* 39 (1961): 631–46.

11. Ibid., 645–46.

12. Norman B. Ryder, "Nuptiality as a Variable in the Demographic Transition," paper presented at the annual meeting of the American Sociological Association, New York City, August 31, 1960, 10.

13. Ibid., 9.

14. I thank Holly Brewer for conversations about the Cambridge Group for the History of Population and Social Structure.

15. See J. W. Leasure, "Malthus, Marriage, and Multiplication," *Milbank Memorial Fund Quarterly* 41, no. 4, part 1 (1963): 419–35; and J. J. Spengler, "Was Malthus Right?," *Southern Economic Journal* 33 (1966): 17–34.

16. Richard Symonds and Michael Carder, *The United Nations and the Population Question: 1945–1970* (New York: Praeger, 1973), 190.

17. Oscar Harkavy and Krishna Roy, "Emergence of the Indian National Family Planning Program," in *The Global Family Planning Revolution: Three Decades of Population Policies*, ed. Warren Robinson and John A. Ross (Washington, DC: World Bank, 2007), 301–24.

18. For an account of Besant's early positions, see Mytheli Sreenivasan, "Birth Control in the Shadow of Empire: The Trials of Annie Besant, 1877–1878," *Feminist Studies* 41, no. 3 (2015): 509–37. Besant changed her views after she came into closer contact with Gandhi's antipathy to contraceptives, after moving to India. On this point, see Ahluwalia, *Reproductive Restraints*, 91–92.

19. Rahul Nair, "The Construction of a 'Population Problem' in Colonial India 1919–1947," *Journal of Imperial and Commonwealth History* 39, no. 2 (2011): 227–47.

20. Ahluwalia, *Reproductive Restraints*.

21. Ibid., 29–31.

22. See Nair, "Construction of a 'Population Problem,'" 239; and Ahluwalia, *Reproductive Restraints*, 133–42.

23. For more on how Prime Minister Nehru drew heavily on US advisers funded by the Ford Foundation, see Nikos Sackley, "Foundation in the Field: Ford Foundation's New Delhi Office and the Constriction of Development Knowledge, 1951–1970," *American Foundations and the Coproduction of the World Order in the Twentieth Century*, ed. J. Klige and H. Rausch (Gottingen, Germany: Vandenhoeck and Ruprecht, 2012), 232–60.

24. Connelly, *Fatal Misconception*, 199–200.

25. See Sarah H. Heil, Dianna Gaalema, and Evan Herrmann, "Incentives to Promote Family Planning," supplement, *Preventive Medicine* 55 (2012): s106–12.

26. See J. P. Elder and J. D. Estey, "Behavior Change Strategies for Family Planning," *Social Science and Medicine* 35 (1992): 1065–76.

27. See Sackley, "Foundation in the Field."

28. Coale and Hoover, *Population Growth*.

29. See S. N. Agarwala, "Raising the Marriage Age for Women: A Means to Lower the Birth Rate," *Economic and Political Weekly*, December 24, 1966, 797–98; K. G. Basavarajappa and M. I. Belvalgidad, "Changes in Age at Marriage of Females and Their Effect on the Birth Rate in India," *Eugenics Quarterly* 14, no. 1 (1967): 14–26; C. R. Malakar, "Female Age at Marriage and the Birth Rate in India," *Social Biology* 19, no. 3 (1972): 297–301; C. Chandrasekaran, "The Mysore Study," *Population Bulletin of the United Nations* 19–20 (1986): 6–13.

30. Harkavy and Roy, "Emergence," 307.

NOTES TO CHAPTER 5

31. S. N. Agarwala, "The Age at Marriage in India," *Population Index* 23, no. 2 (1957): 96–107; see also S. N. Agarwala, *Age at Marriage in India* (Allahabad, India: Kitab Mahal, 1962).

32. S. N. Agarwala, "Birth Rate Can Be Halved," *Yojana* 8, no. 7 (1964): 2–3. Agarwala later went on to direct a major demographic research center in New Delhi and a World Bank project to reduce fertility in Lucknow, India. Agarwala, *Raising Marriage Age*, 1, and *Indian Population Problems* (New Delhi: Tata McGraw Hill, 1974), 129.

33. United Nations Department of Economic and Social Affairs, *The Population Debate: Dimensions and Perspectives Papers of the World Population Conference Bucharest 1974* (New York: United Nations, 1975), 172.

34. S. N. Agarwala, "Raising the Marriage Age," 797–98.

35. Basavarajappa and Belvalgidad, "Changes in Age," 25.

36. P. P. Talwar, "A Note on the Changes in Age at Marriage of Females and Their Effect on the Birth Rate in India," *Eugenics Quarterly* 14, no. 4 (1967): 294.

37. P. Krishnan, "A Note on Changes in Age at Marriage of Females and Their Effect on the Birth Rate in India," *Social Biology* 18, no. 2 (1971): 201.

38. Malakar, "Female Age at Marriage," 301.

39. United Nations, *Regional Seminar on the Status of Women and Family Planning for Countries within the Economic Commission for Asia and the Far East Region, Jogjakarta, Indonesia, June 20–30, 1973* (New York: United Nations, 1974), 102.

40. UN Department of Economic and Social Affairs, *Population Debate*, 32.

41. Symonds and Carder, *United Nations*, 140.

42. Kumudini Dandekar, "Age at Marriage of Women," *Economic and Political Weekly* 9, no. 22 (1974): 867.

43. "India Set to Raise Age for Marriage," *New York Times*, August 11, 1974.

44. Connelly, *Fatal Misconception*.

45. "Proposal to Raise Marriageable Age," *Times of India*, August 6, 1974; "Move to Make Child Marriages a Cognizable Offense," *Times of India*, April 23, 1975, 1a.

46. S. Johnson, *World Population—Turning the Tide: Three Decades of Progress* (London: Graham and Trotman, 1994), 114.

47. Karan Singh, "National Population Policy," *Population and Development Review* 2, no. 2 (1976): 310, para. 5. Emphasis in original.

48. Ibid., 311–12.

49. Connelly, *Fatal Misconception*, 323.

50. Harkavy and Roy, "Emergence."

51. Connelly, *Fatal Misconception*, 326.

52. Harkavy and Roy, "Global Family Planning Revolution."

53. "Move to Make Child Marriage"; "Minimum Age for Marriage Raised," *Times of India*, September 21, 1978, 15b.

54. Their example was noted and praised by the Committee on the Status of Women in India, which recommended in 1974 that the central government emulate the example of Gujarat. This committee, whose positions are elaborated in the next section, called for "all offenses under the Child Marriage Restraint Act to be made cognizable and Special Officers

NOTES TO CHAPTER 5

be appointed to enforce the law." See CSW, *Status of Women in India: A Synopsis of the Report of the National Committee on the Status of Women, 1971–74* (New Delhi: Indian Council of Social Science Research, 1975), 43.

55. S. N. Agarwala, "Some Aspects of Family Planning Programme," *Journal of Family Welfare* 12, no 4 (1966): 1.

56. S. N. Agarwala, "Family Planning Programme and Management Tools," *Indian Journal of Public Health* 18, no. 3 (1974): 129.

57. Harkavy and Roy, "Emergence."

58. Sonia Correa and Rosalind Petchesky were among the most prominent voices making this argument. See Sonia Correa and Rosalind Petchesky, "Reproductive and Sexual Rights: A Feminist Perspective," *Population Policies Reconsidered: Health, Empowerment, and Rights*, ed. Gita Sen, Adrienne Germain, and Lincoln Chen (Boston: Harvard Center for Population and Development Studies, 1994), 107–23.

59. See also Ahluwalia, *Reproductive Restraints*.

60. Malini Karkal, "Age at Marriage," *Journal of Family Welfare* (March 1968): 51.

61. Ibid., 56.

62. In an announcement of Karkal's death in 2002, feminist activists from the Forum for Women's Health in Mumbai fondly appraised her professional stance, which often ran counter to the mainstream of her field: "Dr. Karkal worked for many years at the International Institute for Population Sciences, Bombay. She was a demographer who looked at human beings and not merely the numbers counting them. She also constantly emphasized the importance of looking at quality of life rather than talk in terms of numbers while discussing the issue of population." https://web.archive.org/web/20040211064329/, accessed on October 30, 2012.

63. Dandekar, "Age at Marriage," 871.

64. Ibid., 871, 874.

65. CSW, "National Committee on the Status of Women (India)," *Towards Equality* (New Delhi: Government of India, 1974), 323.

66. Ibid., 322. Italics mine.

67. Ibid., 326–330.

68. Ibid., 23.

69. CSW, *Status of Women in India*, 27.

70. Ibid.

71. Ibid., 360.

72. Sagade, *Child Marriage*, 46–47. Emphasis mine.

73. Forbes, "Women and Modernity," 416.

74. Sagade, *Child Marriage*.

75. The practice of child marriage typically was a two-stage process, with betrothals occurring before puberty and the actual move from the natal to the conjugal home taking place after puberty. (There were class, caste, and regional differences in the practice, of course.)

76. Sagade, *Child Marriage*, 35.

77. Ibid., 42.

78. For details, see Whitehead, "Modernising the Motherhood Archetype."

Chapter 6. Investing in the Girl Child, 1989–2015

1. Article 1 defines a child as "every human being below the age of eighteen years unless, under the law applicable to the child, majority is attained earlier." United Nations, "Convention on the Rights of the Child," *Treaty Series, Treaties and International Agreements Registered or Filed and Recorded with the Secretariat of the United Nations*, 1990, 46–61, https://goo.gl/p4eAnu.

2. For a list of signatories and the terms of their acceptance, see United Nations Treaty Collection, *Convention on the Rights of the Child*, New York, November 20, 1989, https://goo.gl/cjq2Gf.

3. See, for instance, the following research on the girl child by Indian academics: Meera Chatterjee, *Both Age and Gender against Them*, mimeo (New Delhi: NIPCCD, 1988); Neera Burra, "Sight Unseen: Reflections on the Female Working Child," paper presented at the National Workshop on the Girl Child, New Delhi, 1987; Rami Chhabra et al., "Health and Demographic Consequences of Early Marriage and Fertility," *Social Change* 17, no. 3 (1987): 4–26.

4. See, for instance, Kumudini Dandekar, "Why Has the Proportion of Women in India's Population Been Declining?" *Economic and Political Weekly* 10, no. 42 (1975): 1663–67.

5. Amartya Sen, "More Than 100 Million Women Are Missing," *New York Review of Books*, December 1990.

6. UNICEF, *The Girl Child: An Investment in the Future* (New York: United Nations Children's Fund, 1991), 28.

7. UNICEF, *Report of the Executive Board, 16–27, April 1990*, E/ICEF/1990/I3, 58.

8. Neera Kuckreja Sohoni, *The Burden of Girlhood: A Global Inquiry into the Status of Girls* (Oakland, CA: Third Party, 1995).

9. See the bibliographic index, UNICEF, *Girl Child*.

10. This index, like other UN sources mentioned in this chapter, can be accessed at the repository of UN documents in the Newspapers and Periodicals Room, Library of Congress, Washington, DC.

11. The subject categories "child" and "children" are found in the UNDOC Current Subject Index through the 1980s, but they do not cross-reference "girl" until 1991. There is a steady increase in the entries under the category "children," particularly as 1990 approaches, when the Convention on the Rights of the Child was organized. A new subject category appears, "child prostitution," as an addition to "child abuse," "child development," "child health," "child labor," and "child welfare" in 1990, since prostitution was one node of the increasing official interest in girls.

12. UN, *The Girl Child: Report of the Secretary-General*, August 24, 2007, A/62/297, 4.

13. As an example, in its November 1949 congress in Moscow, the UN consultative group Women's International Democratic Federation established an International Day for Protection of Children, observed in many countries as Children's Day, on June 1.

NOTES TO CHAPTER 6

14. UN, "Children, Youth, and Aging Persons," *United Nations Yearbook 1990*, vol. 44, ch. 14 (1990), 79.

15. The goals are listed as follows: special attention to the health and nutrition of the female child and to pregnant and lactating women; access by all couples to information and services to prevent pregnancies that are too early, too closely spaced, too late, or too many; access by all pregnant women to prenatal care, trained attendants during childbirth, and referral facilities for high-risk pregnancies and obstetric emergencies; and universal access to primary education with special emphasis for girls and accelerated literacy programs for women. See UNICEF. "Goals for Children and Development in the 1990s," http://www.unicef.org/wsc/goals.htm#, accessed June 7, 2015.

16. UNICEF, *Girl Child*, 8–10.

17. Digumarti Bhaskara Rao, *Status and Advancement of Women* (Delhi: APH, 2000), 190.

18. Ibid.

19. Michelle Murphy notes the influence of Larry Summers's 1992 clarion call as chief economist of the World Bank in elevating the policy of educating girls. Murphy, "Mergers."

20. UNICEF, "Achievements Made in the Implementation of the UNICEF Policy on Women in Development, including the Situation of the Girl Child," (1992), E/ICEF/1992/L.5.

21. Ibid., esp. 11–19.

22. Mary Purcell, "The Working Group on Girls Is Founded," *Action for Girls: Newsletter of the Working Group on Girls (WGG) and Its International Network for Girls* 3, no. 19 (2015), https://goo.gl/NgrUxJ.

23. Convention on the Rights of the Child, "Report Adopted by the Committee at Its 209th Meeting on 27 January 1995, Committee on the Rights of the Child, Report on the Eighth Session," Geneva, 1995, CRC/C/38, 72–73.

24. These action items are listed using either strong or weak opening verbs, such as "urges," "encourages," "requests," or "stresses."

25. UN General Assembly, *The Girl Child: Resolution Adopted by the General Assembly*, 18 December 2007, A/RES/62/140, February 19, 2008.

26. Ibid., *Girl Child: . . . 21 December 1995*, A/RES/50/154, February 15, 1996.

27. Ibid., *Girl Child . . . 12 December 1996*, A/RES/51/76, February 20, 1997, 3.

28. Ibid.

29. At its fiftieth session in February 2006, the CSW identified the girl child as its "priority theme," and it collaborated with UNICEF to organize an expert group meeting on the girl child and build momentum toward creating an International Day of the Girl Child.

30. The first secretary-general's report on the girl child explains, "At the 10-year review and appraisal of the Beijing Platform for Action in 2005, Member States reported that, despite the achievements made, particularly in relation to the enactment of legislation, the protection of the rights of the girl child had not been fully achieved." UN ECOSOC, *The Elimination of All Forms of Discrimination and Violence against the Girl Child, Report of the Secretary-General*, December 12, 2006, E/CN.6/2007/2, esp. 4.

31. The secretary-general occupies the preeminent role in the UN bureaucracy as chairperson of the UN system and is responsible for coordinating the chief executives of all UN organizations.

32. UN ECOSOC, *The Elimination of All Forms of Discrimination and Violence against the Girl Child, Report of the Secretary-General*, December 12, 2006, E/CN.6/2007/2, 6.

33. UN, *Forced Marriage of the Girl Child: Report of the Secretary-General* (New York: UN, 2007). The CSW spurred this focus on forced marriage at its fifty-first session in its resolution 51/3, asking all member states to prevent forced marriages of girls and asking the secretary-general to report on the implementation of this resolution.

34. Ibid., 3.

35. UN Inter-Agency Task Force on Adolescent Girls, "Girl Power and Potential: A Joint Programming Framework for Fulfilling the Rights of Marginalized Adolescent Girls," 2009, https://www.unicef.org/adolescence/files/FINAL-UNJointFramewokrpdf.pdf.

36. UNICEF, "The Multiplier Effect of Educating Girls," *State of the World's Children Report, 2004*, https://www.unicef.org/sowc04/sowc04_multiplier_effect.html.

37. UN Foundation, "Investing in Adolescent Girls," May 26, 2011, https://goo.gl/VuVVyG.

38. The short overview YouTube clip of the Girl Effect campaign makes clear this causal logic. "The Girl Effect: The Clock Is Ticking," *girleffect*, September 13, 2010, https://www.youtube.com/watch?v=1e8xgFoJtVg.

39. See Girl Up's homepage, https://www.girlup.org/.

40. A Celebration of Women: The Butterfly Effect Has Begun, "'Greatest Return Comes from Investing in Girls and Women' Says UN Chief," April 23, 2013, https://goo.gl/H1BBVD.

41. Nina Easton, "Melinda Gates on Bill, Ending Poverty, and Her Plans to Invest in Women and Girls," *Fortune*, May 21, 2015, http://fortune.com.

42. Ellen Johnson Sirleaf, "'Africa Rising?' Not Really, Unless We Invest More in Girls," *CNN World*, 2015, http://www.cnn.com.

43. For a good discussion of this point, see Murphy, "Girl."

44. For a critique of the instrumental dimension of girl-focused campaigns, see ibid., and Kathryn Moeller, *The Gender Effect: Capitalism, Feminism, and the Corporate Politics of Development* (Berkeley: University of California, 2018). For an analysis of how girls have been instrumentally mobilized in US military counterinsurgency campaigns, see Molly Geidel, "Building the Counterinsurgent Girl," *Feminist Studies* 44, no. 3 (2018): 635–65.

45. For a recent review of this history, see Hester Eisenstein, *Feminism Seduced: How Global Elites Use Women's Labor and Ideas to Exploit the World* (New York: Routledge, 2015). See also Linda Y. C. Lim, *The Globalization Debate: Issues and Challenges* (Geneva: ILO, 2001).

46. See Kathryn Moeller's 2014 ethnography of Nike's Brazil campaign, "Searching for Adolescent Girls in Brazil: The Transnational Politics of Poverty in 'The Girl Effect,'" *Feminist Studies* 40, no. 3 (2014): 575–601.

47. "Haryana's Apni Beti Apna Dhan Scheme Starts Paying Off," *Observer Political Bureau*, December 18, 1997, http://www.hvk.org/1997/1297/0049.html.

48. UN Population Fund–India, *Special Financial Incentive Schemes for the Girl Child in India: Review of Select Themes*, https://www.unfpa.org/sites/default/files/resource-pdf/UNFPA_Publication-39772.pdf, accessed December 20, 2015.

49. HAQ, Center for Child Rights, "Child Marriage in India: Achievements, Gaps, Challenges," New Delhi, HAQ, 20, https://goo.gl/Nw7GqN.

50. Ministry of Women and Child Development, "National Strategy Document on Prevention of Child Marriage," February 14, 2013, http://vikaspedia.in/social-welfare/women-and-child-development/strategy-child-marriage.

51. Anand Krishnan et al., "'No One Says 'No' to Money'—a Mixed Methods Approach for Evaluating Conditional Cash Transfer Schemes to Improve Girl Children's Status in Haryana, India," *International Journal for Equity in Health* 13, no. 11 (2014): 1–10, https://goo.gl/nBiawN.

52. Priya Nanda et al., "Do Conditional Cash Transfers Have an Effect on Girls' Delayed Age of Marriage Status? Findings from an Evaluation Study in North India," abstract for the Population Association of America 2015 meeting, http://paa2015.princeton.edu/uploads/152563. This study is also reported in http://www.indiaspend.com/cover-story/in-haryana-a-pioneering-incentive-fails-young-women-15271, accessed December 20, 2017.

Chapter 7. Curtailing Parents?

1. "Current Marital Status," NFHS-1, 1992–93, sec. 4.2, 74, http://www.dhsprogram.com/pubs/pdf/FRIND1/FRIND1.pdf, accessed June 22, 2015.

2. Ibid., xxiv.

3. "Age at First Marriage," NFHS-2, 1998–99, 55, https://dhsprogram.com/pubs/pdf/frind2/frind2.pdf, accessed December 20, 2017.

4. "Age at First Marriage," NFHS-3, 2005–6. 163, http://www.nfhsindia.org/, accessed June 22, 2015.

5. For a discussion of the various symbolic and economic factors shaping age of marriage in contemporary India, see Sonalde Desai and Lester Andrist, "Gender Scripts and Age at Marriage in India," *Demography* 47, no. 3 (2010): 667–87.

6. Sagade, *Child Marriage*.

7. "Thirteenth Report on the Prevention of Child Marriage Bill, 2004," presented to the Rajya Sabha by Department-Related Parliamentary Standing Committee on Personnel, Public Grievances, Law and Justice, November 29, 2005, https://goo.gl/b7kLGE, accessed December 29, 2017.

8. Sagade, *Child Marriage*.

9. *National Report on 'A World Fit for Children,'* Ministry of Women and Child Development, Government of India, 2007, https://www.unicef.org/worldfitforchildren/files/India_WFFC5_Report.pdf, accessed December 29, 2017.

NOTES TO CHAPTER 7

10. *Handbook on the Prohibition of the Child Marriage Act*, Ministry of Women and Child Development, UNESCO, and HAQ, 2006, https://goo.gl/FfHgQ4, accessed December 24, 2017.

11. Prohibition of Child Marriage Act, 2006, *Gazette of India*, https://www.childline india.org.in/pdf/Child-Marriage-handbook.pdf, accessed December 23, 2017.

12. In one high-profile 1992 case, Bhanwari Devi, a grassroots worker in Rajasthan who reported a child marriage in a high-caste family, was gang-raped by men of that family as punishment. For a short biographical sketch, see Maduli Thaosen, "Bhanwari Devi: A Hero We Failed," *Indian Women in History*, March 3, 2017, https://feminisminindia .com/2017/03/03/bhanwari-devi-essay/, accessed December 30, 2017.

13. "Proposal to Amend the Prohibition of Child Marriage Act, Law Commission of India, 2006, and Other Allied Laws," 2008, http://lawcommissionofindia.nic.in/reports/ report205.pdf, accessed December 25, 2017.

14. Legal correspondent, "SC Lauds Karnataka for Declaring Child Marriage Void," *Hindu*, October 11, 2017, https://goo.gl/TiwrjL, accessed December 25, 2017.

15. "Child Marriage in India: Achievements, Gaps, and Challenges," Center for Child Rights, HAQ, 2012, https://goo.gl/KuopzH, accessed December 25, 2017.

16. "Child Marriage: Lok Sabha Unstarred Question 1372, to Be Answered on 22-12-17," Ministry of Women and Child Development, Government of India, 2017, http://164 .100.47.190/loksabhaquestions/annex/13/AU1372.pdf, accessed January 3, 2019.

17. "India Fact Sheet," NFHS-4, 2015–16, 2017, 2, https://goo.gl/YK5T9A, accessed December 25, 2017.

18. See examples of cases listed in Kirti Singh, *Law and Son Preference: A Reality Check* (New Delhi: United Nations Population Fund [UNFPA], 2013), 108–9.

19. See Flavia Agnes, "Controversy over Age of Consent," *Economic and Political Weekly* 48, no. 9 (2013): 12, http://www.epw.in/journal/2013/29/commentary/controversy-over -age-consent.html, accessed August 13, 2013.

20. Protection of Children from Sexual Offences Act (No. 32 of 2012, June 2012), Government of India, 2012, 10–11, https://childlineindia.org.in/pdf/POCSO-ACT-Gazette .pdf, accessed January 3, 2019.

21. "The Criminal Law (Amendment) Bill, 2013: Facts and Myths," *Feminists India*, March 17, 2013, http://feministsindia.com/tag/age-of-consent/, accessed July 3, 2013.

22. Agnes, "Controversy."

23. Soutik Biswas, "Should India Lower the Age of Consent?," BBC, March 16, 2013, https://goo.gl/fBFkn8, accessed July 3, 2013.

24. Pratiksha Baxi, "Complicated Terms of Engagement," *Hindu*, October 25, 2017, https://goo.gl/y488zG, accessed December 20, 2017.

25. For an excellent analysis of this practice, see Srimati Dasu, "Sexual Property: Staging Rape and Marriage in Indian Law and Feminist Theory," *Feminist Studies* 37, no. 1 (2011): 185–211.

26. Brewer, *By Birth or Consent*, 296.

27. Singh, *Law and Son Preference*, 107–9.

28. "Sexual Health of Adolescents in India: A Female Scenario from NFHS-3," *National Family Health Survey*, http://epc2012.princeton.edu/papers/120793, accessed December 20, 2017.

29. Mridu Khullar, "In India, Banking on the 'Morning After' Pill," *Time*, May 26, 2010, http://content.time.com/time/world/. See also Sanchita Sharma, "Emergency Pill Safe Only If Used as Directed," *Hindustan Times*, 2011, http://www.hindustantimes.com/, accessed June 20, 2015.

Conclusion

1. The consensus figure used to account for the number of child marriages is 700 million; it is cited across UN documents from 2014 and 2015; is mentioned in the *General Assembly Resolution on Child, Early, and Forced Marriage*, December 18, 2014, General Assembly, January 22, 2015, A/RES/69/I56, and appears in the third paragraph of the UNICEF webpage on child marriage, http://www.unicef.org/protection/57929_58008.html, accessed August 18, 2015.

2. The US Congress passed the 2012 International Protecting Girls by Preventing Child Marriage Act (S.414), which authorized such spending. For examples of organizations with broad mandates advocating on this topic, see International Center for Research on Women, http://www.icrw.org/preventing-child-marriage; the US Global Health Initiative; and Chanel Hasty, Medical Sciences for Health (MSH), "US Senate Passes Child Marriage Prevention Act, Global Momentum to Protect Girls Growing," June 1, 2012, http://msh.org.blog.

Index

abolitionism, 43, 88–93
abortion, 113, 116, 123, 130
abduction, 63, 64, 68, 69, 71, 74, 78
activism and advocacy, 4–5, 87; antitrafficking (*see* antitrafficking); birth control, 44, 103, 106–7, 171n8; child welfare, 31, 142, 147; girls, 122, 124, 127–28, 130, 138, 142, 149; marriage age, 77, 82, 85, 94–95, 98, 103, 142, 144–45, 177n81; reproductive rights, 103, 114, 115, 118. *See also* NGOs; population control
adolescence, 51; and girlhood, 49–60, 95, 130, 152; in India, 39–49; in psychology, 4–18, 37–39
adulthood: age of majority, 62; attributes, 35–41; and marital status, 8–15, 99
advertising, 6
Advisory Committee for the Protection of the Welfare of Children and Young People (League of Nations), 23
Advisory Committee on Traffic in Women and Children (League of Nations), 23

Agarwala, S. N., 101, 108–15
Age at Marriage in India, The (Agarwala), 108
agency (concept), 70, 75, 106, 114, 170n3, 174n33
Age of Consent Committee (India), 41, 64, 78–81, 119, 177n85
Agnes, Flavia, 146
All India Women's Conference (AIWC), 77, 118, 168n24, 177n80
American Journal of Psychology, 37
American Psychological Association, 37
American Social Hygiene Council, 43
androcentrism, 5, 40, 45, 49, 127. *See also* boys and boyhood: as a norm
Annan, Kofi, 133
Antislavery Society for the Protection of Human Rights, 95
antitrafficking: Anglocentric standards, 29; Dadabhoy Bill, 68; international campaigns and standards, 10, 23, 64, 67, 72, 74, 83–84, 127 (*see also* League of Nations); PCMA and, 144; sexual maturity and, 18; travel and 32–33, 63, 72;

antitrafficking (*continued*): UN and, 124, 131–32; US initiative, 11
Apni Beti Apna Dhan (program), 138–40
Ariès, Philippe, 5, 56

bai (term), 10
baiko (term), 10
Ban Ki-Moon, 133
Beardon, M. O'Brien, 178n87
Because I Am a Girl (movement/campaign), 11
Bihar (state), 111, 139, 176n69
Bill and Melinda Gates Foundation, 135
biology, 12, 38, 108
biopolitics, 29–34, 157n1
birth control: emergency contraception used as, 149; eugenics and, 103, 106, 114, 179n102; feminism and, 114, 171n8; health and, 116; promoting, 43–44, 106–7; testing, 3. *See also* family planning; population control
Bloch, Iwan, 27
Bombay, 22, 71, 79
Boutros-Ghali, Boutros, 87, 180
boys and boyhood: as a norm, 5–9, 39–44, 49; relative to girlhood, 37, 81–82, 111–12, 121–34, 145, 150, 183n1
BRAC (organization), 135
British Association for Moral and Social Hygiene, 43, 46

Cambridge Group for the History of Population and Social Structure, 105
Central Legislative Assembly, India, 61, 65–66, 72, 177n85
childhood: and adolescence, 35–37, 159n14; in European history, 5–8, 164n25; for girls, 62, 69, 82; in India, 5–8, 40–41; and innocence, 5–9, 45, 98; legal definitions of, 69, 82, 92, 98, 150; scholarship on, 5–9, 35–37, 40–45, 56, 62, 69

child labor, forced, 5, 8–9, 89, 117, 129, 131, 158n12, 187n11
child marriage, 192nn1–2; in Britain, 7, 30, 63, 82, 181n25, 182n39; in colonial America, 182n39; in India, 3, 63, 86, 143, 157n3, 157n6, 175n52, 177n77, 177n85, 179n102, 190–91; reporting on, 191n12; revivalists and reformists on, 170n3; scripture and, 6, 42, 159n22; as two-stage process, 186n75
Child Marriage Prohibition Officers, 145
Child Marriage Restraint Act (CMRA, India, 1929), 41, 77–78, 81, 83, 102, 104, 118–20, 185n54
Child Marriage Restraint Act Amendment (India, 1978), 59, 101–3, 110, 112–14, 117–20, 143–44, 153
children: human rights of, 21–23, 31–36, 87, 121–41; idealization of, 55; as objects of love, 42–48; power over, 62–69, 72–80, 94–100, 144–49; as property, 42–48
class, socioeconomic: adolescence and, 36–37, 38; complexity of, in India, 154; education and, 59, 79; innocence and, 8; marriage age and, 116, 186n75; "ordinary," 83; parental protectiveness and, 14; power and, 65–66; of *Stree* readers, 50; in US, 6
climate, 27, 164n32; heredity vs., 26; laws and, 32, 96; puberty and, 12, 13, 18–19, 24, 25–26, 27–29, 30–31, 40, 43, 155; race and, 19–20, 24–25, 26, 34; sexual practices and, 19, 23–24, 25, 27. *See also* tropical exceptionalism
climatology, 19, 40
Coale, Ansley J., 104–9, 113
Codes of Misconduct (Tambe), 2, 11
Cold War, 40, 48, 94, 155
colonialism, 26, 155; and marriage, 18–19, 65, 66, 92, 99
coming-of-age ceremonies, 17
commercial sex, 1, 34, 62, 170n4. *See also* prostitution

Index

Commission on the Status of Women, UN (CSW), 87, 115, 181n31
Committee on the Status of Women (India), 115
Committee on Traffic in Women and Children, 21, 23
concubinage, 68–71, 83, 174n30, 175n44
conditional cash transfer schemes (CCTs), 138–40, 141, 151
Connelly, Mathew, 3, 107
consent, sexual, age of: abduction and, 63, 64, 68, 69, 71, 74, 78; changing norms, 3, 7, 32, 74; climate, geography, and, 14, 23–24, 29–30, 42, 72; for concubinage (see concubinage); country shaming and, 32, 42; feminism and, 146–48, 149; girlhood and, 7, 61–62, 81, 153; for girls vs. boys, 2; health and, 81; international context and, 20, 21, 33, 63, 73, 77, 82; internationalizing, 14, 20; for marital sex, 61–62, 67, 69, 74, 76–77, 81; nationalism and, 11, 14, 32, 62, 63, 66, 72, 73, 77, 83–84, 154–55; for nonmarital sex, 61–63, 68, 69, 71, 74, 76, 78–84; parental control (see parents); for prostitution (see prostitution); puberty and, 30–31, 97–99, 152, 155, 159n22; religion and, 62, 66–67, 69, 73, 84; varying by context, 2, 7, 14, 61–64, 67–70. See also Age of Consent Committee (India); sexual age standards
"Consent to Marriage and Age of Marriage" (UN), 93
contraception. See birth control
Convention on Consent to Marriage, Minimum Age of Marriage, and Registration of Marriage, UN (1962), 85–87, 97, 98
Convention on the Elimination of Discrimination against Women, UN (CEDAW), 127, 144
Convention on the Rights of the Child, UN (CRC), 121, 127, 187n11

Copenhagen Summit on Social Development, UN (1995), 132
Covenant of the League of Nations, 21
Criminal Law Amendment Ordinance of February 2013 (India), 147
CSW (UN Commission on the Status of Women), 87, 115, 181n31

Dadabhoy, Manicekji B., 68, 174n30
Dadabhoy Bill, 64, 67–71, 174n30, 174n33
Darwin, Charles, 26, 28
daughters, 6, 11, 64, 68, 75–76, 78–80, 146, 148. See also girl (concept); girlhood; parents
debt bondage, 88–89
Declaration of the Rights of the Child, League of Nations (1924), 91
Declaration of the Rights of the Child, UN (1959), 91, 98
Declaration on Human Rights, UN (Vienna, 1989), 132
DeLuzio, Crista, 5, 6, 38
demographic imagination, 30–31
demographic transition theory, 104, 183n5
demography, 12, 130; feminist, 102, 114–15, 186n62; Indian experts, 14, 122, 185n32; and population control, 102, 104–11, 113, 114, 120, 152–53, 155; research on marriage age, 59; research on puberty, 28
Descent of Man (Darwin), 26
devadasis (temple dancers), 172n19, 176n76
Development Alternatives with Women for a New Era, 118
development studies, 121
Dhanalakshmi (program), 139
Divatia, N. B., 69
Driscoll, Catherine, 5, 36, 38

Economic and Social Council (ECOSOC), 86, 88, 91, 93, 95
Edelman, Lee, 8

195

Educating Girls and Women (World Bank), 128
education, of girls, 59–60, 63, 73, 79–80, 83, 141; childbearing and, 11, 111, 112, 113, 114–17; class and rural-urban differences, 59, 79, 154, 178n95; initiatives and policies, 123, 128–35, 175n52, 188n15; marriage and, 42, 59, 94–95, 98, 115, 116–17, 152, 177n80; progressive ideas, 47; as protection from procurers, 73; as a right, 98; single-sex vs. coeducational, 38, 48, 178n94; in US, 6, 38–39. *See also* sex education
Edwardes, Stephen Meredyth, 17–18, 19, 22–23, 63, 72
elitism. *See* eugenics
Ellis, Havelock, 44
empowerment, of women and girls, 133, 138–39
eugenics, 103, 108, 114, 178–79n102
Eugenics Quarterly (later *Social Biology*), 108

family: children in, 46, 104–7, 143–48; welfare, 112–16
family planning, 103, 107, 109–10, 112, 113–16. *See also* birth control; population control
feminism: and birth control, 114, 171n8; in demography, 102, 114–15, 186n62; and sexual consent age, 146–48, 149; transnational, 2–5, 154, 157n7
feticide, female, 130
Food and Agricultural Organization (FAO), 86, 132
Ford Foundation, 104, 107, 184n23

gender: and girlhood, 2, 5–15, 35, 58–60, 152–55, 159n17, 159n23 (*see also* boys and boyhood); oppression based on, 144
General Assembly Resolution on Child, Early, and Forced Marriage, UN (2014), 192n1
General Assembly Resolution on the Girl Child, UN (1995), 126, 132–33

Geneva Declaration of the Rights of the Child (League of Nations, 1924), 91
genital mutilation/cutting, 88, 124, 126–27, 130–32
girl (concept). *See* gender; girlhood
Girl Child, The (UNICEF), 124, 127, 129, 131, 187
Girl Effect (campaign), 11, 135–36, 138, 161n36, 189n38
girlhood: and age standards, 6, 35, 41–42, 58–60, 67–76, 82, 101–2; attributes of, 5–15, 116–20, 151–54; campaigns featuring, 11, 121–29, 131–40, 189n28, 189n44, 189n46; and girl children, 61–64, 81–83; and girl power, 10; visualization of, 49–60
Girl Up (campaign), 11, 136–37, 189n39
Global Partnership for Education, 135
Gour, Hari Singh, 76
Grossberg, Michael, 7
Gujarat (state), 112–13, 139, 185n54
gynecology, 27–28, 34, 41

Hailey, Malcolm, 75–77
Halberstam, Jack, 8
Hall, G. Stanley, 37
Haryana (state), 138–39
heterosexuality, framing of, 7
Hippocrates, 25
Human Rights Law Network, 144

Imperial Legislative Council, 67
Indian Association for Moral and Social Hygiene, 46
Indian Institute of Public Administration, 48
Indian Majority Act (1875), 69
Indian Ministry of Health and Family Planning, 110
Indian Penal Code, on age of consent, 66–68; and kidnapping, 68, 71–72, 74, 78, 163n14; for marital sexual relations, 66, 76, 173n23; for nonmarital sexual relations, 68, 71, 78; for prostitution, 67,

Index

68, 78, 83, 163n14, 174n29. *See also* Child Marriage Restraint Act (CMRA, India, 1929); Child Marriage Restraint Act Amendment (India, 1978); Prohibition of Child Marriage Act (PCMA, India, 2006)
Indian Social Institute, 47
infanticide, female, 5, 123, 132, 138
infantilization, 9, 128
innocence (concept), 8, 56; childhood and, 5–9, 45, 98
Inter-Agency Task Force for Adolescent Girls, UN, 134
International Alliance of Women, 87, 95, 180n4
International Association for Social and Moral Hygiene, 22
International Council of Women, 180n4
International Court of Justice, UN (ICJ), 86
International Day of the Girl Child, 123, 188n29
International Federation of Women Lawyers, 96
International Journal of Sexology, 44
International Labor Organization (ILO), 134
International Protecting Girls by Preventing Child Marriage Act, 11, 192n2
International Society for the Suppression of White Slave Traffic, 64, 67
International Union for the Protection of Girls, 17, 22
International Women's Health Movement, 118

Jewish Association for the Protection of Girls and Women, 21
Jinarajadasa, Dorothy, 76
Jinnah, Mohammad Ali, 75
Joint Meeting of the Committees on Traffic and Child Welfare, League of Nations, 23
Joint UN Programme on HIV/AIDS (UNAIDS), 134
Joshi, Ganesh Vyankatesh, 70
Joshi, N. M., 72, 74

kanya (term), 36
Karnataka (state), 107, 139, 145
Kasliwal, Nemi Chandra, 97, 182n46
kidnapping, 63, 64, 68, 69, 71, 74, 78
Kinsey, Alfred, 44
Kishori Shakti Yojana (Female Youth's Strength Scheme), 139
Krishnan, J., 43
kumar (term), 36
kumarika (term), 36
kunku, 50–51, 53–54

Law Commission of India, 145
laws: age of consent, 62–63, 82–83, 109–13, 132, 142–43; enforcement of, 13, 65, 94, 111–12, 117, 132, 134, 143–44; UN resolutions, 87–89; women in India, 65–66. *See also* Indian Penal Code; marriage, age of: international standards and laws
League of Nations: advisory committees, 23; antitrafficking, 5, 17–22, 29, 31–34, 35, 63, 71, 74, 92, 152; antitrafficking conventions, 17, 19, 20, 34, 74, 161n2; Covenant, 71–74; Convention on the Abolition of Slavery (1926), 88; history, 17–22; impact, 3–5, 31–34, 83–90; organizational structure, 162n12, 166–67n76
Leclerc, Louis, Comte de Buffon, 25
legal age of marriage. *See* marriage, age of; marriage, age of, in India
Lesko, Nancy, 39
Lesser Child, The (report), 123
Lyon, I. B., 41

Madge Bill, 67
Madhya Pradhesh (state), 139
Maharashtra (state), 49, 66, 123, 169n52, 173n23
Malabari, Behramji, 66
Malaviya, Madan Mohan, 61
Malthus, Thomas Robert, 3, 101, 103–7. *See also* population control

Index

mangalsutra (necklace), 50–51, 53–54, 56
Marathi language, 10, 49–50, 106, 169n52
marital rape, 76, 173n23
marriage: forced, 85–91, 127, 134, 179n1, 189n33; free, 89; voluntary, 146, 148–49
marriage, age of: concepts shaping changes in, 2–3, 32, 59–60; enforcement, 13, 65, 94, 111–12, 117, 132, 134, 143–44; for girls vs. boys, 41–42, 81–82, 93–94, 96, 102, 111, 145, 183n1; outside India, 23, 30, 32, 71, 82, 96, 98; international debates, 2–3, 18–19, 92, 96, 98 (*see also* United Nations); international standards and laws, 3, 7, 11, 14, 86, 88–89, 94–95; vs. prostitution age, 7, 62 (*see also* prostitution); puberty and, 6, 30, 41–42, 81, 99; religion and, 42, 61, 66, 73, 78; social shifts, 1, 59–60, 68, 83, 94, 146; vs. statutory rape age, 2, 7 (*see also* rape: and age). *See also* consent, sexual, age of: for marital sex; population control
marriage, age of, in India, 2, 6, 11, 143, 145–46, 152–55; 1891, 62, 66–67, 68–69, 102, 159n24; 1911–29 debates, 64, 67–68, 82–83, 152; 1949, 102; 1960s–70s discussions, 101, 108, 113, 114, 152–53 (*see also* population control); feminism and, 62–63, 77, 101–2, 103, 114–15, 117–18, 146–49. *See also* Child Marriage Restraint Act (CMRA, India, 1929); Child Marriage Restraint Act Amendment (India, 1978); Prohibition of Child Marriage Act (PCMA, India, 2006)
Marriage Hygiene (journal), 44
Mathias, Theo, 47–48
maturity: emotional, 35–37; intellectual, 35, 42, 69–70; physiological, 37, 42, 69; sexual, 1–2, 17–22, 34, 36, 39, 61, 70, 151–52. *See also* menarche; puberty
Medical Jurisprudence (Lyon), 41
medical science, 12–13, 48. *See also specific topics*
menarche: adolescence and, 35, 37, 49; climate, geography, and, 19, 25–28, 34; and marriage, 17, 41, 49; puberty and, 162n4; as sexual threshold, 17–18, 41
menstruation, 25, 42, 81. *See also* menarche
Milbank Memorial Fund, 104
Modern Girl around the World Project, 6
motherhood, 2, 77, 153, 178–79n102
Mother India (Mayo), 77, 157, 172–73n20, 177n81
Muddiman, Alexander, 77
Mukerjea, Moni John, 45–46
multiplier effect (economic concept), 135
Mysore (state). *See* Karnataka
Mysore Study, 101, 107

National Christian Council, 43, 45, 168n31
National Council of Women in India, 76, 176–77n77
National Family Health Survey, 143, 192n28
National Human Rights Commission, 144
nationalism, and sexual consent age in India, 14–15, 63, 155; and colonialism, 66, 83–84; drama around reforms, 62, 69; and international reputation, 11, 32, 72–73, 77
National Population Policy (NPP) statement, 110–11, 119
National Strategy Document on Prevention of Child Marriage, 139
Natu, Vishnu Raghunath, 70
Nehru, Jawaharlal, 107, 184n23
Nehru, Rameshwari, 168n24, 177n85, 178n87
NGOs: and child marriage, 87, 94–96, 98, 139, 144, 151; and chil-

dren's rights, 122, 144; and CSW, 87, 94–96, 98; on the girl child, 122, 126, 127–28; interagency networks, 128–29, 134, 142, 144; investing in girls, 128–29, 138, 152
Nike, 11, 135, 137–38, 189n46
Nirmala Niketan College, 48
nongovernmental organizations. *See* NGOs
nonmarital sex, age of consent for, 61–63, 68, 69, 71, 74, 76, 78–84
Notestein, Frank, 105–7
Novo Foundation, 135
Nutrition Programme for Adolescent Girls (NPAG), 139

Obama, Barack, 11
obstetrics, 19, 28, 35, 41
On Uterine and Ovarian Inflammation (Tilt), 26

Pandey, Jyoti Singh, 147
parents: children as property of, 45–49, 96–99, 138–40; and marriage, 63–66, 70, 75–83, 93, 146–50, 182n39, 183n1
patriarchy, 61, 73, 118, 149
petite fille, la (term), 127
Pillay, A. P., 44, 107, 168n34
Platform for Action, 131, 133, 188n30
Population Bomb, The (Ehrlich), 103
population control, 3, 101–3; aggressive, 110–12; birth control and, 97, 114, 119; discourses about, 103, 109–10, 113, 120, 141, 154–55; feminism and, 101, 103, 114–16, 118; funding for efforts, 107, 109; and marriage age, 102, 103, 106–9, 146, 152; UN and, 97, 101, 104, 106, 120; and women's well-being, 109, 114–15, 117 (*see also* reproductive rights)
population growth, 13, 103–10, 113, 117–18, 120, 153
Population Growth and Economic Development in Low-Income Countries (Coale and Hoover), 104, 107, 183n7
poverty: and birth rates, 106, 114; as cause of early marriage, 143, 148; and education, 79; effect on girls, 129; girls as key to ending, 135–36; and health, 103; and subsidies for girl children, 138
pregnancy, 2, 133; age of first, 42; early, 104, 111, 113, 127; physical health and, 81, 104, 111, 188n15; repeated, 103, 188n15
Prohibition of Child Marriage Act (PCMA, India, 2006), 144–45
prostitution: abolition movement, 22, 29, 33, 34, 43, 162n13; cross-border vs. national, 21, 33, 63, 67; girls born into, 67, 173n26; and health, 171n7; vs. "immoral sexual relations," 63, 75–76, 82–83; laws and regulations, 65, 68, 71–72, 78, 163n14, 172n20, 174nn29–30; questionnaires about, 31–32, 163n14; and rehabilitation, 31, 33, 166n75; religion and, 172n20, 176n76; sexual autonomy and, 34, 61, 163n17; state control of, 18, 22, 29; terminology, 161n1, 170n4, 174n34, 187n11; violence and, 134. *See also* antitrafficking; concubinage
psychologists: Anglo-American, 35, 38, 44; Indian, 45–47, 60
puberty: age of, 42, 87, 89, 95, 164n30; and climate, 12–13, 19, 24, 28, 30; as consent, 97–99, 152, 155, 159; and marriage age, 6, 30, 41–42, 81, 99; racialized assumptions about, 169n38; and two-stage marriages, 186n75
Purcell, Mary, 131
Pushpaben Committee, 113

queer theory, 7, 160n30

race: as concept, 19–20, 24, 28, 46, 60; science, 19–20, 24, 28–29, 34, 40, 155

Index

racism, 13, 100, 154
Rajiv Gandhi Scheme for Empowerment of Adolescent Girls (Sabla), 139–40
Rao, B. K., 47
rape: adultery and, 174n33; and age (statutory rape), 2, 7, 18, 63, 68, 71, 74, 83, 146–47, 175n50; marital, 76, 80–81, 173n23; and parental control, 64, 78, 149; protections from, 147, 148; as punishment, 191n10; victims of, 7, 82–83, 148, 170n5
Rathbone, Eleanor, 29–30, 32, 82, 165n54
Reddi, Muthulakshmi, 176n76
religion, 65, 69, 73; and girls' agency, 75, 183n1; and marriage age, 6, 42, 61, 66, 73, 78, 159n22; and prostitution, 172n20, 176n76; and sexual consent age, 62, 66–67, 69, 73, 84
Report of the Age of Consent Committee, 41, 64
reproductive rights, 97, 100, 103, 114, 115, 118, 182n50
Resolution on the Girl Child, UN (2005), 126, 131–33
Rockefeller Foundation, 107, 183n7

Sabla scheme, 139–40
Sagade, Jaya, 40, 117–19, 144
Samaj Swasthya (magazine), 106–7
Samarth, N. M, 73
Sanger, Margaret, 103, 106
Sarda, Harbilas, 177n85
Sarda Act. *See* Child Marriage Restraint Act (CMRA, India, 1929)
sati (practice), 84, 179n114
science: activists using, 41; of adolescence and puberty, 29, 48, 152; climatology, 19, 40; and female feticide, 123; geography, 27; hygiene, 44; population, 106, 108 (*see also* demography; population control). *See also* race: science; social science

secretary-general, League of Nations, 71
secretary-general, UN, 189n31; Ban Ki-Moon, 133; Boutros Boutros-Ghali, 87; reports from, 93, 94, 122, 127, 133–34, 135; statements by, 136–37; statements to, 95; U Thant, 97
Sen, Satadru, 5, 67
sex education, 43–44, 46, 48–49
sexology, 27, 44
sexual abuse, 119
sexual age standards, 2–5; climate, geography, and, 17–18, 20, 22–23, 30, 34; ideal heterosexuality, 7; innocence, 8; internationalizing, 3, 11, 20, 77; morality and, 3, 19. *See also* consent, sexual, age of
sexuality: colonial, 162n5; and fertility and health, 119; influence of Western media, 46; in *Marriage Hygiene*, 44; and power, 34, 146
sexual maturity, 1–2, 17–22, 34, 36, 39, 61, 70, 151–52. *See also* menarche; puberty
sex work, 170n4, 171n7. *See also* prostitution
Shafi, Muhammad, 73
Siam, 21, 23, 33
Simmons, LaKisha, 5–6, 38, 159n14
Singh, Karan (minister), 110–11
Sirleaf, Ellen Johnson, 137
slavery, chattel, 89, 91. *See also* transatlantic slave trade
social science, 40, 49, 105, 155
Society for the Protection of Children in Western India, 69
South Asian Association for Regional Cooperation (SAARC), 123–24
South Asian history, 5, 6, 7, 8, 172n15
Special Body of Experts on Traffic in Women and Children, 31
statutory rape. *See* consent, sexual, age of; rape: and age (statutory rape)
sterilization, 107, 111–13, 116

200

Index

St. Joan's International Social and Political Alliance, 94–96, 180n4
Stockton, Kathryn Bond, 8
Stoler, Ann, 24
Stree (magazine), 9, 11, 13, 49–60
Subrahmanyam, C. S., 73
Summers, Larry, 129
Supplementary Convention on Slavery, UN (1956), 88, 90, 93, 99
Suppression of White Slave Traffic protocols, 21, 64, 67

teenager (concept), 36, 56–60, 146–49
teen pregnancy, 133. *See also* pregnancy: early
temple dancers (*devadasis*), 172n19, 176n76
Tilak, B. G., 66
Tilt, Edward, 26
Towards Equality (report), 115–17
transatlantic slave trade, 87, 91, 99–100
transnational feminism, 2–5, 154
tropical exceptions, 96. *See also* climate
tropics and tropicalism, scientific, 24–25
Tye, C. Y., 104–5, 109

UK AID, 135
UN. *See* United Nations (UN)
UNAIDS, 134
UN Commission on the Status of Women (CSW), 87, 115, 181n31
UN Convention on the Rights of the Child (UNCRC, 1989), 121, 127, 187n11
UN Development Program (UNDP), 86
UN Educational, Scientific, and Cultural Organization (UNESCO), 132, 134
UN Foundation, 11
UN Fund for Population Activities (UNFPA), 104, 106, 134
UN Girls Education Initiative, 135

UN High Commission on Refugees (UNHCR), 86
UNICEF: on child marriage, 144, 151; on the girl child, 121–22, 124–27, 128–33, 135–36; State of the World's Children Report (2004), 135, 157n3; World Summit for Children (1990), 128–29
United Nations (UN): action orientation, 128–29, 131–34, 140–41; on adolescent girls, 132–33, 134–35; on children generally, 121, 122, 128–29, 135; General Assembly resolutions, 126, 131–33; on the girl child, 121–22, 124–25, 128–33, 135–36; India and, 3, 18–19; marriage and consent laws, 18–19, 85–87, 89–92, 94, 97–100, 144, 151–52; maturation debates in, 95; NGOs and, 157n8; political differences in, 4, 94, 98; population matters, 104, 106, 107, 109–10; records and publications, 13, 89–90, 94, 125–27, 187n10; research by, 94, 99, 107, 116, 151; secretary-general (*see* secretary-general, UN); social and economic goals, 33, 86, 88, 89, 91, 99, 115
Universal Declaration of Human Rights, UN (1948), 88–89, 97
U Thant, 97, 182n50

"venereal disease," 29, 43, 162–63n13
Vienna Declaration on Human Rights (UN, 1989), 132
Vincent, William H., 72–74, 175n58
Vishindas, Harchandrai, 73

Wheeler, Henry, 69
women (category): activism on behalf of girls, 22–24, 79–82, 87, 123–40; age boundaries of, 49–56, 146–50. *See also* girlhood; puberty
Women's Indian Association (WIA), 71, 76–77, 79, 118, 175n52, 177n81

Index

Working Group on the Girl Child, UNICEF, 131
World Conference on Women, UN (Fourth, Beijing 1995), 126, 132
World Declaration and Plan of Action for the Survival, Protection, and Development of Children, 128
World Health Organization (WHO), 86, 132, 134
World Summit for Children, 128–29
World War I, 21
World War II, 5, 14–15, 28, 33, 84–85, 89

Year of the Girl Child, 123–24
Year of the Woman, 5
Yousafzai, Malala, 11, 161n37
youth (category), 36–38, 44–48. *See also* adolescence; puberty; teenager
yuva (term), 36

zamindari (socioeconomic class), 66

ASHWINI TAMBE is an associate professor of women's studies at the University of Maryland College Park, where she is also affiliate faculty in history and Asian American studies. She is the author of *Codes of Misconduct: Regulating Prostitution in Late Colonial Bombay.*

The University of Illinois Press
is a founding member of the
Association of University Presses.

———————————

Composed in 10.75/13 Arno Pro
with Adrianna Extended Pro display
by Lisa Connery
at the University of Illinois Press
Cover designed by Megan McCausland
Cover illustration: Young woman/girl with double braids
by M. R. Achrekar (1936). Used for *Stree* cover, May 1956.
Courtesy former editor Mukundrao Kirloskar.

University of Illinois Press
1325 South Oak Street
Champaign, IL 61820-6903
www.press.uillinois.edu